D0276964

# On the Wilder Shores of Love

A Bohemian Life

# On the Wilder Shores of Love

## A Bohemian Life

LESLEY BLANCH

*Edited by* Georgia de Chamberet

virago

VIRAGO

First published in Great Britain in 2015 by Virago Press

Copyright © Georgia de Chamberet, 2015

For permission to reproduce copyright material by Lesley Blanch please
contact the Estate of Lesley Blanch on email archive@lesleyblanch.com

A CIP catalogue record for this book
is available from the British Library.

ISBN 978-0-349-00544-7

Typeset in Sabon by M Rules
Printed and bound in Great Britain by
Clays Ltd, St Ives plc

3 5 7 9 10 8 6 4 2

Papers used by Virago are from well-managed forests
and other responsible sources.

MIX
Paper from
responsible sources
FSC® C104740

Virago Press
An imprint of
Little, Brown Book Group
100 Victoria Embankment
London EC4Y 0DY

An Hachette UK Company
www.hachette.co.uk

www.virago.co.uk

# Contents

'I don't write fiction because I can't invent. For biography I have to remember, and then work round a character. In biography you don't invent anything, but you interpret. However, that doesn't mean that you don't use your imagination.'

*Lesley Blanch*

# On the Wilder Shores of Love

# Lesley Blanch Remembered –

## Georgia de Chamberet

*The Wilder Shores of Love* – about four nineteenth-century European women who found love and adventure in the Middle East – became an instant classic when it was published in 1954. Lesley Blanch would remark, with pleasure: *my title coined a phrase which I still hear people use, or sometimes see in the press – 'the wilder shores of Westminster' in a piece on stormy politics, or 'the wilder shores of romanticism' on a new fashion.* Marianne Faithfull wrote a song called 'The Wilder Shores of Love'. Cy Twombly's painting *Wilder Shores of Love* was used to promote his solo retrospective at Tate Modern.

Author and traveller, racy yet scholarly romantic, Lesley Blanch inspired generations of writers, readers and critics. Her most famous book was about those four women *escaping the boredom of convention* – a succinct summary of her own life. She left England in 1946, never to return, except as a visitor, and died in the South of France, aged 103, in 2007. Having lived to such a great age, she went from being a household name to a mysterious and neglected living legend.

## ALADDIN'S CAVE

My earliest memories are of Lesley in her little house in medi-
aeval Roquebrune which perched high up over pencil-straight
cypresses and the Mediterranean. After skidding along a maze
of narrow cobbled streets leading to a thirteenth-century keep,
a blue door at the end of a dark alleyway was flung open in a
blaze of sunshine, fragrant patchouli, and welcoming exclam-
ations. Lesley and my mother, Gael Elton Mayo, met through
their Russian husbands in New York after the Second World
War. They remained close despite their peripatetic lifestyles.
Lesley was my godmother. She was a frequent visitor to my
parents' flat in the sixties and adored my French father (my
mother's third husband), who she nicknamed 'Growler'
because of his deep, velvety voice like the Russian opera singer
Chaliapin.

In the seventies Lesley gave her house in Roquebrune to her
late housekeeper's daughter who was getting a divorce and
had a young daughter to bring up. She moved along the coast,
into a small, pink-washed villa submerged in foliage on a hill-
side beside the bay of Garavan on the French-Italian border.
It was near the tiny station built by Queen Victoria, and con-
versation was punctuated by the occasional passing train.
When my mother died of cancer in 1992, Lesley became home
from home and I visited her often. She was admired by her
friends for her eclectic decorating style which was a blend of
the exotic and intimate – Russian ikons, samovars, Qajar
paintings, Turkish waterpipes, portraits of striking bearded
men, turbaned ladies enlaced in the arms of their lovers, por-
traits of cats painted over the faces of Bengal Lancers on
horseback, a pair of black and white Staffordshire dogs,
Mogul toys, Damascene furniture inlaid with mother-of-pearl,

*Lesley Blanch and Georgia de Chamberet, Garavan, 1971.*

Caucasian rugs, Persian embroideries, a low English chair from her nursery and other bric-à-brac – all blending into a harmonious whole.

She chose to wear clothes from the countries where she had travelled – from eighteenth-century museum pieces to bargains found in the souks of the Persian Gulf, or Istanbul – since they were made for comfort. During the day she might dress in a shirt and trousers, but in the evening she would change into a brocaded robe, or a cotton caftan, with a winding turban and velvet slippers; and a necklace of enormous uncut stones and bracelets like cuffs. She could turn the most ordinary of objects, the most normal of rooms, or the most humdrum of incidents into a story. Lesley made a home for her imagination and was happy in her little house filled with treasures from her travels. It was an entrancing retreat from having lived a life of high intensity on many a wilder shore.

## A Determined Romantic

The last of a kind, Lesley Blanch brought to a close that elegant line of woman traveller-writer-romantic scholar: Isabelle Eberhardt, Jane Digby, Aimée Dubucq de Rivery, Isabel Burton, Laurence Hope and Lise Cristiani, travelling across the frozen expanses of Siberia.

She had a soft spot for Russian men, was mad about the Orient, and very open-minded. Lesley's early journalism brings to life the artistic melting pot that was London between the two world wars. Her later writing evokes the Middle East as it once was, before bombs and fundamentalism became daily news. Intense scholarship about those cultures which obsessed her underpins her books.

'Bohemian' may be a hackneyed term, but it serves her well.

*Lesley's desk in Garavan,* circa 1981.

She escaped from Edwardian suburbia and moved between worlds and places. The world and its books were Lesley's education, not school. Lesley was a paradox: fascinated by past vanished worlds, yet a forward-looking trailblazer. She was a product of her time: an innovator, not a slave to fashion. To the historian Philip Mansel, she was: 'not a school, a trend, or a fashion, but a true original'.

She liked to alternate long, serious books with short, light ones. *The Wilder Shores of Love* was followed by a cookbook, *Round the World in 80 Dishes*, and her introduction to Regency courtesan Harriette Wilson's *Memoirs*. *The Sabres of Paradise: Conquest and Vengeance in the Caucasus* was followed by *Under a Lilac-bleeding Star: Travels and Travellers* and her only novel, *The Nine Tiger Man: A Tale of Low Behaviour in High Places*. Her autobiography *Journey into the Mind's Eye: Fragments of an Autobiography* was followed by *Pavilions of the Heart: The Four Walls of Love*. The biography *Pierre Loti: Portrait of an Escapist* was followed by *From Wilder Shores: The Tables of My Travels*. The last book she wrote, specifically for a French readership, was her memoir about her husband, *Romain: A Private View*. The only one of her books to have been written on the basis of a commission was the biography *Farah, Shahbanou of Iran*. Lesley's reputation now rests primarily on two great works of narrative non-fiction, a biography and her autobiography.

A WRITER'S RETREAT

Lesley wrote at a desk in her living room amidst a harmonious assembly of esoteric objects from distant corners of the earth. French windows opened on to cool green shade. Ring doves flew about the terrace festooned with honeysuckle and jasmine, and a superb toad occasionally came and sat on the threshold (he was ignored by the cats). She had a particular affection for him, as she did all creatures. Lesley wrote in long-hand, late into the night, or in the morning after breakfast, with numerous domestic interruptions in between. Her research notes and initial drafts were written in lined exercise books. She wrote and rewrote obsessively; as much as ten or fifteen times. Her work was thrown into wicker baskets for safekeeping. At the draft typescript stage she would cut-and-scotch-tape the pages back together again into a better sequence. Susan Train, bureau chief of American *Vogue* in Paris, first met Lesley in the sixties through *Vogue* photographer Henry Clarke, and they remained lifelong friends. She usually arranged for one of her secretaries to type up Lesley's handwritten manuscript before delivery to the publisher, and they would discuss editorial improvements.

On one of my visits in June 2001, Lesley was fretting about the late delivery of an introduction for a reprint of Isabelle Eberhardt's *Journals*. So I deciphered her graceful writing and typed it up on my laptop at the table in my bedroom, the smell of datura drifting in through the window. This led to my help-ing with her memoirs – which are published in Part One of this volume for the first time – when I returned to see her in September that year. I occasionally made comments and asked questions, initially received with a certain sharp-edged reserve, but then we began to look forward to our time together. As well as new writing, she began to search out pieces she'd writ-ten before. After breakfast on the first morning of my stay, she would hand me something she had written about New York in the early fifties, a vignette about Marlene Dietrich, or an amusing traveller's tale about Afghanistan, saying: *I've got this ready for you.*

I became fascinated by the many lives she had led and the

different worlds she had known. And I hoped to find out about The Traveller who had fired her imagination, so that later she kicked off the dust of England and left it all behind.


## THE TRAVELLER

Born in Chiswick in 1904, Lesley was an only child. Her father was cultivated, clever but idle, and spent his time in museums and galleries, while her elegant, loving mother longed to travel, but never did. For a while, it was her mother's money that kept the family in style. After St Paul's Girls' School and the Slade School of Fine Art, it fell to Lesley to earn a living so she could support herself and her parents. She became a working woman at a time when few women had careers. Although she did illustrations for Illustrated Newspapers Ltd, as well as private commissions, portraits and book jackets, the income was insufficient.

Theodore Komisarjevsky brought Director's Theatre to England. A friend of Lesley's parents, he was a welcome visitor to the family home. Her mother and father *loved him in spite of themselves, accepting his comings and goings like the flight of some strange bird, a rather disturbing creature whose irruptions into their life brought drama, colour and confusion. I loved him unreservedly: for his strangeness and for the climate of danger that I sensed around him – as adventurer, and as the man of whom, even unconsciously, in my earliest childhood I had been desperately aware.*

The opening night of his production of Borodin's *Prince Igor* for Sir Thomas Beecham at Covent Garden on 4 November 1919 was a triumph. A great *metteur en scène*, an inspiring teacher, and a master of theatrical orchestration, his approach to acting was partly based on Stanislavsky's theories. His sister Vera, who died of smallpox in 1910, created the role of Nina in Chekhov's *The Seagull* and was considered to be the greatest actress of the time. As Wagner had done with opera and Diaghilev with ballet, Komisarjevsky dreamed of creating a universal model of theatre with drama. He directed John Gielgud, Edith Evans, Charles Laughton, Alec Guinness and Peggy Ashcroft, all of whom acknowledged their debt to him. Mysterious and cynical with a perverse and impish sense of humour, he was an unpredictable but fascinating character.

In 1921 Lesley was seventeen and Komisarjevsky was thirty-nine. Her relationship with him was, she said, *heart-warming through hard times*. An older, worldly-wise man, he was sustaining not only emotionally, but also by way of her eventual collaboration with him as a scenic and costume designer. Yet she never talked about him, choosing instead to immortalise him as 'The Traveller' in her autobiography, *Journey into the Mind's Eye*. She wrote: *the Traveller acted disgracefully, abusing every canon of honour. He not only seduced a minor, but the daughter of old friends who had entrusted her to his care while abroad. Yet neither of us had the slightest qualm, nor were we ever found out. The Traveller conducted the whole affair with what was, I suspect, practised care.*

As her 'mentor', he offered an escape route out of bourgeois suburbia. They travelled together to Paris, or into the provinces. Lesley may have been an unconventional, free spirit, but her instinct for self-preservation was strong.

I asked Lesley about Komisarjevsky the last time I saw her in 2007. She answered: *Peggy Ashcroft took him off me.*

☪

Lesley was a talented artist. Her portfolio *circa* 1923–35 came to light in January 2014. It contains seventy theatre designs, book illustrations, caricature-portraits, artwork for wall panels, and whimsical line drawings of animals. Some are originals and some black-and-white photographs of her work. Eight were included alongside designs by Oliver Messel and C. Lovat Fraser to represent England in New York's Museum of Modern Art, Theatre Art International Exhibition in 1934. There are scenic and costume sketches for three of Komisarjevsky's productions: Cimarosa's *Giannina et Bernardone* performed at the Théâtre Pigalle in Paris in 1931; *The Merchant of Venice* performed at Stratford in 1932; and his production of *Macbeth* in 1933. Lesley's portfolio raises as many questions as it answers: two costume designs are for the Balanchine–Ravel ballet *Daphnis et Chloé*. On one, the name 'Lydia Lopokova' appears. Three sketches are for a Massine ballet with a terpsi-

*Scenic design by Lesley Blanch for Komisarjevsky's production of Cimarosa's* Giannina et Bernardone, *Théâtre Pigalle, Paris, May–June 1931.*

chorean theme titled *Baroque*. On one is written the name 'Toumanova', and on another is 'Delaroria: dance with Shabelevsky'. There are also two designs for Massine's ballet *Rouge et Noir* – the sketch for 'The King' was included in the MOMA Exhibition. She also created the costumes for David Lichine's two-act ballet *Les Imaginaires*, which premiered at the Théâtre des Champs Elysées in Paris and came on to the Royal Opera House, Covent Garden, in August 1934.

Lesley's designs for Ashley Dukes and his wife, Polish-born 'Mim' Rambert, are racy, baroque and beautiful. The Mercury Theatre (home of the Ballet Club, later the Ballet Rambert) in Notting Hill was like a European alternative to the Bloomsbury group.

## BRITISH *VOGUE*

Lesley turned to journalism since, in her view, she expressed herself better in writing. Articles such as her profile of Pushkin for *Time and Tide*, and also for *Harper's Bazaar*, were remarked. She joined British *Vogue* and became features editor in 1937. During the Second World War she was on the front line of women journalists covering a wide range of topics, and documented the lives of women in the Forces. She collaborated with Lee Miller and the journalist Anne Scott-James, who described Lesley in her thinly disguised autobiographical novel *In the Mink*: 'Everything about her was abundant; her talents; her talk; her friendships; her travels; her experiences. Even her appearance was rococo. With her rounded figure, wide innocent eyes and golden curling hair, she reminded you irresistibly of a gilded cupid, knowing neither vice nor virtue, but playful and loving, pouring out affection, humour, ideas, plans, stories, words from her rich cornucopia of personality.'

Lesley left *Vogue* in 1945, and briefly wrote a column for the *Daily Mail*, but fell out with the commissioning editor, her love for all things Slav not chiming well with its conventional readership. Edward Hulton hired Lesley to write profiles about the cinema and its stars for *The Leader* – a journal of current affairs and the arts which was complementary to his successful photojournalist magazine, *Picture Post*.

## ROMAIN GARY

In 1944, Lesley met Romain Gary, born Kacew – a young Russian-born French navigator with General de Gaulle's Free French Forces. It was a *coup de foudre*, and it was mutual. She arranged for Lee Miller and Germaine Kanova to photograph Gary in his military uniform and wrote in *Vogue*, in January 1945, about his first novel, *Forest of Anger*, which portrayed the Partisan groups in Poland – *men and idealists, fighting on for men and ideals, as they do everywhere* – and the horrors of war, *the little people everywhere, caught up in the maw of world destruction, pitting their ants' struggle against vast forces.* Her concluding words were prescient: *for those who are interested in the new writers, here is one of significance.*

Lesley was living with friends Eden Box, the artist, and Helen Mansell, in a tall house in St Leonard's Terrace overlooking the Royal Hospital Chelsea grounds. Gary moved in. The couple married on 4 April 1945, and celebrated at Prunier's restaurant. She was 41, and he 31. A marriage of minds, their love story has echoes of Flaubert's *Sentimental Education* and Stendhal's *The Red and the Black*. Gary was posted to Sofia in Bulgaria where Lesley joined him. Life in the French Diplomatic Service took them from the Balkans to Paris, Berne, New York and

Los Angeles. From these home bases they extended their travels further – to Turkey, North Africa, Mexico, Central America. Gary spent every available hour writing, and went on to receive France's most prestigious literary award, the Prix Goncourt, under his own name in 1956, and the pseudonym Emile Ajar in 1975. Under the statutes of the prize to win it twice is not allowed: his literary hoax caused a scandal. Today, he is considered by many in the French literary world to be a more modern writer than Sartre.

Theirs was an unconventional marriage. Lesley travelled alone to wild places to satisfy her wanderlust and research her books which Romain accepted, unlike other husbands in the fifties who expected a wife to be at home cooking dinner every night. She accepted his need for women and sex. Anne Scott-James wrote: 'They were both of them capable of being loving and sympathetic, or of being absolute hell, and by a miracle the marriage worked out. They were both so damnably intelligent that they must have either got on well or killed each other within a week; luckily, it was the former.'

When not travelling or socialising, the couple would sit snug in dressing gowns, writing their books in longhand as neither one had learned to type. By the time they reached Hollywood their writing careers had taken off. Her success with *The Wilder Shores of Love* in 1954 was followed by his Goncourt-winning novel *The Roots of Heaven*. As bestselling authors, the couple were invited everywhere. Lesley talked about how much they enjoyed it, *we knew everybody: Aldous and Maria Huxley, Igor Stravinsky and his wife Vera, George Cukor, who became a great friend, Gary Cooper, Charles Boyer – everyone interesting. James Mason, Sophia Loren, David Selznick ... Grand Hollywood parties? Oh no, there was never enough money for us to do that. But we had a Russian cook, and it was sometimes very amusing to give a dinner for, oh, Cecil Beaton and Laurence Olivier and Peter Ustinov and Leslie Caron, who was one of the few intriguing women there at that time.*

According to those who knew them as a couple, they had a special affinity and similar interests, and were extremely entertaining. They shared a love of books and ideas, as well as animals. My mother used to say that there is a great difference between loving and liking a man, and would cite Lesley's words about her husband: *I'm madly in love with him, but he's unbearable!*

Gary became notorious for his womanising. In her 1957 Diary, Anaïs Nin writes, 'I met his wife Lesley Blanch, author of *The Wilder Shores of Love*. She was at first on the defensive – I did not know why. Later I realised it was because Romain Gary is a Don Juan.' When Jean Seberg, the young star of Jean-Luc Godard's film *Breathless*, came with her

*Lesley with Smiley, Garavan,* circa 1981.

husband to one of the Garys' star-studded suppers, it marked the beginning of the end of two marriages.

## A ROMANTIC TRAGEDY

Lesley's greatest love was Theodore Komisarjevsky. Of her love for Romain Gary, she would say: *he was Russian by birth, and I found The Traveller again in him.* Both were exceptionally talented Slav exiles, each a creative mastermind in his realm: one theatre, the other fiction. Their restless spirit appealed to Lesley's gypsy side which longed *to escape the boredom of convention.* Each man had a mesmeric effect on her, as though casting a spell. Each man was a faithful friend and fickle lover. Komisarjevsky and Gary were unwittingly cruel to their women, however much they professed to love them.

Like all good storytellers, Lesley mined that rich seam between imagination and reality. She plundered her life and her passions and turned tragedy into beauty, and believed that: *learning how to deal with pain is the most important thing in life.*

## NOW EAST, NOW WEST

Divorce from Romain Gary was finalised in 1963. Lesley made Paris her base – dividing her time between a little top-floor flat in Avenue Mozart and Roquebrune on the south coast – when not travelling. She crossed Siberia on the Trans-Siberian Express; roamed through Outer Mongolia, Turkey, Iran, Samarkand, Afghanistan, Egypt, Oman; and returned to the Sahara which had inspired *The Wilder Shores of Love*. In

Paris she saw old friends – Nancy Mitford, Violet Trefusis, Rebecca West and the Windsors: *Wallis was a very nice person and I don't mind what anyone said, he was highly intelligent.*

The arrival of the jet plane in the sixties made travel easier and cheaper. This new internationalism found expression in fashion magazines – shoots in exotic, natural locations could now be arranged. Henry Clarke suggested to Diana Vreeland (editor-in-chief of American *Vogue* from 1963 until 1971) that Lesley write the accompanying text to his photographs of Arabia, Turkey and Persia which were perfect for feature articles. Lesley's way of enveloping the Middle East and Islamic world with a poetic aura of mystery and beauty chimed with Vreeland wanting to show readers new horizons.

The April 1965 issue 'Scheherazaderie for the Sheikh at home' displayed a Western vision of the Orient with models in dramatic poses inspired by Diaghilev's Ballets Russes and paintings by Matisse. Vreeland wrote in her 'Editor's Note' for this issue: 'Lesley Blanch is an adventurous woman, mentally uninhibited. She has proved that in her six books, beginning with *The Wilder Shores of Love* ... Part of the Blanch effectiveness as a writer lies in her first-hand research, her pleasure in sensuous details, her spread of knowledge, and her understanding of love.'

Lesley also did commissions for *The Sunday Times*. She particularly relished travelling to Afghanistan, the Arab Emirates and Egypt with Eve Arnold to write the accompanying text for the series *Behind the Veil and Womanhood*. It later became a film for the BBC and NBC. Philip Mansel writes: 'For [Lesley Blanch], the veil, especially the all-covering *burqa* of the Afghans, is a means of female self-protection, equalisation, independence, even seduction, the garb of convenience, privacy and honour – rather than part of the mechanics of male domination.'

In Afghanistan, while Arnold was captivated by women and children, Lesley followed The Traveller's advice: 'Always explore a new town on an empty stomach, it sharpens the vision.' 'Leave the main thoroughfare immediately.' 'Spend your time dawdling or just sitting. Let the town come to you.' 'Forget monuments. Look at daily life first, it was this which made the men and the events which the monuments commemorate.'

## THE OUTSIDER

As Michael Ratcliffe said of Lesley: 'Scratch any of her more rapturous epithets and you will find, just underneath, a balancing detachment, an unsentimental toughness that has much in common with Nancy Mitford and Rebecca West.'

At times her approach to personalities and events reads like a novel, even though she was a serious writer. She combines rhapsodic abandon, empathy and admiration, alongside historical perspective and scholarly detail. Like Isabelle Eberhardt – one of her more memorable heroines – Lesley rejected conventional European morality. Romain Gary's quip that, 'Lesley doesn't mind my infidelities, she is very eighteenth-century!' did not mean that she herself was as wanton as he was, but that she was tolerant. Lesley often said that she had *always detested conventions, although I greatly respect traditions, being both iconoclastic and traditional.* There was a time when, as a woman, to live unconventionally – *wild and free* – and completely on the outside was the only way to escape a repressed society and humdrum domesticity. Sexual freedom meant emancipation.

A Sheherazade figure, Lesley was a masterly mythmaker. The mistress of reinvention, she remained studiedly private.

Writing of The Traveller, she could be describing herself: *secrecy was with him a fine art, something he enjoyed practising for its own sake.*

C⋆

Yves Agid, the oldest son of Dr René Agid and his Swedish wife Sylvia who were close friends of Romain Gary's, described to me why Lesley had made such an impact on him as a young man: 'People didn't know much in the fifties having lived in isolation because of the war; they were not spoiled as we are now. Lesley was a very different, original person, and was married to a man whom I adored. A writer and an intellectual who had travelled, she was ambitious and dynamic. She had a powerful personality: on the one hand almost masculine, and on the other very feminine. There was a space between the assertive, tough, selfish woman; and the feminine and sensual woman. She had an ambivalent, paradoxical quality. On the one hand, she was truly a woman of the twentieth century, yet she wanted to be in a harem. I often wondered to what extent the heroines in her books were projections of herself. She was both strong and submissive, which was disconcerting.'

The Lesley I knew was seductively glamorous, witty, fiercely intelligent and overwhelmingly well-read with eclectic tastes; and much loved by her friends. She was great fun; age did not matter. A good listener, she held her own in conversation; and never lost her curiosity about life.

A great storyteller, her stories were invariably bloodcurdling (severed heads outside the gates of Samarkand) or romantic (Sultan Murad's room in Topkapi Palace). She dramatised her emotions to great effect; and the domestic irritations of life would be given a theatrical twist – comic or tragic, all depending. People who did not know her invariably misunderstood and took her adventurous humour seriously. *Darling Self* was referred to with a gleeful sense of fun, and the telephone answered with a long drawn out, world-weary: *Ouiiii* ... then her voice would brighten up.

She could also be waspish. I remember – with amusement now – a catfight we had about painting the outside wall leading up to her front door a very particular shade of pink: Lesley was a perfectionist. She had a strong autocratic streak, and relished the company of the great and the powerful. She was vitriolic about her enemies and loyal to her friends.

Her cornflower-blue eyes stayed clear and her mind alert to the end. Her skin was peachy soft when you kissed good morning, and she always smelled delicious – jasmine, patchouli, Serge Lutens' 'Arabie'. She preferred the company of men and understood what they wanted, although her life was a celebration of the power of female friendship.

She was coquettish and seductive, drawing a person into her beautiful bubble as though by magic. If they were cast out, it was like being jilted by a lover. Friends and admirers were of all ages and backgrounds: *I liked having adventures in far away, wild countries. Everywhere I travelled I collected lots of friends, and yes, I did have lovers too.*

Hugo Vickers first met Lesley in 1981: 'Delicious tea was served and we had a long talk. I knew we would get on before I saw her – she said later that she knew as soon as she saw me at the gate. We were on the same wavelength ... She gets many visitors, but turns most away. Usually they ask about "all those Arabs as lovers". But Shirley Conran was allowed in. She came with flowers. Now they see each other and recently Shirley Conran wrote asking for details about Arab lovers for a novel. Lesley said, "She should have gone out there and found one for herself."' Shirley Conran tells me she took this advice. And that she was given insights into Arab culture for her novel *Lace* by Lesley and the late King of Jordan.

She saw a great deal of Gore Vidal and Howard Austen when they lived on the Italian coast near Ravello. They also talked for hours on the telephone. Vidal said to me: 'Lesley was the Queen of the Middle East. She was divine.'

Turi Munthe remembers a special relationship: 'I first met her when I was fifteen. She was staying with my parents, who were out for the evening and asked me to look after her. I was long-haired and adolescent, and furious about having to waste my time with her. Hours later, when my parents came home, they found the two of us singing reggae together. In the meantime, I'd discovered Imam Shamyl, between-wars London and Lady Ellenborough. I'd also slightly fallen in love. And I think she had too. I serenaded her. She told me stories to make a lusty fifteen-year-old boy's eyelashes curl. And so began one of those deeply privileged friendships between generations. I made her a little younger, and her attention to me made me feel more a man. When I think of Lesley, I see her sitting at home in a turban, but mostly I have a pitch-perfect memory of her voice. I can hear her English, like a foreign language, unlike and better than anyone else's. These trans-generational relationships are rare. I have had really only one or two.'

A VANISHED WORLD

The work we had begun on Lesley's memoirs in 2001 stopped just as we were reaching her early working life in London's bookish and theatrical worlds. She was generally supportive of biographers and historians researching the lives of her better-known late friends – Nancy Mitford, Cecil Beaton and Violet Trefusis among them. Her late ex-husband had become a cult literary figure in France and she always welcomed his biographers into her home, helping them with their research. So when *Romain Gary: le caméléon* was published in Paris, in March 2004, certain statements and errors made in the book came as a terrible shock. Lesley was completely undone: *Do I have to just sit and take it?* Susan Train acted as a go-between for her and the lawyers and made claims against the French publisher and author, who were obliged to make a great many corrections for subsequent editions and printings. Although vindicated, Lesley was so disheartened and exhausted, work on her memoir was not resumed. She died aged 103, on 7 May 2007.

This book, *On the Wilder Shores of Love: Sketches from a Bohemian Life*, completes the work we started on Lesley's memoirs. Part One, *Scenes from Childhood*, is about her early years in Edwardian Chiswick, and ends with *A London Life* which is based on her preparatory notes for a chapter about the twenties and thirties. Part Two, *Scenes from the Home Front*, is a selection of her writing for British *Vogue* during the Second World War. Part Three, *Scenes from a Marriage*, is Lesley's pithy narrative about her husband, *Romain: A Private View*, which was written specifically for a French readership and has never before appeared in English. Part Four, *Faraway Lands*, and Part Five, *The Eastern Eye*, are a medley of travel pieces, vignettes about people and places, some dating from the sixties and others written between 2001 and 2004.

A seductive and scholarly rebel who was quite happy to own up to having spent a lifetime running away from the shadow of the suburbs, Lesley Blanch lived her dream.

# Far to Go and Many to Love —

*Lesley Blanch*

'FAR TO GO and many to love,' said the gypsy woman insinuating her blowsy bulk, shawls, basket and baby into the doorway from where I was buying wooden clothes pegs, and bargaining for a probably stolen honeycomb. I must have been about sixteen at the time and had always found the gypsy people irresistible. They seemed to breathe another air, all far distances and adventure. Their glittering eyes, by turns melting or savage, could cast spells, or see ahead into the future, it was believed.

Today, as I look back over my long life, I see that the gypsy's sibylline utterances have pretty well summed it up. I see a fragmented whole, many shifting patterns and ways of living, merge, break, form, and re-form. There is no consecutive line or abiding pattern. It is not so much untidy, as restless, forever to new pastures, new emotions or shifting horizons. Were there never any anchors or *points d'appui*? Yes. Animals and plants, music and books and the gift of being able to look – to observe – which has enriched me along the way.

But where to begin? As I was once, I am no more, either outwardly or inwardly. The patterns of my life were forever changing, forming and re-forming, adapting and developing, a *perpetuum mobile* of great journeys, biting poverty, nomadic uprootings and agitating romantic interludes. All these different states of being produced a number of different women, among whom I occasionally recognised something of myself, with the fundamental self lurking beneath the latest façade. Then something would happen and the climate would change, the pace quicken, and I would be off again towards some other facet of living and see another self emerging beneath the now rather worn façade. It was a restless life. Indeed, much as the gypsy foretold.

Yet beneath all these alter-ego ladies that slid easily from one state to another – scatterbrain teenager, bookworm, romantic Miss, would-be scholar, painter, breadwinner, journalist, mistress, housewife, traveller and traveller again – there lurked yet another self, some suppressed gene that caused me to long for a house with its land and a roof and rooms, in which to take root. All of my other selves still longed for distant shores, for the eternal Elsewhere, but one self still yearned to unpack and stay put within four walls.

The house in which I now live has gradually acquired subtle qualities which defy or evade strictures of time, distance, or substance. Which is just as well, for at the age of one hundred, one might otherwise be described as washed up on the shores of time. These four walls – pinkwashed in the tradition of the surrounding countryside, the Ligurian coast – have each assumed a special character and evoke different aspects, climates, events or emotions of my long life, as if to compensate for the desolation and loss of almost all my possessions one fatal night in April 1994, when my house and almost everything in it was burnt to the ground. Next morning, standing among the ashes, wearing an odd selection of garments supplied by my kind neighbours who had sheltered me in my nightdress, I realised that I must start life all over again at eighty-something. It was a desolate thought and a desolate scene. Only the blackened, scorched branches that used to brush the windows were still standing against such sooty bricks and beams as still remained. Everything seemed to shiver, still dripping from the hose-pipes of the firemen. Suddenly a feeling of warmth returned as I saw my two cats crawling towards me from some obscure hiding place, to which they must have fled in the night. They were bewildered, hungry and rather resentful. As I stood knee deep in charred debris and broken masonry, they suddenly ran at and up me, clawing as if I was a tree trunk. I realised that I must make some sort of decision, to go or to stay, and rebuild – I stayed.

*The Nancy Mitford memorial window, Garavan.*

☾⋆

The narrow north wall reveals little, being only a frame for my front door, which sometimes admits, besides friends, a chill draught recalling the climate of my English childhood. It is perforated by several wide arches which reveal the hillside above, crowned by a four-hundred-year-old olive tree in all its majesty. Nevertheless a few crumbling recesses in the old stones seem to hold traces of a nursery wall stacked with dog blankets, a rabbit's hutch and a commodious cage where my white mice scuttled to and fro.

The east wall, the long wall of the living room, is all light and warmth, that radiant and revitalising light of eastern lands – the smiling morning of my travels. I call them the Years of the Minarets – sacred and profane merge harmoniously here. The frost-bound cupolas of an Orthodox Church in Siberia become the crumbling walls of Balkh in Afghanistan's 'Mother of cities' to past ages. The sumptuous golden domes of the Most Holy Meshed dissolve and become a high-prowed dhow sailing to Zanzibar, which in turn dissolves into Tamerlain's jade tomb at Samarkand, while the Nile becomes a remote Saharan horizon or the Pont Neuf. Across that eastern wall, the 'Sweete Thames' of my earliest years still runs softly before turning into the Orontes or filling a well chunked out of rose red rocks at Petra, the city 'half as old as time'. It is now ringed by hotels and motels, but when I was there I slept in a cave and it was all part of that splendid morning. My eastern wall is a long one, and on it much is written.

The south wall tells of languorous, timeless hours, hours of stillness, breathing musk and jasmine and the heavy breath of the Sirocco, mingling with the datura from outside my window. I hear again the rattle of tric-trac counters, as an oil lamp sways flickering across a whitewashed wall where lizards scuttle, or plop on to my pillow. Here are shadowy paths and soft footsteps in the sand.

This south wall is pierced by a low window which is set above a narrow *takht*, or divan, and is known as the Nancy Mitford memorial window, made possible by the legacy she left me. This enabled me to acquire an ancient longed-for Cairene *moucharabiyeh* – one of those traditional, delicately carved, latticework screens through which the inmates of the harem could peer at the world outside. Dear Nancy! How she would have screamed, being represented by a *moucharabiyeh*; 'Oh darling! Why must you always give us such terrible words to pronounce,' she would say, when I went on about Caucasian tribes or the bazaars of Zanzibar. Dear Nancy, some of my darkest days in Paris were lighted by her friendship.

The west wall is not the sunset scene one might suppose, rather, it is that glimmering sheen or luminosity which suffuses the Nile at evening and is known as the Afterglow – 'And he says much, who says evening'.

☪

Although the walls which surround me now are not those of the old house, they still glow for me as though from elsewhere. Those old walls, which seemed to welcome me and absorb my traveller's tales when I returned from journeys, had become the rhythm of my life. There were many halts in many lands when I was *en poste* with Romain, my Russian-French husband – something like eleven major moves across the world in eighteen years, and these walls had come to shelter the harvest of my wandering years. So many homes, in so many lands, so many treasures, beautiful, rare or considered worthless, found along the way and cherished. Crude Afghan hangings, beautiful Caucasian carpets, *toiles de Jouy*, Persian tiles, Arab robes, many ikons, a brightly coloured lamp from a brothel in Cairo, a Spode teacup for my nursery supper, a magnificent Qajar painting of the court of Fath Ali Shah, and a mysterious Shaman's wand from Siberia, its black magic stoutly refuted by my mother's Regency silver teapot. As my possessions accumulated, almost by the hour it seemed, there was a need for more and more space, shelves piled on shelves until there was only the floor left for leaning towers of print.

Above all there were my books, largely concentrated on Russia or the Middle East, but sprawling widely over central Asia, along with everything I had managed to find about the Afghan Wars. I was proud of my library and happy when Oxford's oldest college, New College, accepted to house it after my death, together with a number of boxes containing notes and letters of research I had made in the Caucasus and Turkey when I was writing *The Sabres of Paradise*. So many other subjects too: Venetian music, Victorian needlework, folk art, old playing cards from China to Peru – all gone, all lost in the fire.

*Part One*

# SCENES FROM CHILDHOOD

# 1. Chiswick

BY THE CALENDAR, I was an Edwardian child: that is, having been born in 1904 my first six years were spent in that easy-minded era before the death of King Edward VII in 1910. I recall very little of that time, yet I have kept a curiously clear remembrance of its end. My father was in his dressing room brewing his breakfast coffee, an inviolate ritual which even I knew must be respected. No other hand was ever allowed near the contraption which now puffed and chugged at his bidding. I was fidgeting round, hoping to get a story before he settled down to *The Times*. But he disappeared behind its crackling façade and I was about to go back to the nursery when he put the paper down and said very slowly and clearly, 'Go and tell your mother the King is dead,' so I trotted off to my mother's room where she was, as usual, breakfasting in bed with her companion-cat beside her and a book in her hand. She always refused newspapers at breakfast, 'Time for them later,' she would say. I repeated the message parrot-like, at which my mother said, 'Oh dear!' and pushed aside the cat, the book, and the breakfast tray and went to join my father. For the rest of the day she wore what I called her sadly face and both of them were noticeably glum.

I could not know then, as they did, that the King's death marked, before all else, the passing of a whole way of life. My family were not interested in the royal family, or in any way connected with Court life, but they were historically minded,

and essentially still Victorians. Walter Blanch and Martha
Mabel Thorpe married in 1901. He was, I believe, born in
1863, she in 1876. Thus this brief Edwardian reign had linked
them, and myself less directly, with the vast panorama of
Victorian England. Never again that quiet certainty that
England was almighty, unquestioned, ruling over much of the
map. To be British was enough – that is, if you accepted, rather
than questioned any disturbing doubts. My parents did not
probe too deeply, for comfort's sake, which was essentially an
Edwardian outlook.

I was born in Chiswick in a house now long destroyed,
where my parents, greatly disturbed by my approaching
arrival, were living in temporary accommodation while wait-
ing to obtain more comfortable living quarters in Strand on
the Green nearby. This fascinating tumble of old houses, all
sizes, centuries and styles, from fishermen's cottages to the
lordly house where Zoffany had lived and received his sitters,
all opened on to a narrow footpath running beside the river
which, at certain seasons and tides, became flooded and
impassable. The extraordinary charm of this place had over-
come both my father's wish to remain in London and my
mother's longing for the country. Nevertheless to obtain a
house on that coveted strand was frustrating, a waiting game,
or a game of chance. Some houses were eaten with wood dis-
ease, some had drainage problems, all were damp, yet rarely
obtainable. So my parents decided to wait for a chance which
was never to come their way and settled close at hand in
Grove Park near the station, in temporary quarters which
gradually became a permanency, thus perfectly expressing
their basic Oblomovism, or inertia; call it what you will, they
were drifters.

The Chiswick into which they had drifted was, in fact, one
of the three Chiswicks of that name, for although they

merged, they were each of a different character and aspect. There was the Chiswick which ran beside the High Road on the way west out of London, an ugly commercial area of clanging trams and mean side streets. But at Turnham Green some trim villas and trees began, with a small pompous Town Hall, a public library, tennis courts, shady avenues and a few blocks of flats, telling of the orderly suburban life lived there: this was the second Chiswick. The third Chiswick, that of my childhood, was quite otherwise. It spread between the two cardinal points of Strand on the Green and Old Chiswick with its historic highlights of Devonshire (now Chiswick) House and the riverside Mall. It was an odd, pear-shaped dollop of land, much of it still meadowland with clumps of elms and a certain carefree air as if thumbing or disregarding any threats of development. It was essentially a countrified scene still not much encroached upon by the few tree-lined sandy roads of Grove Park, or its architectural jumble of solid Victorian houses for solid mid-Victorian families, which often stood empty, not yet cut up into flats, or 'studios'. There were one or two lines of elegant little villas, their gardens trim with laburnum and lilac and, here and there, a fine old house standing aloof among its ancient cedars, with stables from which a now rather seedy-looking carriage and pair would emerge for some ancient figures (in bundles of black shawls) to take the air. Our doctor still bowled about in a brougham which lent a certain air of importance to the slightest ailments. It was a leisurely way of life, curiously time-warped: only one small line of shops – a dairy, a butcher and a confectioner – sounded a commercial note. Tradesmen still made their morning rounds from door to door. The baker's van was heralded by delicious wafts of fresh-baked buns and bread. The greengrocer's cart, pulled by a piebald pony called Saucy, brought round fresh fruit and vegetables which were weighed out on huge brass scales. At that time nothing so exotic as kiwi or avocados was known and fruits kept to their seasons, so we were spared forced strawberries or unripe grapes. Milk was fetched from the little dairy where it stood in a huge white china pail, ladled out into the customer's jug or mug. Only the butcher's boy disturbed the even tenor of our ways by his frantic antics on a scarlet bike. He tore about headlong, our orders of joints, chops and such in a basket fixed to his handlebars, barely covered by bits of paper; when the wind scattered them they looked distressingly naked. Very few households boasted their own telephone and one or two old-fashioned ones still employed a uniformed page boy, or 'Buttons', to run messages or answer the door. The new-fangled telephone booth, when at last it was installed on an inconvenient crossroads, was rarely used and considered difficult as it required tuppence to operate. Perhaps I have been unjust to the practical resources of Grove Park: there was in fact a small cardboard-like station, with a booking office and a porter. Now and again, a branch line of the L.S.W. ran a rattle-box train which connected us with Waterloo Station and Clapham Junction *en route*. What a curiously remote scene I evoke – nearer to the eighteenth century than to the life around me today – but it might be described as cosy.

My parents never made a secret of the fact that my arrival had been a shock. They had not planned on a family, for that would have put a stop to their singularly harmonious life *à deux*. 'I don't think we are quite used to you yet,' they would sometimes say, in a teasing way. They never made me feel unwanted, or an intruder – just a surprising addition. My father had sombre, Malthusian views on reproducing the species. Profoundly pessimistic by nature, he saw no reason to do so and, unlike most men, had no urge to see himself reproduced. When cornered by conventional arguments such as,

'Well, the world's got to go on, hasn't it?' he would say, 'Why?' which damped down further discussion.

My mother was fundamentally, and in secret, almost as pessimistic. Totally absorbed in her love for him, she had never been known to express any maternal urges. Once, many years later, she spoke of my unexpected arrival and admitted that although she adored my father, he was not really suited to the parent role. In those days, there were no morning-after pills or 'easy' abortions, so she had to accept the situation, and presently decided to see it as an interesting challenge – how to bring up a child on entirely new, personal lines, away from all conventional ideas – 'And then,' she added, almost unwillingly, 'perhaps I was beginning to get a little bit bored.' She did not enlarge on the way my father was starting to live more and more on his own terms, increasingly withdrawn into some limboland where she could not follow. He was clamping down on so many of their former diversions – concerts, the theatre, visits to friends, discovering some unknown little restaurant. Travel, she had early discovered, was out of the question. It was easy to understand that so lively and enquiring a nature as my mother's, with an almost childish sense of enjoyment, had gradually become frustrated.

Her emotions were lavished on her animals and plants with whom she talked on equal terms, believing that they needed such expressions of affection to flourish. The animals repaid her with ecstatic dialogues of squeaks and grunts, while the plants had their own way of communicating, and it was obvious they flourished on her care.

They must have been what today are called 'loners', a self-generating, self-sufficient pair, he with his books and rare objects, she with her paint-box and piano, each in their own private sphere from which they communicated with each other, or me, and perhaps with some outside space – a beyond – of which I knew nothing. They never spoke of their own families, if indeed they had ever possessed such. They might have been a pair of miraculously conceived orphans. But, come to that, did I ever ask them the usual childish questions: where did you live when you were little? Did you have lots of brothers and sisters – a dog, a horse and so on. My father and mother seemed to me quite a different species to other fathers and mothers. In the first place, I saw mine floating, not walking, and each living in their own remote airy

*Martha Mabel Blanch née Thorpe.*

soap-bubble, where there would have been little room for relatives, let alone ancestors. The uncles and aunts and cousins and grandparents of whom other children spoke were lacking in my life; family life, as such, I have never experienced.

I think it must have been quite a long time before my parents assumed positive or human form. In the beginning I have a cloudy recollection of them as a luminous presence which floated in and out of my line of vision and with which I seemed to communicate vaguely. Soon I discovered that I too was floating in a bubble-like realm of my own; it was smaller than the other one, but very snug, and I could make it float off wherever I wanted, far, near, high, low, to and fro, though to what and from where, I have no idea ... Now I see myself quitting my bubble-sphere and making a rather daring descent into more solidified surroundings, where I can sense that my mother and father are somewhere around, though I do not see them, or indeed have any idea how they look. But Nanny May, my nurse, is emerging in detail, although she left us when I was about four. She is all pink, a pink dress and a round pink face with freckles. She is not like the nannies I see where I go to play. Nanny May laughs a lot and likes to run the pram along at a terrifying speed – I am screaming with joy – My mother is also screaming, and running after us frantically.

When at last I become aware of the two beings who are my father and mother, they are still impersonal, faceless images: my father in a Harris tweed jacket, rough to touch, and his cigarettes (Latakiych) make me cough. My mother is more approachable and congenial, a mysterious fragrance floats around her, which comes back to me as I write. It is *Essence de Jasmine* which I was to rediscover for myself thirty or more years later, in a Tunisian souk, sold there in little painted wooden phials, drenchingly sweet. My mother is soft to touch and seems to diffuse a warm glow, which later I recognised as charm. I suppose these two separate beings were also recognisable by their voices, but I have no recollection of any spoken words, only a soft silence around them when I was taken to join them and told not to make a noise. Gradually my mother is coming clear, she is a tall, tall presence, her head seems a long way away from the floor where I am sitting. She is waltzing round and round whistling to a canary which is balanced on her finger and cheeping back merrily. Is it now or later that I recognise the man stretched out on the sofa as my father? He is reading a book, and a rabbit called Ermyntrude is sitting inside his jacket, her big ears are sticking out and twitching every time my father groans at what he is reading – politics perhaps. He was a fascinating talker if he wished to talk. But I must not allow myself hindsight.

## 2. Earliest Memories

ANIMALS ALWAYS PLAYED a great part in our household which to my infant eyes was a sort of animal kingdom, inhabited in time by many kinds of creatures, furry, leathery, feathered or prickly with a few scalies such as lizards or geckos, beside stray cats or mongrel dogs. They shared our board, and some my bed. Only the hedgehog presented certain difficulties. He would trot up to the bedside and squeak pathetically, but though I was willing, it did not work out for the best, and I think we both felt the loss.

As I look back over a lifetime of loved and lost animal companions, I know that they have been dearer to me than most people. My tangled tropical garden at Garavan, from where I write this, has come to shelter a sad little line of graves, 'Watered by a Mother's Tears' as crumbling tombstones have it in ancient Turkish cemeteries.

☪

Earliest memories? A few bright-coloured fragments like a shattered porcelain bowl that will not piece together. I am angry, banging my head on the floor, again and again in suicidal fury because I cannot get my own way – about what, I have no idea: but I can still recall the hot vibrations of pain and rage. I was a violent child.

Now something shining and golden comes into view, it is

beautiful and I want it. But it is out of reach and I begin to yell. I am lifted up close to the object of my desire and I still cannot get at it. This object was in fact a sixteenth-century Flemish offertory plate, part of my father's collection of rare objects, Chinese porcelain, a Seljuk prayer rug and all else, so that looking back, it seems that my lifelong craving to acquire heterogeneous objects of all ages, lands, and kinds was manifested early.

One last fragment of the shattered bowl: someone is holding me up to a small window to watch a lot of rabbits scampering about a field. It is getting dark, but their white tails still show when they run, 'They always play like that before they go to bed,' says a voice beside me, whose voice? Why are we in this strange place? But it is my bedtime too, and I am put to sleep in a large bed with curtains all round, and I don't remember any more.

Of people, as recognisable beings, I have no very early remembrance: only a series of blurred, passing forms which come and go around me. But I have a clear recollection of an enormous cat which used to jump into my cot and settle down beside me. I can still remember how her whiskers tickled, as she purred a roaring purr of bliss. Nubby, or Nubia, was my mother's adored companion-cat, a sumptuous tabby who had transferred her affections to myself, which, my mother told me later, had been hard to bear. 'I think she thought you were the kitten that had been taken away from her, years before, and she wanted to keep you close. You seemed so happy together, so I never listened to all the busybodies who said you'd be overlaid, suffocated, mauled, or pick up some awful germ.'

☾⋆

It was a memorable day when I discovered that I was no longer always the centre of attention. What was the matter? What should I do to get back on that comfortable footing? I had not realised that my father, who had yielded briefly to my infant exigencies, now intended to regain his old, unquestioned supremacy. Set against that resolve, my efforts were puny, though it was not for nothing that Nanny May said I had become a proper handful. At last, my father admitted I had beaten him at his own game, but there must be no more of it.

*Lesley Blanch, aged three.*

Looking back, I see that he was, without doubt, the most entirely selfish being that I ever encountered. Unless he was getting his own way without questions, he withdrew to his dressing room, not so much in dudgeon as in silent reproof. Perhaps this was the male equivalent of the sofa-and-sick-headache syndrome so useful to many generations of thwarted women. In any case, co-operation as such was unknown to him, unless it coincided with his own wishes. He flatly refused to be pinned down to any commitment or plans. Everything had to happen at the moment he wished it to, as if a spontaneous expression of his mood. My poor mother might be struggling to discover if she should accept or refuse some invitation, decide a menu for the day, or even book reservations for a holiday for which she longed. But his answer was always the same, 'My darling girl, how can you expect me to say, here and now, what I shall feel like, so far ahead?'

So my mother gave up making plans for family holidays and since Nanny May took hers with her family on their farm, my mother, who believed firmly in the benefits of sea air, took me off to Frinton, or Worthing or anywhere with a good beach. Those weeks cannot have been much of a holiday for her, alone with an obstreperous child, given to unpredictable pranks.

There had been that awful never-to-be-forgotten occasion on the beach at Dawlish, when she had become engrossed in *Silas Marner* and was roused from its pages by wild cries from an angry crowd gathered round a rock pool where I stood, a furious four-year-old clutched at and condemned by angry strangers. It seems I had wandered off and, encountering another child about my own age and size, had hurled her head first into one of the many rock pools, from where she was retrieved, soaked, shivering, screaming and bleeding from several nasty cuts. 'Poor little Vera, poor little mite,' moaned her anxious nanny, who was also clearly to blame for inattention to her charge.

My mother was overcome with shame and dragged me away amid hostile murmurs. 'Whatever made you do such a thing?' she kept demanding, to which I would only reply that I did not like little Vera. I was not taken to the beach again, and we returned home almost at once. When this disagreeable incident was reported to my father he said, 'Homicidal instincts – I have them myself sometimes,' adding, 'I wonder if you will ever understand? That child is like me, she doesn't like the human race.'

These remarks were to further exasperate my mother and still rankled, I believe, when she recounted them to me, half a lifetime later. Moreover, disagreeable as they had been, they were presently borne out by further unfortunate incidents which I remember clearly enough and which I enjoyed creating. I had begun to relish naughtiness – bad behaviour for its own sake, with deliberate aggravation brought to a fine art. Eventually, the family doctor was consulted. He prescribed soothing syrups and persuaded my mother that I would soon grow out of my tiresome ways.

☾

Is first hatred remembered as keenly as first love? More so, I believe. First love is like some charming toy we still recall in a rosy haze, but first hatred, once roused, stores itself away; cold poison. It was my father who roused my first, fierce hatred.

The cause was Ermyntrude, the large black and white rabbit who lived among us as one of the family. She was extremely clever and had early established habits of hygiene which doubly endeared her. Two hutches on a balcony were her special territory. One she slept in, the other she reserved as her loo, to which she repaired unfailingly in moments of need. She was, in short, a self-trained, house-trained rabbit. She got on well with all the other animals who came and went about our house, but she clearly preferred human society, sometimes on my mother's lap, or tucked inside my father's coat, as I have described earlier, or she would lollop about the nursery, playing marbles with me, or allowed herself to be wheeled around in the dolls' perambulator. Some of my happiest memories are of festive tea parties where our animals and the toy kind – my mixed-up menagerie – all sat round the table and Joseph, the chameleon in his coat of many colours, strayed about between the plates; Nubia had to be restrained from pouncing – she never really cared for poor turncoat Jos. On these occasions, Ermyntrude was the life and soul of the tea party, her long floppy ears always twitching. She was given a lettuce sandwich and a saucer of milk and when she wanted what Nanny May called 'seconds', she would thump her strong hind legs impatiently. Once, not getting any attention, she made a real rabbit leap and, seizing the milk jug by its spout, was about to jump down to help herself freely when disaster was averted.

Sweet Ermyntrude! She had many accomplishments, and enjoyed scrabbling her paws across the strings of a banjo, or thumping a drum by kicking out with those strong, flat hind legs. She enjoyed showing off and there was always a rapturous audience. One dark day she developed a sudden passion for gnawing at the legs of the furniture. Nothing was sacred: my father's most prized Jacobean chest, my mother's treasured walnut writing desk, the kitchen table, alike were all disfigured – devalued as my father remarked coldly. That damned rabbit! What to do? Every reeking remedy or deterrent was applied: Ermyntrude was smacked and lectured, but just went on gnawing.

At last, my father struck: Ermyntrude must go! Neither my mother's pleadings nor my frantic cries moved him. Though usually rather remote, or indifferent, he now proved implacable. In helpless bewilderment I saw Ermyntrude being stuffed into a basket and taken out of my life for ever. She was given to the neighbours whose garden contained several hutches full of rabbits. 'She'll settle down, she'll have lots of friends here,' said the neighbours, kindly, as my mother's sobs redoubled. A week later we learned that Ermyntrude had remained

*Walter Blanch.*

crouched in a corner and refused to eat and soon was dead. Better so. But now I realised that furniture – objects of value – had counted more than all Ermyntrude's love, companionship and trust and a wave of hatred choked me, blinded me. I attacked my father, raining furious, ineffectual blows, kicking and biting, till I was dragged off and locked up to cool off. Such was my first experience of hatred. Over the years it has not been an emotion I cherished: but I keep a good bit handy, for good causes.

# 3. Treat Outings

FROM THE BEGINNING, I was brought up to the English ritual of The Walk. Rain or shine, Nanny May and I, or any of her successors, set forth in the afternoon, generally heading across Duke's Meadows for Old Chiswick which offered many diversions. The Walk assumed capital status when it was understood that I should choose our destination. Each day some special goal was to be achieved, a point in history or legend as recounted by my father; there were many such and it was in this way that I came, early, to know something of that third Chiswick which stretched between two fabled cardinal points: Strand on the Green and Old Chiswick, with its celebrated Mall.

Devonshire House was the splendid Palladian villa which Lord Burlington, an eighteenth-century aesthete, had created, stone by stone, as an exact replica of the famous Villa Malcontenta, one of Palladio's celebrated palazzos along the Brenta, near Venice. There, among the ornamental gardens, statues and waterways, groves of ilex and cypress, the beautiful Georgiana, Duchess of Devonshire, liked to ruralise. She would dash down from her residence on Piccadilly and give al fresco routs and fêtes to entertain the great figures of her day at her bidding. Princes, statesmen, Fox, the poet Moore, fops, musicians and diplomats all rolled down from London in great swaying coaches. Only seven miles from the turnpike at Hyde Park Corner, they found Arcadia, with Venus presiding.

But when Nanny and I passed by, Devonshire House stood sealed away; the high walls over which only the tips of the cypress could be seen revealed nothing of past glories. A great silence had fallen over the place; there was no sound of revelry by night. It had become a lunatic asylum, where Dr Tuke, the distinguished alienist, lived sequestered beside a few of his special cases. They were said to be a quiet lot. Only the peacocks that strutted the grounds shrieked – a raucous, chilling sound.

Sometimes our Walk followed a lane to the river, past the crouched-down, ancient, whitewashed inn – was it the Burlington Arms? – where it was held the young Shakespeare had sometimes come up river for a day of carousing with cronies, far from the clamour of Deptford. Old Chiswick was full of such legends. Behind the small parish church, shadowed by its yew trees, where the road took a sharp left turn and Chiswick Mall began its splendid sweep, a few rusted, broken-down railings enclosed a lonely, lichen-covered tombstone, lurching forlornly on an odd, pinched little triangle of land edging the river. According to almost illegible wording – a Latin inscription? Some dates? – this was still the only memorial to the greatest of England's eighteenth-century painters: William Hogarth. Why it was there, so curiously placed and dilapidated, I never discovered. But Hogarth was what might be described as an uncomfortable artist – raw and bitter. His tragic, grotesque pictures reflected Georgian London life in all its horror and humour, cruelty and greed, which it had been thought better to forget and was indigestible to the sleek taste of mid-Victorians – or so I imagine. In my childhood I could not see further than the lonely tombstone of a man whose pictures were familiar to me from an old book of engravings over which I loved to pore. I felt sad for the painter of the pictures that enthralled me and so liked to push a bouquet of squashed-up dandelions or wild flowers through the railings, where they lay wilting on the brown earth. Very unhealthy, Nanny thought, but my mother sympathised and said something ought to be done about the neglected headstone. Hogarth and his brown mongrel dog (he has left a portrait of them together) lived near the centre of Old Chiswick Village, where his house stood, a narrow sliver of dun-coloured brick, almost as abandoned as his grave. (On a road map of this area as it is today, which I regard with bewilderment, it seems to be included in the grounds of Chiswick House.) Certainly the house where he lived and died has now been restored and classified a national treasure, but to my mind looks just as forlorn, standing close to a turn in the A4, as cars and airline coaches roar past on their way to Heathrow.

Chiswick Mall offered a less melancholy spectacle for the walker. A line of stately houses of all dimensions and dates stood amid ancient trees, set back from the river by gardens and a narrow road – the Mall – which had to be crossed if a householder wished to reach a little bankside plot giving direct access to the river where a dinghy might be moored alongside, or a table and chairs set out under a parasol. In summer, one of the pleasures of our walk was to catch sight of a flustered parlour maid teetering out from a house bearing a tea-tray loaded with cups and saucers, kettles and cakes. I enjoyed making a sudden run at her if I could. Rarely, all too rarely, for a child's delight, there would be a knock-about spill with the parlour maid in hysterics as she was given notice on the spot; and myself chastised for making trouble.

Many celebrated people had lived along the Mall. Each house had its own tale to tell, of former owners, or lingering ghosts. William Morris, the bearded father-figure among his Pre-Raphaelite flock, was one. I knew about him from the art books and old numbers of *The Studio* which my mother showed me. Here he designed and wove those strange and beautiful fabrics and made furniture, or was busy at his printing press, surrounded by his disciples and full-skirted, halo-haired sitters: all responded to that Mediaeval or Biblical urge which also inspired Rossetti. Here too, a little further along, was the house to which Lady Castlemaine had withdrawn, to weep, when no longer one of King Charles II's fabled favourites, immortalised by Lely's paintbrush. Centuries-old gossip still lingered here, telling how she was consoled by the attentions of a celebrated tightrope walker, known as Jacob, who lived nearby in Hammersmith.

In the sixties a famous thespian family settled in the Mall, the press ever buzzing around, for they were the Redgrave family, en bloc. Michael, as celebrated in theatre as in film, a subtle and perfected actor, beside him his wife Rachel Kempson. I first knew them when they were filming at Elstree, or opening in a new play along Shaftesbury Avenue. Both passed on their fine talents to their children, headed by Vanessa. I came to know them in the 1930s when Komisarjevsky was producing *The Merchant of Venice* at Stratford and I was designing the costumes. We had decided to break away from the classic Venetian clothing and I vaguely remember it all became Spanish, with Rachel in the huge stiff hoop and ruff of a Velázquez lady. But let us return from this wild leap out of sequence to my childhood walks in Old Chiswick.

After a pleasing half mile or so, where several large houses and spreading trees stood, unthreatened by the axe or electric saw, Chiswick Mall became Hammersmith Mall which remained much in the same pattern, except there were fewer gardens as it narrowed towards a celebrated pub called The Dove which stands to this day. Certain Theosophists met and lectured from these large houses, Mrs Besant among them, my mother said, attending the lectures diligently. There were all kinds of creeds or beliefs and forms of worship aired along the riverside, at that time, or so I heard the grown-ups saying to each other, suggesting they might consult the Bishop, whoever he was. To a child's eye, the general overall pattern of life along the two Malls appeared pretty much unchanged. I should remind readers that these Malls are in no way connected to those tawdry shopping centres called Malls which now proliferate about our cities in slavish imitation of America's commercial way of life.

All scraps of marginal history delighted my father and mother, who loved to come on them, often by chance, in musty old volumes from unknown sources, which often proved more reliable than later official volumes. But I knew nothing of all that and just listened and looked as I walked through a part of Chiswick which, at that time, was still curiously time-warped. Every house had a history.

Nanny had special points of interest too. One of these was the Home for Inebriates, a beautiful Georgian house of rosy brick, where Nanny's friend Mr Tug was porter at the gates and always regaled us with an indescribably sweet kind of cream bun. 'Keeps them inside from 'ankering arter the 'ard stuff,' he would say, stuffing a last sticky treat in my pocket.

I longed to meet one of those mysterious-sounding inebriates. 'What are they? How do they look, eat, talk?' I would ask.

'Same as the ones outside. This place ain't a zoo,' Mr Tug would reply.

I remained baffled.

☪

From the beginning my parents were determined that I should be familiar with the finest in art and literature. Thus I was

early acquainted with characters and incidents described by
Dickens, Thackeray, Chaucer, or the unknown authors of the
*Arabian Nights Entertainment*. Defoe's Man Friday jostled in
my mind with the Crusaders, Oliver Twist, a peg-legged John
Silver, or Lancelot. Perhaps I didn't understand any of it, but
like the poetry that was read to me I loved the sound of the
words. Such words!

> 'The Assyrian came down like a wolf on the fold
> and his cohorts were gleaming with purple and
> gold ...'

Then my father might fall silent, savouring the splendour of
such images, or he might cite some softer strain, perhaps one
of Herrick's rustic verses or Marvell's 'green thoughts in a
green shade'. Oddly, Shakespeare had no place in those evening
readings since my parents considered his language – the speech
of his time – too difficult for a small child to follow. They
strongly disapproved of any concessions, such as watered-
down 'Tales From ...' which they thought an insult to both
author and reader, so Shakespearian thunders had to wait.
Curiously, fairy tales too were not on the menu then. It was
only much later that I discovered Hans Andersen or the
Grimm brothers' dark northern Muse.

My mother would read me verses inspired by Mediaeval life
in romantic terms – love and chivalry, the knight and his lady,
Keats's Isabella mourning over the pot of basil containing the
head of her dead lover, or the knight slain in battle, falling
from his charger ... 'Between the saddle and the ground,
Mercy he sought and mercy found ...' Poetry of all kinds was
part of my childhood, long before I could read: intoxicated by
the rhythm, I would intone Macaulay's *Lays of Ancient
Rome* – 'Lars Porsena of Clusium, by the Nine Gods he

swore' – as enthusiastically as lines such as those on Byron's lady who 'walks in beauty like the night'.

Some evenings, all those magical words gave place to the picture-books and paintings that my mother showed me and I enjoyed the colours and shapes and images she revealed to me, sometimes lifting down a picture from where it was hanging for me to look at it closely. Together, she and I pored over a mixed bag, Italian Primitives one night, Tiepolo's carnival scenes the next, Madonnas or martyrs, beside Chardin's quiet interiors, followed by a luscious still-life painted by a Spanish monk. My mother never applied moral strictures to art: if it was beautiful or interesting, it could not be unsuitable for a child. Therefore, Aubrey Beardsley's illustrations in *The Yellow Book* – all decadence, and much admired by her generation – were also part of this raree-show. Contrasts were stimulating to my imagination, she believed, so riotous baroque or austere Egyptian temples were gulped down alike; 'magic casements opening wide'.

I never remember a time when I was not obsessed by a longing to travel, to reach some remote horizon. That nebulous Elsewhere was an ever-present shimmering dream nourished by the rituals of bedtime stories, not always of the most usual kind, but I would have no others. 'I'll sing thee songs of Araby and tales of far Kashmir ...' my father would intone as he settled down to read me something about such characters as Pocahontas, Lalla Rookh, or Lord Byron. These romantic-sounding figures moved across a shadowy background: that 'Abroad' which was already forming in my infant mind. I saw it as a magical state which I would one day attain by the equally magical act of going – of setting out – in short, of travelling.

☪

A cumbersome and rather grand edifice known as a Pollock Theatre was a splendid acquisition for any nursery or, come to that, any home. Its elaborately decorated cardboard structures, all pilasters and cornices, were accompanied by curtains which rose and fell, as good as any theatre in London. There were also a number of paper backcloths, scenes of the countryside and perspectives of city streets. My joy was now unconfined as I scuffled through dozens of brilliantly coloured sheets of paper containing gothic castles, the ogre's lair, a gypsy encampment and some richly upholstered interiors with fringed love seats, palms and a piano. Here numbers of characters disported at my will. They had all arrived in a box massed with separate sheets. Columbine, Jack the giant killer, a pilgrim monk, Salome and Saruddin and such. All you had to do was to cut them out and stick them on to cardboard and then cut round so that you had a large variety of solid actors for your theatre. Trying to make Dick Turpin stick on his famous black mare, Bess, led me a merry dance. There were some mysterious characters among the rest, turbaned and flamboyantly moustached. I thought one particularly intriguing; he was labelled Saladin, but he might just as well have been labelled Shamyl, whose stand against the Tsar had once aroused much interest in England and was later to arouse in me the most violent emotion which led to my researching and writing one of the only books in English about this extraordinary character who held the Tsar's army at bay and abducted two Russian princesses. But I anticipate. It was easier to play Columbine and Desdemona as I made both of them partner the Moor. Once I sent Columbine and Othello off for a trip on a schooner manned by a number of blue-coats all dancing a jig. Mr Pollock did not favour tragedies and almost all his characters were robustly cheerful. I have since wondered what he would have done if confronted with the characters of *Wuthering Heights*, a book which the public still much enjoyed before it became rich material for film versions.

When many years later I called on Mr Pollock to thank him for the many pleasures he had given me, I found him still living at Hoxton behind the same little shop in a dingy little parlour where his two daughters, the Misses Pollock, were still colouring the play sheets with a little kettle wheezing on the hob for tea. This was the first of many visits to this house of delights. I had to be very careful to bring a little trade into my visit and not always be there just to ask questions about the old play sheets. So I found myself buying innumerable packets of long bronze hairpins, or disgusting bundles of liquorice sticks and there were horrible objects called sugar babies which were gelatine, to be sucked; nauseating hours spent relishing his family's memorials of a long-vanished world where famous stars strutted before ha'penny dipped footlights, 'None of them electrics,' said Mr Pollock firmly and his daughters nodded. 'We used to do wig-work on the side,' they told me, 'tricky work it was, with curling irons and ringlets brushed round and round hoop-sticks, before being given a shine with pork fat. Once a sea captain of a whaler brought us some blubber but it was too heavy and smelled something awful.'

'You have to be careful in this business,' their father added, though once he acceded to my pleas for some fine moustachios and a little pot of glue, the whole being designed to give my father a turn when he so mercilessly wakened me at 7 a.m. for school at 9, and the glue stuck firm and very much delayed my departure. How much I relished causing him these annoyances. I was not a loving child and not at all obliging in daily life.

C⋆

I never went to school until I was ten: both kindergarten and nursery school were unknown to me except for one brief moment between Nanny May's leaving and another nanny's arrival. I can vaguely remember an odd establishment kept by two old sisters. We sang nursery rhymes, learned to curtsey and do elementary stitching – darning in particular, with an old stocking stretched tight over a mushroom-shaped piece of wood. Mending and darning were part of life then, before consumer-goods plenty. But that short spell with the Misses Peeke has lingered in my mind for the curious manner in which it linked me with the Crimean War.

The old ladies' father, Sergeant Henry J., had been an orderly attached to one of the field hospitals during that dreadful campaign, or so my mother learned when she asked the origin of the long yellowing strips of linen upon which we children stitched laboriously. Yes, they had been part of a supply of bandages destined to be dispatched to Miss Nightingale's hospital at Scutari. Likewise the oddly-shaped brown woollen hood or cagoule, known as a Balaclava from the battle of that name, was something the soldiers adopted during the appalling cold of a Crimean winter, and it was on the felty surface of this historic object that I was learning to feather-stitch, an accomplishment which has been of little use to me since. But my mother was enchanted by the idea of such a link: she called it 'living history'.

My education, in a strictly scholastic sense, was both fitful and unorthodox. My mother invented an original method of teaching me by rolling history, geography, poetry, music and art into one huge tangled ball which we unravelled strand by strand, era by era. A sequence of English Kings would be identified not only by their likeness, but by some outstanding event or artistic achievement. Thus Henry VIII, as portrayed by Holbein, was associated not only with the Field of the Cloth of Gold, but with a madrigal he had written and which my mother picked out for me on the piano. Nowadays there would be marvellous television documentaries to whet a child's appetite for knowledge; still, my mother's idea of associative learning (rather advanced, in those days) did give me a certain kaleidoscopic awareness of continuity and the essential flavour of each country or century as time passed.

Such lively methods of instruction were furthered by the astute manner in which my parents soon began to combine my first educative outings with their own expeditions about old, old London, of which much then remained. It was important to catch me young, even if I could hardly walk steadily, so, clutching a hand, I would stagger about from, perhaps, the Inns of Court to the Elgin Marbles or Wapping Old Stairs, where a restorative round of winkles were eaten traditionally, though dangerously, being speared on a pin, 'Cockles and Mussels, Alive! Alive O!' – as the song went and soon I was singing it. Sometimes we headed for the Tower, largely for me to feed the ravens (time enough later for the Traitors' Gate), or made a special trip by cab to what was left of China Town in Limehouse.

My mother would buy her tea from no other source than one big trading centre where she could talk tea with the experts. At the centre, or depot, there were still a few ancient pig-tailed figures who smiled toothlessly and waggled a shiny yellow pate as they wrapped up neat little packets of various delicate brews: Lapsang, Lapsang Soo Chow, Orange Pekoe, Bohea, Green Tea or Black which were the same leaf, but treated differently, the ancients explained. In any case, these visits and the rather hushed atmosphere lingered in my mind and I have grown to nurture an almost reverential attitude towards tea-drinking, while I cherish an abhorrence of the teabag, or mug.

How much I enjoyed those outings! The big tea warehouse stood a little way from one of the many wharves where the Clipper ships used to moor and unload their huge cargoes of mysterious-looking leather sacks, brass-bound wooden boxes and painted metal trunks. Big business it may have been, but to me it was pure exoticism – had I known the meaning of the word then. The small grey-painted box-like rooms, 'tea-parlours' said one of the ancients, were where various teas could be sampled and transactions conducted. It was in one of these that we were always received with elegant formality. Low wooden seats ran round the walls, and above, there were dozens of little cupboards which opened to reveal lead-lined tea caddies of precious teas, which I was allowed to sniff. It was better than any of the museums we visited so regularly.

In the corner a small brass kettle steamed, and one of the ancients brewed samples which we sipped from minuscule porcelain bowls. I was always included in this ceremony which was delightfully flattering to my infant ego. A lot of bowing and expressions of rapture were exchanged during these visits and had we worn Mandarin robes it could have been a subject for Chinnery's paint brush.

Then, one day, all was spoiled. Perhaps I had been chattering too much, but I was suddenly presented with a large, illustrated book of Chinese Tortures, in all their grisly detail. It was just the thing to keep a child quiet – children being known to feast on horrors. I can remember turning each page with rapt attention. It was very puzzling. There were men without heads, their heads were on the ground beside them, and there were men with no arms or legs hanging on hooks over a fire. All of a sudden my mother swooped down and tore the book away from me and, shouting angrily, banged it over the shiny yellow head of an ancient. My lovely picture book! I rushed to get it back from the mystified ancient, but it broke apart in my hands, the brilliant coloured pages (lots of red) fluttered moth-like about the little tea-parlour, while I howled with rage and the ancients stood round cackling with unrestrained laughter. Disaster, like pain, is always said to be irresistibly entertaining to the Chinese.

Another of these expeditions, or Treat Outings as they came to be known, was one I particularly enjoyed, for I was by now a little older and more able to walk around without a guiding hand. This particular outing to Covent Garden Market demanded a very early start. Sometimes on a summer morning we would set out about six o'clock, by a local train to Waterloo. The expedition proper always began at Apsley House, No. 1 London, the splendid mansion which had been the Duke of Wellington's London house, at Hyde Park Corner. Here my father always made a ritual bow towards its grim façade, for he admired the Iron Duke and was fond of recalling the great man's opinion that railways – then very new-fangled – would only encourage people to move about unnecessarily. As we went along Piccadilly, beside the fluffy early green of the Park, all was quiet, almost empty at that hour. There was little commerce, and many fine private houses still shuttered. We walked on through a still sleepy Leicester Square, plunging into a twist of little streets surrounding the Market which, as we drew near, seemed to roar and rattle and bang, with raucous cries and the neighing of horses. Then, suddenly, there it was, the Market – with its Piazza, the Opera House and the beautiful honey-coloured stone arcades vibrating in blasts of cabbage, spices and dung.

Sumptuous piles of fruit and vegetables glowed; barrow boys and porters uttering strange cries wove through the jostling shouting crowds carrying towering stacks of baskets on their heads. Spiky tufted pineapples or peaches and bloomy purple grapes were wrapped in pretty pink paper. What were then great novelties, scarlet peppers, or a golden newcomer called grapefruit were exciting to see; but there all was excitement, colour and beauty. The flower stalls seemed overloaded by unnameable hot-house blooms beside the lupins and Sweet Williams I knew from my walks with Nanny May.

At Covent Garden I saw strange-looking straw-hatted and shawled women lurk in the shadows waiting to scrabble for leftover flowers with which to make up the little nosegays or buttonholes they offered passers-by at street corners, or from their perches round the Eros statue at Piccadilly Circus. My father knew many of them by name, from earlier bachelor days, and he would call out, 'Hello! Bessie,' or 'Maudie', or 'Gertie', and seeing me they would shout back, 'That your little nipper?' Something of London's timeless tradition was around us, on those early expeditions. Then my mother might widen further horizons, saying, 'See those little pink roses over there? They come all the way from Damascus and make a most beautiful perfume called Attar of Roses, and their petals make Jam! Rose-leaf Jam! You shall have some, one day,' she promised. And so I did, with my bread and butter nursery supper.

Occasionally my father would strike a darker note and chill me by describing how frightful serpents could lurk in crates coming from tropical shores. Then I would have a sudden vision of a great high-masted barque, the kind I had been shown at the London Docks and all of it connected like pieces of a puzzle: the Piazza, the Docks and that strange dark world from where the serpent came. Abroad! Then my father, at his most impressive, added that if the crate was opened carelessly, terrible things would happen. The serpent, disturbed in its sleep, would rear up swaying and hissing, defying all attempts at capture. Once a big bell was rung and a megaphoned voice gave warning that some particularly dangerous spider had escaped from a box labelled 'Zoo', and was on the loose. So my mother hurried us away, our feet slithering on the wet cobbles and refuse, where at that very moment the spider was probably straying. I longed to linger, for danger was already becoming an irresistible attraction.

Sometimes we went Steeple-chasing, my father's waggish name for expeditions devoted to visiting the lovely old steepled churches of Wren's London, Hawksmoor's city too, where spire upon spire of creamy stone soared above the narrow streets in a beauty that was at once majestic and intimate. These churches have poetic names that recall their history: St Mary-le-Bow, St Bride, St Andrew-by-the-Wardrobe and so on. Eight of the fifty churches built by Sir Christopher Wren were to perish during the Blitz in the Second World War. Some rose again, in part, some remained as ghostly memories, some were recalled only by a plaque; phantoms trapped in the canyons of tower blocks, offices and apartments now considered new chic living.

My father's unfathomable past did not intrigue me in those early days: I just went along with it, delighted with whatever outing he suggested. A rare one, from which my mother held aloof, was when I went with him to visit old ringside friends. He had boxed a lot in his youth, spending much time among the bruisers, though boxing, he took care to insist, was a noble art and not just bashing. Thus, from time to time I would find myself peering through the ropes of a practice ring at some rather rough and ready, but very professional, set-up at Blackfriars when young trainees or 'likely-looking lads' were being put through their paces by old champions turned coach. I loved watching those light tapping, almost dancing steps, the ritual and niceties of an upper cut. 'Well Miss, your Pa 'ad a proper left 'imself,' they said and I glowed, but wondered – how was it that my father, moving so delicately among his treasures, could suddenly seem another person? Could one person become people?

I could not know, then, that all my parents' expeditions were in fact measures of escapism, a brief refuge from an oncoming future of progress and change – all things which they dreaded. Looking back, I realise that lingering for a little while among the traces of another age gave them a feeling that they were still part of that scene – so much more pleasant to them than the present. It was inevitable that I too should become affected with this preference for the past.

My parents were dyed-in-the-wool Dickensians, often launching into long sessions out-quoting each other from those immortal pages. Soon, I too had set up as an infant Dickensian. Even before I could read I used to hang over Cruikshank's marvellous illustrations to Dickens' earliest writings, fascinated by the *Comic Almanack* and *Sketches by Boz*, so that all that teeming caricatural world was forever fixed in my infant mind; an immortal crew of Londoners as the immortal draughtsman has left them for our delectation. Sam Weller, Sergeant Buzz-Fuzz, a drab in The Gin Palace at Seven Dials, or holiday makers on the excursion steamer to Greenwich – 'Villikins and his Dinah', Paterfamilias and his brood – all seemed more real to me than the people around me.

Even today, Cruikshank's London still closes round me. The diverse new population has not banished it. I no longer live in England, but foreign television sometimes gives me snatches of London – a scarlet bus, an incident with the police, royal figures on a balcony, or some huge political demonstration – a field of faces, speckled brown, black, pink, white, light and dark and suddenly among them, a face that Cruikshank drew, a true Cockney face, weasel-sharp or slobber-fat, creased and kind, or cold and closed, but a *Londoner's* face. Then I go back to the years of my childhood when my parents took me about the streets and squares and alleys I liked to re-people with Cruikshank's characters. (No subsequent illustrators ever evoked that magic.) Sometimes I felt they were so near that I would surely come on them round the next corner, lurking along Cheapside, in Threadneedle Street, or anywhere about that great city that still rang to the sound of Bow bells.

Thus, although I was a child rusticating in Chiswick and came to live most of my adult life abroad, I still regard myself as a Londoner; and Chance, that 'sweet chance that led my steps abroad', also led me to live, briefly, in two of London's most legendary places. First in Albany, with its rakish Regency flavour, its long roofed 'cat walk' and top-hatted porters at the gates; later at St Leonard's Terrace, a charming row of small eighteenth-century houses overlooking the green expanses of the Chelsea Pensioners' historic quarters. Here, during the worst years of the Second World War, when every variety of bombs rained down, rents were almost token fees and I was able to lease No. 32, which was to become the setting for an especially romantic part of my life.

But I am skipping ahead chronologically – I must now return to my infant self, standing at a corner of Seven Dials, then not much changed since Dickens and Cruikshank portrayed it. The infant voyeur is getting cold and suddenly wants to go home and find Joseph the chameleon or any other pet and sit by a roaring fire, toasting crumpets, or making 'dripping' toast; particularly Dickensian occupations – pre-radiator delights.

# 4. Magic of Magics: The Traveller

I CANNOT PLACE the precise moment when I became aware of the extraordinary man known to my family as The Traveller. He comes into focus slowly, trailing a shimmer of sparks, like a comet, quickening till I see a face, a yellowish face, and a bald, shaven pate, like one of the Chinamen on the painted tea caddy in the kitchen, though he does not have a pig-tail, as they do, and I am disappointed. This strange figure was a Russian and I have written at length in another book, *Journey into the Mind's Eye*, about the overwhelming effect he was to have on my life. He came and went fleetingly – his sudden arrivals and disappearances had a kind of conjuror's magic about them; now you see him, now you don't. He was unlike anyone I had ever encountered and in my mind's eye he has remained unique.

His impact on our daily life was galvanic. Suddenly everything was different. The hours we kept were designed to suit his erratic timetable. At his request I was allowed to sit up late and have a place beside him at dinner. Even the food we ate changed for he brought with him the most exciting extras like caviar, in large quantities (which he ate with a small spoon), and a variety of tropical fruits then unknown in England. He also brought me the most unlikely objects in place of toys. A *kinjal*, or dagger, from the Caucasus, a little ikon, with its own lampada to hang over my bed, and one Easter, a beautiful little blue enamel Easter Egg – Fabergé, I heard later, but as my mother said, when she appropriated it, really too precious to play with.

He had known my parents long ago, before their marriage, where, or in what circumstances I never discovered as they seldom spoke of old times. His dazzling flow of talk was in easy English, though strongly accented and flavoured by that centrifugally deep tone I came to know was unmistakably Russian. The subjects he touched on ranged widely – wildly even, like the adventures he recounted. Sometimes he worked himself into a state of furious altercation with my father

when international politics were on the boil, at which point my mother made frantic efforts to get him back to stories of his travels. 'Abroad' was her favourite subject, and soon mine too. Poor Mama! She had resigned herself to becoming a stay-at-home, since my father flatly declined to set foot outside England. We never knew why, but I slowly became aware that he too had his own 'Abroad', a state of immobility, which he said allowed his brain to travel for him. No doubt the illusion of exotic distances was strengthened by that intricately carved wooden *moucharabiyeh*, or window screen – from Cairo, he said – which he had placed across the door of his dressing room. My mother's only escape to distant lands was by books, or The Traveller's fabulous talk – his special magic.

For myself it was different. Listening to those tales of the faraway places he had known, the seas he had sailed and journeys on trains such as the Trans-Siberian fired me to make a sudden and violent decision. I too would become a Traveller. Magic of magics! I would reach all the places he described. Nothing was going to stop me. I was not going to get stuck at home.

'Don't put silly ideas into her head,' said my father, when I whined to go on the Trans-Siberian, the legendary train which ran for seven days and nights before grinding to a halt at Vladivostock. The Traveller had told me all about it, '*verst by verst*', inflaming my imagination with accounts of its special characteristics. 'The passengers like to pray as well as look out of the window, or drink tea endlessly,' he said, so a little chapel was attached to the train with a pope, or priest, who rang a bell for mass every now and then. But he didn't add that the train always carried a coffin or two – provision against sudden deaths – natural or unnatural, I wondered, when much later I was preparing to make the journey myself.

I remembered The Traveller had also described certain luxuries reserved for first-class passengers: a piano, and a library – of sorts – though little of what was later called railway-fiction, I imagine. In pre-Revolutionary days, Russians who could read preferred French novels for whiling away time, their own authors being on the sombre side, while for those who could not read there was always someone with a guitar, at which the whole carriage would set up a mournful chant, just as they might sink into one of those timeless states of being, of nothingness, or passivity, so close to the Arabs' fatalism, *Nichevo* or *Mektoub*, being as one. Alphonse de Custine, in his critical account of a journey made through Russia in 1839, remarked on this similarity: 'The Russians,' he wrote, 'were blond Arabs, Orientals, who in their former migrations, lost their road, and whose chiefs, by mistake, led towards the North a people born to live in the sun.' Another observer remarked, 'The contour of their manner is purely Asiatic.'

☪

But I knew nothing about that then – I was simply obsessed by every detail of the legendary train, that one day (Magic of Magics) would transport me to Siberia. I knew exactly what I was going to do when I got there. I wasn't going to get out till I reached the halfway point, at Irkutsk. Then, on the shores of Lake Baikal, I was going to eat a special kind of fish called *omul* and then go far into the impenetrable forests of the Taiga where, perhaps, I'd meet some escaped convicts and help them – how, I had not worked out. 'Some of my family …' said The Traveller, as I rattled on, but my mother said it was romantic rubbish to pretend he was from Siberia as everyone knew he came from Moscow.

'Alas! I am only a Muscovite,' he told me apologetically. I think he must have been amused by the place Siberia occupied in my infant mind. 'There are other places just as far away, with other big trains that go just as slow,' he teased. 'Why not go somewhere warmer? Try Lake Van, where there are those white cats that swim like eels. I was there myself not long ago,' he said and I believed him, as I always did. His comings and goings were all part of the mystery with which he surrounded himself. Soon after, he disappeared and was gone for a long while. But I had been fired. All that counted now was to become a great traveller as soon as possible, and to discover 'Abroad', which also contained that mythical Siberia.

I made a start by lugging a heavy atlas to the nursery where I could mark out future journeys undisturbed. The yellowing pages had coloured decorations of tribes and palm trees, spouting whales and pagodas. The large, rather empty space next to Russia was marked Siberia and was illustrated by a huge white bear fighting a man who held a knife and I felt worried about the bear. I had heard that 'Abroad' people were often very unkind to animals.

☪

A small bicycle, given me on my sixth birthday, got me going. Pedalling furiously along a quiet lane behind our house I was making for the Hindu Kush, or perhaps the Hoggar (neither ideal for biking), or any other destination I fancied that afternoon. Admittedly my bike was no ordinary machine. It had a way of tackling enormous distances – to the far side of Asia even – so long as I was back in time for tea.

This was sometimes difficult, for once in the saddle, mountains and forests sped past, mighty rivers were bridged miraculously, and the towers of secret cities rose, mirage-like, as I made for some destination which the old atlas had revealed. As I learned to disentangle the alphabet, my imagination was further inflamed by the strange-sounding place-names spelled out in it – some more alluring than others – and I rolled them over my tongue voluptuously. Shenandoah, Shiraz, Shirvan, Rocamadur, Orontes, Laredo, Timbuctu: beautiful sounds that became a sort of lullaby I intoned each night in bed. Some names were strangely forbidding – the Taklamakan desert, for example, had a harsh sound and was also very difficult to pronounce. Yet even when I had it pat, I never tried to reach its sandy wastes, which was odd, because the Sahara was just as sandy but seemed more inviting, becoming an almost everyday outing, like Nizhny Novgorod. Was I unconsciously recalling some fearsome incident The Traveller had told of the Taklamakan? I little knew then that one day I would straggle along the outer edge of that awesome desert, frozen and exhausted, awaiting the anti-climax of the local bus. The Taklamakan remains for me part of those magical realms, reached by the equally magical act of setting out – in short of travelling.

In all my sorties about Russia or elsewhere, I never attempted Siberia: that was being kept sacred for the journey on the Trans-Siberian. I knew it would happen, one day. Meanwhile with that astonishing bike I was discovering 'Abroad', a dimension peppered chiefly with Russian place-names because The Traveller had recounted something about them or been there himself – Harbin, Yaroslav, Semipalatinsk. In my own eyes I too had become a Traveller.

'And where did you go today?' my mother would ask, mindful of the bike's magic potential. But I did not always tell and often took care to dissimulate some precise destinations. One had to be careful with grown-ups.

C\*

A year or so on, when the allurements of the magic bike faded, I transferred my fervours to other, scarcely less remarkable journeys beside some of the most outstanding figures of travel literature. I had now become an armchair traveller.

I was in China, following Marco Polo's path. I panted after Richard Burton when he made his astonishing desert pilgrimage to Mecca, circling the Kaaba seven times and ritualistically sipping at the Holy Spring of Zem-Zem. I tagged along behind the young Lord Byron when he called on Ali Pasha the Terrible in his Albanian lair. And then, reaching for yet another horizon (octavo, bound in calf) I was soon in Peru among those asymmetrically veiled ladies of Lima, the 'Cyclop-eyed Tapadas' as Charles Darwin described them in his *Diary of the Voyage of the H.M.S. Beagle*. When I confided some of these new expeditions to The Traveller he was all admiration and suggested I should read about Persia, the 'Turquoise Kingdom', he called it, which was ravishing with its azure domes and minarets. He recommended an account made by Sir Dodmare Cotton, Queen Elizabeth I's envoy to Shah Abbas, 'the Great Sophy, Allah's Shadow on Earth' whose splendours were said to rival those of the Turkish Sultan. He added that the public and private lives and habits of oriental potentates made remarkable reading. 'That account of . . .'

'Please!' said my mother in her most *pas devant* voice. 'Please, Trav'la!' – so I never knew what outrageous snippet of Central Asian gossip was lost to me. She always called him Trav'la, in a curious way, as if it meant something special to them, but to my father and myself he was simply 'The Traveller'. His own name was far too difficult to pronounce, he said. He enjoyed mystery for mystery's sake and once, many years later, cut short any further questioning on the subject by producing three – or was it four? – different passports, all very official-looking, in different shapes and coloured paper, all covered in stamps; one was in Russian, of course, and one I recognised as in an Arabic script, but I was too astonished to do more than gape. He laughed and threw them back into a pouch, saying 'That'll teach you not to pry, Miss.'

If he went under many names, as perhaps he did, he gave me many too, all sorts of odd-sounding ones, 'Pussitchka' was a favourite. 'Changeling' derived from my parents' frequent remarks on how many changes my unexpected arrival had made in their lives. But to The Traveller, I was a true changeling, a Russian *dousha*, or soul, mysteriously interposed in an English nursery.

# 5. Piggy

RECALLING THOSE ENTIRELY carefree years before I was ten and schooling proper took over, I remember lovingly the one really close friendship I ever made with another child of my own age; otherwise it was adults or animals. 'Piggy' entered my life when we were about six and we became inseparable, remaining deeply attached long after we were grown up and life had separated us. She was almost as much an only child as myself. Her brother, Paul, was nine years older and seldom seen, being at the Royal Naval College at Dartmouth, training to enter the Navy.

An old snapshot shows Piggy and me in identical pinafores and sun-hats. I am clasping a struggling hen and Piggy holds a more placid duck. Why she was called Piggy remains a mystery, for she was neither dirty, nor fat, nor greedy as pigs are erroneously said to be. For her, I let down all the guards I put up in my encounters with other children: in winter we went to the same dancing classes, *one, two, three, hop!* wearing identical pleated kilts, white socks and bronze slippers, tied with cross-over elastic. In summer we learned to swim in the river or at the local open-air swimming baths – they were not called pools then, nor were they yet much frequented.

The house where Piggy lived with her father and mother and a Great Dane called Olive, or Ollie, was close to ours, but with the addition of a big rambling garden, ennobled by two

venerable Spanish chestnut trees, said to have been part of an
avenue linking a royal hunting lodge to a royal estate called
Fauconberg, acquired by Oliver Cromwell's daughter. Old
Chiswick was full of such historical links. The garden where
Piggy and I spent so many happy hours was a large spread;
fruit trees, vegetables and flowers flourished there, and chick-
ens and ducks wandered freely as we children did, grubbing
about in all weathers. Although within suburban confines,
living seemed more open, more rustic there and soon it
became my second home where I spent most of my days; my
absence from home ungrudged by my mother who understood
my need for Piggy's companionship and, perhaps, a less rar-
efied atmosphere.

Piggy's family came from Lincolnshire and they kept a cer-
tain rural air about them; a certain careless freedom in the way
they lived and carried themselves and spoke, though there was
no regional accent to detect, only a faint echo of their fore-
bears. They were steeped in country lore, ancient superstitions
and traditions: when to sow and where to prune, the signifi-
cance of a waxing or waning moon, or how the tides flowed.
'Gulls flying upstream this evening,' they might remark,
adding, 'that'll mean a tidy-size storm before midnight.' Next
day after the predicted storm had raged, they would go down
to the river at low tide, where the muddy shore was piled with
driftwood, wrack and quite large logs, which they tied
methodically into bundles and lugged home to dry out for fire-
wood.

They were perfectly indifferent to, or unaware of, the neigh-
bours' disgust when they set out along the quiet roads, armed
with dustpans and long-handled brooms, to scoop up the
gleaming pats of fresh dung dropped by the horses which still
pulled tradesmen's carts going on their house-to-house rounds.
'Fine stuff, this!' they would say, spreading the manure lavishly

about the vegetable garden, where it reeked, though quite pleasantly.

Unlike most country folk, they enjoyed eating out of doors. And how much I too enjoyed those Sunday night thrown-together garden feasts, picking chestnuts out of the embers of a smouldering fire, chomping at a bacon sandwich, or one made of ducks' eggs and fresh-picked dandelion leaves, while Piggy's father told us stories of his Lincolnshire childhood. Generally, he remained a rather remote figure, though it was a different remoteness to that of my father – a more humanised

version perhaps, without that Olympian distance maintained by mine. Piggy's father left early each morning for some job in the City and returned late, usually foul-mouthing over inter-office contretemps, but no one paid any attention. I was aware he did not quite fit in and took refuge in carpentry, though he never got any praise, or even thanks, for the neatly made hen-houses, garden furniture and fences he produced from a small shed stocked with hammers, saws and nails. As a place of refuge, I think it corresponded to my father's dressing room.

Only my mother seemed to be interested and admired his handiwork. She herself cherished secret longings to do like-wise. I remember her fiddling with bits of bricolage. She is sitting at the nursery table, beside her a box labelled 'Carpenter's Kit' and a neat row of miniature tools, a pot of glue balanced on her lap. I see again her long, delicate fingers moving surely, chiselling, joining and generally performing miraculous repairs. She smiles as she works; she is happy. For the moment she has forgotten about household problems, me, or even my father. I am watching her, trying to help, handing her nails, or dropping them so that soon she suggests I go off and play with Piggy, which I have secretly been longing to do.

Beyond the garden where we played, a sandy lane or track petered out into tangles of cow parsley, and elder bushes became flowering trees. Brambles and nettles, a rather painful path, ended in some abandoned gravel-pits, where we clambered and slid rapturously in the gritty sand which to us seemed to sparkle like gold, part of an extra-terrestrial magic with which we invested this wasteland, our kingdom – ours alone – for no one else ever went there.

Occasionally a sudden landslide of gravel would mark the passing of a water rat, who regarded us with profound indif-ference; or a menacing kind of giant seagull, from down-river, round the estuary, would wheel screeching overhead, and our birds, the ones we knew, took refuge in the bushes until the intruder left.

Our near-country life was not something we shared with other Chiswick children who mostly went for tidy walks, or played neatly, and in any case would have been scared out of their nice, clean pinafores by our tumble-di-dee ways. We wandered about alone, free as air, with or without Ollie, and no sinister figure ever approached us. I don't recall our parents showing any particular concern, or warning us of dangerous encounters. In general, people enjoyed a safety now vanished. And we were certainly a pair of innocents, anticipating no evil, nor, fortunately, encountering any.

As time passed there were other dangers which we positively craved. Paddling almost waist-high in the muddy, weedy river's edge, seeing how long we could resist the tides which could sweep strong, was a foolhardy pastime. Once we watched a man struggling to push a woman into the water on the other shore; another time we watched a body float past, quite close, but going fast. We watched dumbly – what could we have done? But we took care not speak of it, at home. If they, the grown-ups, saw all we saw between human and animal life along the, then, deserted shores we should have been forbidden to go there any more.

Sometimes we succeeded in persuading the grown-ups to take us upstream, some miles towards Staines, which appeared to be an open empty countryside threaded by little backwaters. One of these was dominated by a wonderful weir: wonderful to us anyway, as we jumped off it shrieking, to be whirled away on a swirling torrent of water as it rushed towards wider reaches. Whole days were spent plunging down, to be twirled round by the current until we could scramble up a bank and race back and begin all over again.

C*

With what loving forbearance our mothers took it in turns to escort us to other varied delights – the Christmas Panto, Christmas shopping, special children's concerts and shows. They were unflagging on our behalf and we took it all for granted, in the ruthlessly self-centred way of children everywhere.

The bizarre spectacle of Madame Tussaud's waxworks and the celebrated Chamber of Horrors were our special delight. But, best of all, at that time there was a collection of even more remarkable exhibits stemming directly from the Guillotine. As a young woman, Madame Tussaud was celebrated in Paris for her wax models, a kind of portraiture in which she specialised. Her clients were among the most celebrated Parisians of the day and she had been summoned to Versailles to model Queen Marie Antoinette's head and those of the royal family. When the 1789 Revolution hurled France into fury and bloodshed and the Guillotine was busy at work in the Place Vendôme, a Revolutionary Committee engaged Madame Tussaud to make models of its more outstanding victims. There was no way she could refuse. Imagine with what terror and horror she must have stood in her studio, as sacks and baskets of still bleeding heads were brought straight from the Guillotine – the Queen, Madame de Lamballe, Marat and many others, were the terrible trophies some of which by unknown means she kept, and was able to take with her when she fled to England, ultimately to include them in a sort of extra-horrific, grisly Chamber of Horrors. They could be seen, but separately, a rare show which remained a minor, or neglected part of the exhibition. They could hardly be described as an attraction, but they were of passionate interest to those of a historic turn like my parents and myself. There they were: those pale, dead faces, calm or grimacing, just as they were when the blade fell. Madame Tussaud's had a collection of further historic treasures, including one of Napoleon's beds and a carriage if I remember rightly. Alas, all was lost in the fifties in a fire which destroyed much of the famous exhibition. Our horrors were limited, rationed one might say, depending on a special trip to London.

In winter, during the long, dark evenings that set in around three o'clock, we spent more time indoors at home, sampling simple indoor diversions; idiotic card games like the largely forgotten Happy Families were a never-failing joy. We adored those grotesquely presented caricatures, Mr Bung the Brewer, who could be bartered for Miss Bones, the Butcher's daughter, or Master Bones, his saucy son. There were many other childish card games, but I was never any good at cards. Even Beggar My Neighbour seemed too complicated and I was far too slow at Snap, so we moved on, modelling in plasticine, making toffee, or gorging ourselves on 'beef dripping' toast made at the fireside. As a special treat we were allowed a large, iron-bound box of ancient playthings which had been discovered by my father in some antique dealer's cellar. This box had a mysterious quality, like its contents: a painted cup and ball, a baby's silver-gilt rattle with a coral handle, too babyish for us, but its tinkle fascinated the cats. Then there were delicate lengths of crimson silk thread for the intricacies of Cat's Cradle, long rolls of black paper with miniature scissors attached, for cut-out silhouettes, and an only half-filled scrapbook contained beautiful engravings of rustic scenes, sheep penned under a tree, a blackbird on a bough or an ox drinking from a stream – they were Bewick prints had we known it, rare treasures. The scrapbook was inscribed, 'To Sophia St Leger, from her affectionate Governess Honoria Penifold.'

I believe my mother enjoyed those winter evenings even

more than we did. Her long supple fingers had always mod-
elled marvellous plasticine monsters for me, or, with the aid of
a candle, cast shadows on the wall: a church and its steeple, a
dog's head, which became a wolf when its jaws snapped
angrily. Sometimes she played the piano for us to sing 'The
Lincolnshire Poacher', carols and other artless ditties. I can
still catch snatches of the music, but the words are gone.

Just as Piggy's home had come to represent a second home
to me, so her mother came to seem my second mother and I
loved her dearly and cherish her memory still. I see her wan-
dering about the garden, a cigarette dangling from an
earth-stained hand. She never aspired to my mother's quiet
grace, but she had a certain style, in spite of shabby clothes, for
they were then facing hard times (ours were yet to come); in
spite of stockings that were forever wrinkling untidily, and
skirts that dragged and buttons that hung on a thread – 'Blast
it! Why can't one sew and read at the same time,' she would
say, reaching for a book and forgetting the button. She over-
came clumsy shoes and the odd sort of bob she had contrived
by hacking her hair with nail-scissors, at a time when short
hair was not worn. She looked exactly what she was – a
cultivated, country gentlewoman who also possessed the inde-
finable assurance of a woman of the world. This quality had
nothing to do with what is known as a 'worldly' woman, the
kind Somerset Maugham has so perfectly described.

Although essentially very different women, our two moth-
ers enjoyed a warm friendship, though as far as I can
remember, our fathers remained on a more aloof footing. But
at the time of which I write our parents were, to us, just famil-
iar figures, part of home, but not yet the separate beings they
later became – as The Traveller had been, for me, from the
start.

# 6. An Edwardian Child's London

TIME WAS GOING BY and those early expeditions to museums or about old London were widening in scope. My mother and father wanted me to see as many fine plays and great performers as possible, and I remember a few years on, during the First World War, catching rather stilted 'Charity' appearances of both Ellen Terry and Sarah Bernhardt whose throbbing histrionics I found embarrassing beside Ellen Terry's simpler charms. I had not yet reached sufficient sophistication to enjoy 'ham' as such; nor could I comprehend overweight Isadora Duncan's agonised writhings said to represent the sufferings of Poland, or Russia, or other persecuted peoples.

At home, great comics, the gods of the music halls, were considered as seriously as any other internationally fabled artiste: George Robey, Marie Lloyd, Nellie Wallace, Little Tich and others, whose patter and pauses my father used to describe as 'rather near the bone', were all familiar to me, but I missed Dan Leno and many giants of those old music halls so dear to him. Still, the immortal joys of the Pantomime, with all its roots in the *commedia dell'arte* (as if we cared!), presented themselves every Christmas; with its inexplicable idiosyncrasies of Principal Boys acted by buxom girls, the awful Widow Twanky played by a man, and Principal Girls ...

My father had been an ardent theatre-goer in his youth, often playing hookey from school to get a place in the gallery at the Lyceum. Sometimes he would indulge us with imitations (apparently lifelike) of Irving in *The Bells*, with that strange dragging step and curious phrasing. I even believed he had seen Kean: Edmund Kean the thunderous tragic actor no less. But Kean died in 1833 and although my father's date of birth occasionally reached back into some remote era he fancied for the moment, he might as well have claimed to have seen Burbage at the Globe. He was a man who lived in retreat and very much in the past, and perhaps such memories or visions derived from the evocation of older persons upon whose words he hung, as I came to do myself, later on.

☪

Those early years with Piggy slid by happily. There was only one flaw in our friendship: I could not interest her in either the idea of travelling, or the charm of The Traveller, whom she occasionally encountered on one of his rare visits. She said she never wanted to leave the lovely garden which she and her mother were creating. Moreover, she found him ugly!

*Ugly?* But that strange shaven head appalled her! She preferred the tidily brushed heads of the midshipmen whom her brother brought home with him from Dartmouth from time to time and we were packed off with them to watch some International rugger match at Twickenham, a dreadful ordeal for us for we were not interested in rugger, nor yet in boys.

After a while, our reading became a little lopsided. When I set out for the limitless distances of Russian literature, Piggy did not follow me for she became bogged down by the names, finding them difficult to remember and impossible to pronounce. But then she did not have a Traveller to spur her on, to edge her towards Belkin's Tales, or Lermontov's Caucasus. By the time my infatuation with everything Russian had led me even further into the Slav maze, she was immersed in

Dickens, or Kipling where we could meet again at Simla, or 'ford o' Kabul river ...'

Between us we had amassed a long line of heroines with whom to identify. *La Princesse de Clèves* and *Clarissa* had kept us in ferment, until one day we found ourselves drenched, drowned even, by the emotional torrents of *Wuthering Heights* and an overpowering hero: Heathcliff, the darkling demon-lover to put all other pretenders to the hero role out of business – even Prince Andrei. And let there be no more talk of Mr Darcy, who was the beau ideal of some girls we met at our dancing classes.

☪

I must have been edging nine when it was decided I was becoming too obsessed with Russian fantasies. My mother's educational efforts had stopped short at arithmetic and, her French being rather basic, a French governess was engaged. My bookworm hours were curtailed, as were the hours spent with Piggy, since we were in a state of intoxication every time either of us discovered some new horizon of print.

Mlle Ernestine was a dim figure, not young, not really old, not really ugly, yet hardly attractive. We learned that she had been orphaned very young, brought up in a convent, and educated by the nuns. But she was not forthcoming and we knew nothing more of her life or opinions. Soon it was apparent that she was just about as foxed as my mother when it came to multiple fractions, or even long division. So my mother decided it was really far more important for me to speak French fluently. Grammar in the morning and conversational French in the afternoon was the new programme: Mademoiselle and I were to set out every afternoon for long, health-giving walks, where, it was understood, we were to speak nothing but French –

'Conversational' French, my mother insisted, as if she feared Mademoiselle – a Papist – might try religious instruction. The trouble was, we had absolutely nothing to say to each other, after the weather, which had already given Mademoiselle a streaming cold, so we plodded on like funeral mutes. One particularly disagreeable day of cutting east wind, she suddenly broke out, 'Conversational French? *Une conversation dehors, dans la rue? La conversation est pour le salon!*' as she hissed and stomped ahead, bent against the icy blast. I did not know, then, that sex, money or politics are the three topics that will always loosen French tongues in whatever setting.

But one day, one wonderful decisive day, all was changed. We had been walking along Hammersmith Mall and taken a turning in from the river, to find ourselves in an unknown, rather slummy area of small streets. At the end of one stood a small sugar-cake-like building, all curlicue trimmings, iced over with whitewash. It was a cinema. There was no doubt this was the real thing. A large poster outside read: 'CAULDRON OF LOVE. NOW SHOWING. MATINÉES HALF-PRICE.'

As if gripped by some elemental force, we stood there, staring, for how long I have no idea. Not a word was spoken, in either French or English, but suddenly, in a sort of bewildered rush of spinning senses and darkness, I found myself seated beside Mademoiselle in a 'tip-up ninepenny'. I had never been to the cinema before: I suppose my parents thought my outings to the theatre were enough, at that time. Fascinated, I watched a large lady in evening dress who appeared to be angry with a man dressed as a cowboy. They opened and shut their mouths like fishes in a tank, for not a sound was to be heard. But a minute later a ribbon of print ran across the screen saying, 'Velma will not go to Burt's ranch.' This was my first film, black and white and silent, but I was hooked for life.

All the way home, Mademoiselle and I discussed this turgid drama in some sort of mixed-up gab. To hell with French Conversation! I now discovered that Mademoiselle knew all about the cinema and had seen a great many films, though not at the convent. On reaching home, by some tacit agreement we did not mention the agreeable manner in which we had passed the afternoon. But with what duplicity we now set out every day at two o'clock (the picture showed at three) for our tonic conversational walk, calling '*Au revoir!*' or '*A bientôt!*' reassuringly, as we left on our way to perdition; for such our goal must have appeared to my convent-bred governess, responsible for both her own soul and mine.

From those ninepenny tip-ups we saw many famous figures of the silent screen. Some already out of fashion, become back numbers, like Theda Bara, Pauline Frederick or William S. Hart, or another cowboy figure with his horse, Trigger, was it? Lassie was yet to be. There were deathless comics too – swivel-eyed Ben Turpin and Charlie himself – but we preferred heavily emotional dramas. We had no technical knowledge of the medium and were quite unaware that much of the stuff we saw had been made in a day, out of doors, with an improvised plot and dialogue and shot with a primitive crank-handled movie camera. Those are the sort of films that have come to be shown at *Cinémathèques* where the intelligentsia discuss them reverentially.

It was all magic to us and has remained magic to me, even though sometimes I confuse films I saw then with those I saw yesterday on the 'box' or at a special revival. Great directors, unforgettable faces and haunting scenes press round. John Ford, Carl Dreyer, Visconti, Garbo, Mosjoukine, Jacques Tati. Now Mae Marsh or Lillian Gish is struggling across the ice (directed by D. W. Griffith), or better still a stagecoach is plunging hell-for-leather across a stark scrubland. Is it the

Great Plains or Death Valley? No matter, it is the classic land-scape of a Western, blood and bones of the films I first saw then, and would still queue to see, as they are rarities now.

Sometimes I still manage to dream my way back to a ninepenny tip-up beside Mademoiselle, and watch a distant line of horsemen coming closer, closer, till I see them clearly – Apaches? Cherokees? They are in full war-paint with tower-ing feathered headdresses and I seem to hear those terrifying, yelping war cries and the angry beat of their drums (though I am cheating now, for sound only came twenty years later). For Mademoiselle and me, all was silent, a terrible silence, as the Indians streamed towards Dead Man's Gulch, where our hero stood, Colt in hand. He was going to die fighting, of course. But stop! The Indians are wheeling round! They are making straight for us! For Mademoiselle and ME! Clutching each other, eyes shut, we await the scalping knife.

That's cinema; that's 'going to the pictures'.

The cinema! How I loved it, how I love it still. How could I have imagined, then, that nearly forty years ahead I should live in Hollywood, come to know all the stars and directors and eventually, like a homing bird, work at MGM Studios, with the famous director George Cukor, on the only Western he ever made, *Heller in Pink Tights* (the tights worn by Sophia Loren), but that's another story.

☪

For most children, their tenth birthday – a whole decade of living – is an occasion to celebrate, though for me its approach only spelled gloom and apprehension. Long before I reached that fatal milestone I knew it meant being sent to one of those big, new public schools for girls which were springing up everywhere; a hideous prospect, since I had never been to any kind of school after the barely remembered weeks chez the Misses Peeke.

It was not unusual at that time for girls to be educated at home, by a governess or tutors. What was surprising was my mother's decision to supplant them. I do not know at what precise date school became compulsory for girls, but the rather stately phrase 'Educated at Home' still satisfied the Board of Education. I don't recall any official opposition to my mother going it alone.

I can still see us, she and me, seated at the nursery table, in the nursery-become-schoolroom. The table is piled with books and papers, exercise books, dictionaries, maps and even astronomic charts, and I can recall the delightfully imaginative way she approached the various subjects – maths apart, for that foxed both of us. I remember how odd, but thorough, my education was, and how it stood me in good stead when at last I found myself in the cold, competitive classrooms of St Paul's.

Piggy, or rather her parents, had stolen a march on mine, for she was already installed there, a term ahead of me, though with less anguish as she had been, spasmodically, to several local nursery schools before we settled into our carefree alliance. Although her accounts of school life were not enthusiastic, they jolted my parents into action. As I have remarked earlier, they lived in a curiously remote or withdrawn way; they had achieved an indolent state, avoiding anything so positive as making decisions. As a baby I had not disturbed my parents unduly, Nanny May took care of that, and as a prattling little creature I believe they had found me entertaining, but there was no denying the fact that I kept on changing, becoming at last an individual being, representing undreamed-of complications which could no longer be shelved. It became essential that I should be sent to a really good school and I needed to mingle with other girls of my own age. So my parents began belated but feverish efforts to get me enrolled at St Paul's and were profoundly agitated on discovering they must act at once, there being few vacancies left. A bewildering number of official documents had to be presented, innumerable questionnaires filled in and an alarming list of regulation clothing obtained from a specified outfitter in a remote area of London. My father, as usual, had stepped aside from the fray and was unmoved in his dressing room, while my mother paled as she enumerated the items.

'Name tapes – what on earth are name tapes?' she demanded. 'Is all this really necessary in order to be educated?' She spoke in a tone I came to know well, later, when she read my end of term reports, or anything connected with my schooling, to which, oddly, she attached an almost disproportionate importance, as if Holy Writ.

I was not the only problem confronting my father and mother during those soft spring days of 1914. The cloud 'no bigger than a man's hand' was already sighted, by a few. A strange unease, an unspoken tension was spreading across Europe; sinister speculations caused the stock market to quiver uncomfortably. Germany was adopting a most extraordinarily overbearing tone, said my father, reading his evening paper (of a bright yellow colour, I remember) as he drank his whiskey and soda and my mother remarked that Trav'la had always said Germans were the most tiresome people in the world.

Was it at this point, I wonder, that my ostrich parents decided to find some sandy shore in which to bury their heads? Perhaps all those problems – me, my schooling and the appalling possibility of a war – would sort themselves out and go away, if left alone. They had always spoken of Cornwall with a sort of deep, mysterious affection tinged with sadness, or regret. Why had they never thought of settling there, of abandoning themselves to its seductions? But, like Oblomov, the prototype of Russian inertia, they had sunk back on the sofa of immobility.

Now, abruptly, all was changed. My mother announced that we were going to spend the whole month of June in Cornwall. We? Nothing made my father budge from London. Yet he had been persuaded to join us and she had leased a cottage near Bude, on that wonderful wild coast where the seals played and barked and dived. 'This is to be a special birthday present for you – a sort of Treat Outing to celebrate your tenth birthday,' she said, beaming at the prospect of Cornwall, waiting there like some kind of escape hatch from any further problems.

# 7. Cornwall

WE SET OUT FOR Cornwall on June 1st in a horse-drawn cab known as a growler, a kind still much in use about the streets. Motor cars were mostly for the rich, or certain business firms, delivery vans or go-ahead doctors. The few hard-to-come-by taxis were often private cars converted for that purpose and generally unsuited to luggage, of which we had a great deal: my mother's round hat box, her dressing case, my father's book box, a mysterious old-fashioned object called a Gladstone bag, labelled 'Medicine', as well as a couple of small trunks, all of which were piled on to the roof of the cab. No one thought of travelling light. There was world enough and time to travel heavy – and comfortably. At Paddington, ranks of porters rushed about trundling trucks or with loads slung over one shoulder, as our porter was doing. The Cornish Express was awaiting us on platform 2, he said. 'Stow them small bits on the rack, shall I, guv?' enquired this amiable man, before consigning all the rest to the luggage van and touching his cap politely when tipped. Porters, or their absence, were not a problem.

I had never been to a big station before, either as a passenger or to greet or speed a guest. We were not guest-minded. Therefore, I was all agog to see the big steam engine at close quarters and rushed along the platform deaf to my mother's entreaties to return at once.

It stood there in all its majesty, steaming and hissing and

issuing self-important little puffs of smoke. I saw it as some huge mythical beast, like the massive horses ridden by the Bogatyri, giant heroes of Russian legend. I longed to reach up and stroke its fuming flank, but at that moment my father stormed up and dragged me back to our compartment. It was from that first moment of recognition that my abiding love, I might say *tendresse*, for steam engines took root. A surge of love and pride overcame me as I hung out of the window, trying to catch a glimpse of the great monster as it roared ahead. At that moment I was unfaithful to my first, hearsay love, the Trans-Siberian.

It was a lovely journey, that first one – a sort of prelude, or dress rehearsal, for the ultimate Siberian dream. There was to be no rushing to the refreshment room during long stops, no craning from windows for station snacks; my mother had everything organised in our compartment. A potent whiff of methylated spirits rises round me as I write and I see her fiddling with a small kettle and a spirit lamp which flares up dangerously. There is a picnic basket beside her and my father is methodically undoing all the neatly wrapped sandwiches until he finds the kind he prefers. Ham, tongue, egg, cucumber, sardines, honey, 'Ah! Here we are: game pâté,' and he settles to it. My mother tells me to wrap everything up again, 'Just as they were,' she adds, eyeing my father coldly, for she had spent a long time, earlier, making up the packets. But the atmosphere does not cloud over, all three of us are enjoying my birthday treat mile by mile, hour by hour, with our arrival on Cornish soil as its joyous climax.

☾

At Bude, a station wagon rumbled us over the fields broken up by low stone walls, clumps of gorse and stunted, or rather, thwarted small trees, all bent one way against their will by the fearful gales that hurl themselves and giant sprays of sea water across this open countryside. A jagged coastline is broken by headlands which jut out far into the sea swirling angrily below, where enormous seagulls circle and there are seals to be glimpsed flopping about languorously. Such was the Cornwall I now discovered, the North Cornwall my parents loved and had often described to me. It had little to do with the almost tropical charm of St Ives and the south coast, though I came to love that too. But nothing had prepared me for the over-powering emotion I now felt as I gazed around me. Here was wilderness, with an indefinable sense of something hidden; of danger. Did it come from the sinister, silent countryside, towards Bodmin Moor, or the cruel coastline below, with its legends of smugglers, wrecks, and wreckers? But it was every-thing I wanted. In all my life of travel, nowhere else, save Afghanistan, has ever aroused the same profound sense of affiliation, of longing, and belonging.

The cottage my mother had leased was one of two, standing side by side, once used by the coastguards; its thick white-washed stone walls and very small windows imparted an air of snugness, which was reassuring in so bleak a setting. 'Nothing out there till you gets to America,' our driver remarked, indicating a dramatic sweep of Atlantic waters lash-ing against the cliffs below. At this point a curious apparition emerged from the next-door cottage. 'Here's Mrs Penrudock who'll look after you,' our driver continued, as he unloaded our luggage. Her appearance was so strange, so witch-like, that I instantly fancied her brewing spells and stirring caul-drons full of mischief. At first sight she was not prepossessing, being bent and gnarled with a large beaky nose which shel-tered a prickly line of grizzled moustache. But when she smiled, as she did, while curtseying crookedly to my mother, no fangs were revealed, just gums, accompanied by a cackle of jolly laughter. In short, she was a most delightful person and in no time at all had provided Cornish pasties and sloe gin. 'Just the ticket. You won't go wrong with Mrs Penrudock, she's a proper mother to her foreigners,' said our driver, well into his fourth pasty, and I remembered my parents telling me how the Cornish people regarded anyone coming from else-where as being a foreigner. Likewise any Cornish person crossing the boundary river Tamar was said to have 'gone to England' and, returning, was 'back from Abroad'.

Mrs Penrudock did not belie the driver's introduction and we spent some happy days racketing about the countryside in a pony-trap provided by her son-in-law, a nearby farmer. Moreover, learning from my mother that my birthday on the 6th demanded a really splendid cake, she announced she would do better – she would provide a real Cornish treat called Thunder and Lightning. 'Oh, far too rich,' said my mother who recalled this speciality with a certain reserve. But Mrs Penrudock removed herself quickly, thus avoiding any discussion.

On my birthday morning, while I was opening presents, a slight blight was cast by a handsome pen and pencil box intended for schooldays ahead – a nasty reminder. It was only put out of mind when, as if by Magic, the sort of Magic in which The Traveller had encouraged me to believe, a red-faced boy on a bicycle panted up from the Post Office with a telegram announcing The Traveller would be joining us for a few days. Was such bliss possible?

'How on earth did he know we were here?' said my father, who had not quite gauged the power of Magic. 'I'm afraid he'll find Mrs Penrudock's beds aren't very comfortable,' said my mother, who now began to fuss about catering for such an epicure. But I had no doubt the whole thing was Magic and this visit was really his birthday present for me. Magic of Magics! We would go for long walks and talk about Siberia and perhaps he would have something new to tell about Our Train? I felt I would burst with happiness.

We had not seen him for over a year and had no idea where he had been and from where he would be coming. He was reliably unreliable. But true to the telegram he arrived around teatime; 'The Azores,' he said. When at last we settled down to Mrs Penrudock's Thunder and Lightning, I felt life had no more to offer. Perhaps I should explain that Thunder and Lightning was the local treat to end all others, a traditional dish, composed of two large china bowls, one full of that thick yellowish clotted cream found only in Cornwall, the other bowl filled with an equally rich golden honey. A large home-made loaf stood alongside, hunks of which were then torn off and dunked alternately in each bowl. This was not a dish for the queasy but none of us held back. 'My word! You took to it proper, not like most foreigners,' said Mrs Penrudock as she removed the remains.

Perhaps the effects of the Thunder and Lightning had been more powerful than we knew, but something had certainly affected The Traveller. He seemed, if not morose, at least sombre. There were times when he was silent, staring abstractedly as if into another hemisphere, totally withdrawn. He had brought me a beautiful little chess set, with scarlet and white painted chessmen, its folding board shimmering with mother-of-pearl squares, an Indian conceit; but he refused me even one game. 'All those moves – it's too like politics,' he said. Moreover, he avoided plunging into those furious political discussions with my father which they usually enjoyed. Worst of all, he refused to talk to me about Siberia, or Our Train. What had gone wrong?

'Don't you start talking about journeys,' he said sourly, 'I tell you, I've done enough mileage to last me until the next world and beyond ...' He even declined a short walk to visit the seals.

☪

On his last evening we sat late over our supper and the lemon twilight was fading fast. It was very still, only the rooks scuffled in the trees as they settled for the night. Suddenly, almost accusingly, The Traveller turned towards my father. '*Boje Moi!* My God!' he burst out. 'Listen to the peace! Do you realise it? Why don't you stay on here – live here – get out of London – it's finished, anyway. All big cities are. But this is still real.'

My father stared at him curiously. 'If you're so anxious for us to bury ourselves alive, why don't you try it yourself?' he replied. 'Go back to Russia and try the quiet of your estates in Ufa.'

The Traveller shrugged. 'They were confiscated years ago. I've been on the move ever since – cities, streets, deserts. I want to sit down somewhere out of sight of the lot, like it is here,' he added. Almost as an afterthought he announced he would soon be leaving for another long journey – to where he did not say. 'And I don't suppose I shall be seeing you again for some while,' he added, carelessly, lounging away in the darkness towards a light streaming from Mrs Penrudock's window. He had taken a great liking to the old lady and they could be heard cackling and laughing merrily together as she instructed him in the Cornish patois she still spoke.

When he rejoined us, he seemed to have regained his good humour. 'What an old charmer. Must have been quite a beauty,' he said.

'Mrs Penrudock? How about that moustache?' my mother responded.

'A bit bristly, now,' he conceded and went on to tell how much a downy line, the *lèvre ombrée*, or shadowed lip, had been traditionally admired in Persia. 'In Spain too,' he continued, which led us to discuss the amount of Spanish blood that lingered in Cornish veins. The startlingly swarthy complexion and coal-black eyes still to be seen are held to be a legacy from those Spanish seamen cast ashore along the northern coasts of Cornwall and Devon at the time of the Armada in 1588, when the English ships and fearful gales had combined to defeat the massed Spanish galleons of Il Re Felipe II of Spain. Listening to him, we realised that our former story-teller had returned to us with all his old flow of extravagant, unpredictable talk.

Next day he left us, making the sign of the Cross, Russian fashion, over my head while mumbling a prayer, kissing my mother's hand, palm upwards, in his own fashion and embracing my father with unusual warmth. Then, while the station cab (the greengrocer's cart from Bude) waited, snorting, we all sat down for a moment of silence, an old Russian farewell custom he had taught us long before and which always accompanied his departures. Then, suddenly jumping to his feet, and like a dog shaking water off its coat after a plunge, he seemed to shake off the cottage and ourselves; jumping into the cab, suddenly he was gone.

The rest of the holiday fell a little flat. But then The Traveller always left a void and a longing behind him. Still, there was Cornwall as consolation. First the seals, that roared a kind of welcome, or so I thought, when I clambered down a cliff path to make my daily visit and enjoy their aquatic antics. I never tried to go too near, so perhaps that was why I felt accepted. Once or twice some babies flopped near, but I did not attempt to touch them, at which their mothers sank back, eyeing me with languid approval.

We jogged the quiet lanes in the pony-trap, from village to village, where my mother bought beautiful lace from the old ladies who sat at their doorstep with their bobbins and cushions, happy to chat and sell their handiwork, while my father sampled local brews at the inns and I rushed about with the village dogs. We were living exactly the sort of fantasy family life for which, I have come to believe, my mother yearned. My infant notion of soap-bubble spheres where each of us floated in separate states, from which we sometimes communicated with each other, had never appealed to her; it was dismissed as just another of my childish fancies. Perhaps she had never realised how remote, how apart, she and my father had appeared to me as a small child. At any rate, we were now communicating in a more reasonable or normal manner, though – whether by accident or design – we remained, basically, very separate entities, approaching each other warily, with little familiarity – at least where I was concerned. I cannot judge the precise degree of intimacy that existed between them. It was only many years later that I was to learn that my mother's wariness of 'family' was rooted in her own mother's matrimonial follies. My mother had been brought up by her grandparents and kept apart as much as possible from the appalling 'Jackson lot', as my father called them. They were the fruits of my grandmother's second marriage to 'dear William'. A certain time after my mother's marriage, the Jackson lot closed in to claim some of her inheritance left to her by her grandfather, John Stewart, whom she adored. As a result, she was left with considerably less of her grandfather's fortune than he had intended.

Sometimes we went inland, to Bodmin Moor, with its strange granite tors capping the low hills, its creeping mists and curious birdcalls, the flash of a fox across the emptiness, where a hawk wheeled and there was always some insistent

*Lesley Blanch's great-grandfather, John Stewart, who brought up her mother Martha Mabel Thorpe, leaving her most of his fortune.*

sense of foreboding. Not everyone's idea of a holiday outing perhaps, but for me the perfect setting for the sort of dramas I always craved. How different from those sparkling, blue waters of inviting little inlets my mother preferred, where we fished for the mackerel Mrs Penrudock cooked for us in various ways: in oatmeal, in cider, with bacon, or in a pie called Star-Gazey, with the fish-heads sticking out of the pie-crust top, which looked rather cannibalistic.

That first Cornish holiday cast a strange spell over me, and for the rest of my life I have never wanted to go anywhere else – about England, that is. The many-coloured counties of the poet's green and pleasant land left me unmoved, while Cornwall remained that mythical region I sought beyond every far distance I reached on my travels. Had I realised that I had only to cross the Tamar to find it round me, perhaps I might have achieved my parents' dream and taken root there.

☪

Early in July we returned home, in spite of Mrs Penrudock's pleas which echoed those of The Traveller. 'Stay on! Stay here with us – you don't want them cities no more,' she said, wiping her large nose on her apron. But habit had throttled us. Our tickets were taken, our seats reserved and, of course, nothing must stop my going to school.

As if to punish us, it was a chilly grey day and there was none of the charm of our outward journey. As we neared London it began to drizzle and the home counties looked sadly tame after Cornwall. Paddington was sooty, stifling and greasy underfoot. Even the porters seemed less helpful than before. While our luggage was packed into one of the few taxi-cabs, my father bought stacks of daily papers and began attacking them. He read furiously all the way home, throwing them on the floor almost as soon as opened, so that my mother and I were knee-deep in the debris which she gave up trying to sort.

It may seem impossible to believe that for the whole month we spent in Cornwall we knew nothing of the world beyond our cottage windows. We had no letters, or newspapers. Mrs Penrudock could neither read nor write and The Traveller, who had been our only contact with the outside world, had been singularly incommunicative about world events. There was no telephone within miles. In short, we knew nothing of the pace at which political tensions were building up all over Europe. Or had this ostrich pair deliberately closed any windows that might have let in light on the situation? I shall never know.

Everything looked the same on reaching home, except for enormous piles of letters, bills, and such, which were immediately pushed aside to make room for the evening papers. More and more countries seemed to be shouting abuse at each other, with angry threats and alarming ultimatums. What was going on? My parents had no time to explain anything, being glued to the papers, so as soon as I had been reunited with the cats, who were civil, but clearly wished it known that they had not been pleased to be left in the care of the gardener's wife, I rushed off to find Piggy. Her mother knew all about the situation, but didn't want to talk about it, for Piggy's brother the midshipman was still at Dartmouth and likely to be promoted to active service, if— 'If' was a word I kept hearing just then.

The letters and bills which had awaited our return still remained unopened, pushed aside, giving place to relays of the daily papers which now occupied my parents exclusively. There were alarming headlines, printed big and black, about Germany's military superiority and bellicose intentions. My father kept reading them to my mother, who looked dazed. I still did not understand why France was represented as weakling victim – If ...? 'If it comes to war,' my father snapped. War? Russia? Nothing was explained, so once more I returned to Piggy who had much to tell about life at St Paul's, for she had been coming to terms with it while I was in Cornwall.

'Bearable, but no more,' she said and my early forebodings were not calmed. 'You'll hate all those games,' she warned, 'netball, rounders, tennis, gym.' I stuffed my ears and begged her to stop. So we returned to our former pleasures, going to Richmond Park to watch the deer, or photograph them with our box brownies. Sometimes we took Ollie the Great Dane for a swim along the towpath between Kew and Richmond, where a curve in the river bank made an easy stretch for Ollie to splash about. It used to be one of our favourite amusements, in whatever weather. We were a hardy trio and Ollie never hesitated to plunge into the water as long as we threw sticks and shrieked encouragement. But now, all seemed changed. I ached for Cornwall, and wanted to go back there and never leave it, except for Siberia, of course.

Whether it was the fact that those luminously happy hours were spent in Cornwall, or that they came to represent my last perfectly free days of childhood, I cannot judge, from this distance. Yet even now, the sequence of those Cornish hours returns to me, like a brilliantly lit film. There we are, my mother and father, The Traveller, Mrs Penrudock and myself, repeating this strange pantomime of happiness. I have only to 'think Cornwall', and pronounce the old formula, 'Magic of Magics' (which I also used to summon Siberia), to be again on that Cornish shore, our voices mingling with the sound of the sea and the wind across the moor. They still sound for me, beneath the cacophony of this new twenty-first century.

☪

July dragged on while the adult world seethed with speculation and statesmen thundered. There were precipitate troop movements. Reserves were called up and artillery practice rumbled menacingly in the distance. 'Really! We might as well be at war,' some people said, 'but even if we were, it would all be over by Christmas,' said others, firmly ignoring the German nation's grandiose and bloody designs. Nonetheless, a sense of apprehension was apparent even to us children.

There were endless speeches and long close-printed columns in the dailies fed by reporters glued to the House of Commons, the House of Lords, the War Office, the Admiralty, or any other possible source of information. We did not have radios or television bulletins to keep us informed, then.

But on June 28th an Austrian Archduke and his wife were assassinated at Sarajevo, and further talk of treaties or ultimatums was merely delaying the inevitable. On August 2nd the German army invaded Belgium. Britain, allied to Belgium, France and Russia, declared war on Germany on August 4th. The First World War had begun and nothing was ever the same again.

# 8. St Paul's Girls' School

RECALLING MY SCHOOLDAYS, I see that I am inclined to place my own prejudices before the whole. St Paul's was one of the first and finest public schools for girls, an admirable establishment which still proclaimed those lofty standards of idealism which activated THE NEW WOMAN, she who had not so long before risen from the ashes of Suffragette fury. High endeavour, responsibility and the place we were destined to play in the proud future of our country was in the air we breathed – I would not say 'absorbed', for already it seemed to us a little outdated. For myself, endeavour meant endeavouring to leave school as soon as possible, thus becoming grown up – a state which I believed implied freedom. What I was going to do when I was free of school discipline and parental authority was already clear in my mind: I was going to travel, to escape into some glittering limboland of adventure and to hell with the good of my country.

If I was not happy at school, I was not unhappy either. I simply ticked over, but something of my non-conformist upbringing must have been apparent. Without being a disgrace, I was never made a prefect and my end of term reports were not enthusiastic. I never had crushes on other girls, or cherished what was known as 'a pash' for one of the mistresses. I was given to arguing or, at times, questioning a rule. Perhaps Piggy's presence strengthened my isolation, for I cannot recall a single face or name from among that teeming throng – save one brief encounter, which remained firmly rooted.

I was in the Music Wing, a permitted escape from sport, *en route* for one of the small soundproof rooms where one could thump out a march by Schubert or practise scales and arpeggios. On my way I noticed a lonely figure leaning against a window, her face streaked with tears. She was small and dark and had a mild, not-one-of-us look about her. She clutched at me. 'Oh! do help me, you must, I'm so miserable, I can't bear it here ...' she sobbed. 'They've left me here, but I can't, I can't stay ... I must go home. Do help me to get away,' clashing her head against the window pane. Home, I discovered, was somewhere in Ireland and she had been planted at St Paul's as one of the few boarders then accepted.

Her name was Molly – Molly Keane, a name which, oddly, I never forgot as I never forgot the fury of her misery. Presently I had to detach myself and go my way. I never saw her again. I suppose she succeeded in being repatriated, but this encounter came back to me years later, when Molly Keane was a name made famous by the brilliant plays and accounts of Irish life she was writing.

☾

My school days were a sort of void – a space in time between the bright colours of my nursery and the shimmering horizons of the future. Thus I was unable to appreciate the present, the many agreeable, even luxurious, aspects of St Paul's, such as its Music Wing and swimming baths, then not considered requisite to education. The exterior was impressive Norman Shaw style and beautiful natural wood was used lavishly within, on floors, doors and stairways and the panelled Great Hall.

The women who taught us were a later generation than those pioneering ladies who sought higher education as Oxford undergraduates at the first women's college, St Hugh's, under Miss Buss or Miss Beale, but they breathed the same lofty idealism. They sailed about from classroom to classroom, unapproachable figures, sometimes with their academic gowns billowing round them like banners of independence, still not quite equal with their male counterparts at the men's universities to which they were only admitted in 1919. One and all breathed an air of almost missionary fervour. The ethos of high endeavour set the tone of our school song which we dutifully belted out. For myself, I preferred a hymn by Addison which we sometimes sang at morning prayers. His beautiful lines would linger in my ear, softening the chilly routines of the day.

> *The spacious firmament on high,*
> *With all the blue ethereal sky,*
> *And spangled heavens, a shining frame,*
> *Their great Original proclaim.*

But who, precisely, was the great Original? I had remained short on Divine allusions since those early days of penitential churchgoing, and did not care to reveal my ignorance among the many to whom the Bible was an open book. Piggy, while not so totally ignorant as I, was still vague.

☪

Although she and I were in different forms and classrooms, our school life was shared as closely as our life at home. Each morning, a little before eight o'clock, we set out, whatever the weather, on a gruelling journey, originally designed by Piggy's father to ensure we got enough exercise. We began with a brisk trot along more than half a mile of a countrified track leading to Barnes Bridge, which we pelted over to catch a number 9 bus which took us across another more celebrated Thames bridge, the old suspension bridge at Castlenau immortalised by Whistler's painting; this in due course put us down in Hammersmith, where a last panting rush down a side street brought us to Brook Green, just as the school bell was ringing for prayers. This undertaking took well over an hour, morning and evening, and we thought nothing of it, even taking an idiotic pride in always riding on top of the bus, which at that time was not roofed. We scrambled up a twisted iron staircase and if we were lucky got seats, which had quaint little cracked leather aprons that could be hooked over to protect the seats in rainy weather. But nothing was ever any protection against the sleet, gales or rain that beat down on our unprotected heads.

Our silly wilfulness to be always outside – no doubt responsible for so many of the coughs and colds that were an accepted part of winter – was never checked, or remarked upon. If you were out in the fresh air you were all right, it was believed. We were brought up to be hardy. Health was not yet the absorbing topic it has become today, and paediatricians had not yet become indispensable adjuncts to child welfare. Those were spartan days. I remember that when neighbouring children suffered a rather ordinary ailment such as adenoids, they were likely to be operated on at home by the family doctor. Stretched on the specially well-scrubbed kitchen table, they were just told to keep still and take a sniff of chloroform that their nervous mothers proffered on a wad of cotton wool. They seem to have survived without any undue traumas, though we shall never know.

☾

Music held a special place in our life at St Paul's and was, for me, also a lovely let-up from the horrors of sport and gym. Our concert hall was truly admirable with its platform stage and place for an orchestra of thirty, a library of scores, and rows of tiered seats for pupils or audience. There the school orchestra practised or performed at school concerts. Gifted pupils studied extra hours in the music wing, excused from certain classes (and even gym), tackling piano concertos or string quartets, and we all took part in choral practice. The whole was under the aegis of Gustav Holst, no less, and his *St Paul's Suite* was the outcome of his association with the school. We thought the plain timid little figure with the staring eyes of a mystic something of a joke. But when, now, I hear some of his music, such as *The Planets*, I think how stupid most of us were, how wasteful of what was offered us, then.

Some of our music mistresses sounded a note of exoticism by being of Polish or Russian origin and speaking with a rich accent. One was the wife of a well-known contemporary composer, while another I thought particularly fascinating had been, or was said to have been, taught by a pupil of Clara Schumann. This, in my eyes, invested her with a sort of historico-geographic aura (I had been encouraged to read Heine's poetry and Hoffmann's weird tales as a counterbalance to my passion for everything Russian), which evoked the world of German Romantic painters, where unhappy poets or lonely flute players wandered in sombre forests or along some Baltic strand. So I wandered after them and forgot to practise my scales.

I had begun piano lessons early and was considered to be very musical and, admittedly, wonderfully nimble-fingered, showing off with pieces like Sinding's *The Rustle of Spring* or

Grieg's *Papillon*. My poor parents, once such ardent concert-goers, now had to endure my daily hours of practice at the keyboard – scales, arpeggios, Czerny's exercises and more.

From my earliest days at school I was uncomfortably aware that my background, or family life, was not quite like that of other girls and it is from this time that I began to see my parents as parents, like other girls' parents, only somehow different. It was awkward when asked, 'What does your father do?' because my father did nothing I could put a name to, or explain. My father was an expert on furniture, particularly oak, early oak. He would find it for people, or buy it for himself or he'd buy sometimes for museums. He'd make a sort of living now and again. But other fathers were soldiers, lawyers, doctors, in business, or even Parliament; they all *did* something and my painfully truthful answers sounded odd. I was too dumb to invent splendid lies, to say he was on some secret mission, was an inventor, a conjuror – anything – rather than that hateful negation. My father, being well over fifty, was too old to be conscripted and anyhow had shown no wish to do any kind of war work. He simply continued on his familiar nonchalant way. Once, feeling specially embarrassed, I confided in my mother, but she only smiled in a rather pinched manner and said, 'It's really not important – just say he has independent means.' I had no idea what this meant and found the phrase difficult to pronounce. It certainly stifled further questioning.

Only much later, in the cruel future, did I realise the irony of my mother's words. She – or rather her own fortune – was the means that made him independent, that kept him free to spend his days wandering about the city he loved, going from museums to magnificent libraries, from curator to antique dealer, from street markets or junk yards to sales rooms, always on the prowl: seeking and finding strange or beautiful objects, rare pieces, treasures to be delicately repaired, perhaps, to adorn his collection, or to be sold later, traded against an even better toy. It was a leisure which led to ruin. He was perfectly indifferent to my mother's pleas, or tears, when he almost dragged a favourite chair from under her, a charming piece of early eighteenth-century walnut, to return with a splendid Jacobean chest of drawers, expanding on the beauty of chamfered panelling, or the rarity of a piece of Safavid pottery he was after. His extraordinary flair could have been canalised into a lucrative career, but he had absolutely no sense of business; of making it pay. So he drifted, an amateur in the game – a deplorable waster. Such was my father when I gave up trying to explain his activities.

☪

At St Paul's, sport was a moral issue, a religious rite; and the Gymnasium our Temple where we offered ourselves up on the parallel bars and performed other acts of penance. Term after term was made hideous to me as we slithered about the muddy ground. Netball gave me fearful chilblains. Numbed as I was to immobility by the cold, a smart whack from the captain's hockey stick ('play up and play the game') once resulted in weeks of limping and the threat of water on the knee. Dutifully watching the Head Girl's brother playing in some Varsity rugger match at Twickenham meant standing congealed on the touchline in a savage north-easter and brought on pneumonia. We did not have today's comforting range of anoraks and padded outdoor garments. We made do with winter overcoats and woolly scarves. Children did not feel the cold as grown-ups did, or so we were told. Thus, as a sullen spectator, or miserable player, there was never any let-up for me.

Summer was no better. There could be no respite under the one lovely tree in the whole bleak playground. It was an ancient spreading mulberry tree, offering 'green thoughts in a green shade'. Its heavy leaves speckled with ripening fruit awaited the dawdler. But no such luck. A whistle shrilled and we were marshalled to our overcrowded, noisily echoing swimming baths before being directed to the tennis courts where to and fro went that ball and we panted after it. Forty love! Net! Deuce! The hated incantations ring in my ears again. Once, when I was taken as a treat to watch some special tournament during a record heatwave, screwed-up eyes and squinting resulted in conjunctivitis (no one wore dark glasses then, other than blind beggars), with prickly heat thrown in for good measure. Bat and ball, bat and ball was the rhythm of my school days.

I have sometimes wondered how it happened that I became the hardy traveller of later years, wandering in the wildest lands, going from Siberia to the Persian Gulf, without so much as a boil. Were my early sufferings purely psychosomatic, brought on by boredom? I was never bored on my travels, or at home, where, except for some early nineteenth-century prints of celebrated pugilists which my father had collected, or the old classic *Mr Sponge's Sporting Tour*, sport as such was seldom mentioned.

At last I contrived a refuge from the inexorable school timetable and started slinking off to the lavatories, a book stuffed under my gym tunic, like those unfortunate persons trying to conceal an unwanted pregnancy. I had to be very careful about the size and shape of the book, there being no handy paperbacks then. But once safely installed, I was able to read, undisturbed by the rustlings and flushings all around, until some dreaded bell would sound, just as I reached Jane Eyre's first encounter with Mr Rochester, or how the Mongol

hordes took the wailing women by their hair, bending back
their heads to sever the spine more easily, and I would have to
emerge, surreptitiously slide the book into my locker and
exchange it for whichever bat or stick or racquet the forth-
coming game demanded. Piggy was far more sportive than I
and these manoeuvres of mine left her cold.

A less arduous, but inescapable trial during the war years
was our school dinners. We were always hungry, never able to
swallow half the muck set before us. The kitchen staff, or
those responsible for school catering then, must have lacked
the ability and ingenuity to cope with the problems of severe
rationing, insufficient home produce and, above all, the deadly
submarine blockades which paralysed our ports and attacked
our food convoys at sea. When we complained, we rightly got
a sharp answer, 'Don't you know we are at war? Think of all
those starving children in France and Belgium and Russia. If
they could have just one of your dinners ...' Nevertheless I
still shudder recalling those large slabs of some dark-skinned
fish oozing a yellowish fluid, sausages that smelled high, mac-
aroni without cheese, weevily potatoes, wilted cabbage and
puddings that slopped about – tapioca or sago. Margarine
made its appearance at about this time, but portions were
stingy; and we were given one glass of milk every day which
kept us going. Where had suet gone, or fruit? Green apples
were not the answer. We spoke reverently of the dumplings or
lardy cakes of our pre-war nurseries. However restricted, at
home rations were somehow turned into something edible.
Country children did better, but we were Londoners. Food
shortages and casualty lists were part of our daily life.

Just how much we children were aware of the war is diffi-
cult to say. It was just part of that grown-up life to which we
did not belong. It was seldom discussed in class, but some-
times a girl would be called to the Head's room and did not

return: then we knew her father or brother or someone of her family had been killed. Nothing was ever said when she came back some days later, puffy-eyed and wan. Passchendaele and Verdun, Gallipoli and the Somme, were all names that passed over our heads; a sort of litany intoned by the grown-ups, some of whom spent hours moving little red flags over maps of the French battlefields. The full horror of trench warfare was scarcely comprehended.

At this time, patriotism was often expressed rather crudely. An unfortunate young man not wearing uniform was liable to be presented with a white feather – symbol of cowardice – and poor little squirming dachshunds were kicked for being a German breed. The enemy was spoken of as 'Huns' or 'Boches'. Our boys were 'Tommies', immortalised in Bruce Brainfeller's cartoons. Bomb attacks were scarcely known in the First World War, but I did chance to witness a Zeppelin being brought down in flames; bits of its bulk and no doubt some of its crew were flaming fragments, drifting slowly to earth. Piggy and her mother lived in a perpetual state of tension as they followed the battles at sea, for Paul was now serving on a submarine somewhere in the North Sea where battles raged. More and more women were conscripted to work in the munitions factories, or on the land, if they were not needed to look after their orphans and keep the home fire burning. As our losses mounted, a Stygian gloom enveloped the streets which became noticeably empty; the few pedestrians were mostly in black or wore black armbands, denoting mourning, while hand-carts or barrows were taking the place of tradesmen's carts, for all horses had been commandeered by the Army – bloodstock, big dray horses, tradesmen's horses and ponies alike. Once my mother and I were halted at a railway crossing where a long line of cattle trucks were crawling to a stop. Horses were packed side by side, their lovely patient faces looking out across the bars; some were turning their heads from side to side and seemed to be looking for someone. They were a rather shabby lot, part of a convoy being shipped to France. My mother suddenly began to cry. Perhaps, after all, the poor brutes going to be killed on a battlefield were only anticipating their usual end at a slaughterhouse. It was such an unimportant sadness, a mini pathos beside the gigantic scale of suffering everywhere, but it spoke to me in terms I could understand. I cried too.

By 1917 things were bad, very bad, but played down and accepted, in a rather curious manner, by some mothers who noisily proclaimed their pride, their joy even, that they had been able to give a son – two sons, or even three – to die for England. Rupert Brooke's beautiful poem, 'If I should die, think only this of me; That there's some corner of a foreign field, that is for ever England ...' gave comfort to many, but it was all part of our then inbred, unquestioning loyalty which welded us together, as battle after battle went wrong, and, like the appalling casualty lists, could not be explained away, any more than shell-shock or the results of poison gas.

☪

My mother took my end of term reports to heart more than I did. They were a constant disappointment to her, almost a personal affront; a reflection on her own earlier efforts of instruction. Remarks such as, 'Lesley seems to be living in a world of her own', 'Shows no aptitude for science or mathematics', struck deep. We had indeed given these two subjects a miss at the nursery-schoolroom table. In consequence I had at last been sent down to the beginners' class for arithmetic. Sitting among sharp little ten-year-olds, it was hoped, would shame me, a languid fourteen-year-old, into action. But I just sat there, a lacklustre Paulina, as baffled as ever. 'Seems to have no desire to improve' went one report and my mother wilted. But when another read, 'Has a tendency to show off, pretending to have read a number of unsuitable Russian authors', my mother struck. Braving the High Mistress, an intimidating presence, she threw the offending report to the ground saying, 'You find Tolstoy and Gogol unsuitable? Let me tell you *Dead Souls* is Lesley's bedtime reading!'

Overall I believe my hostility to sport and my lack of public (or public-school) spirit went against me; it aroused a kind of chilly suspicion of abnormality, not one of the crowd. And I was derided as being 'booky'. I listened to some of the girls talking about getting married, having babies, or being presented at Court, such were their horizons; so where were all those teachings of higher education? Had it not been for what my father crudely described as 'all that God talk', I might have done better educationally at some more static convent school.

Many years later in my CV for *Who's Who* I put: Educated by listening to the conversation of my elders and betters.

# 9. Post-war Gloom

THE DAYS I HAVE BEEN recalling, the days of my child-
hood before the First World War of 1914–18, in certain
aspects, I think, still linked us with early nineteenth- and even
eighteenth-century ways. Progress advanced at a very meas-
ured pace. We were not constantly bludgeoned by breathless
new inventions. They existed and were adopted gradually, but
were not over-publicised. We were quite accustomed to old
people; some had grandfathers who had walked with a flag
before the first railway engines. The motor car was now a reg-
ular sight in well-to-do areas, though electricity and telephones
were not installed in most of the houses around; but we had
gas lighting and telegrams and a comforting postal service,
with three deliveries a day. War ended.

I left St Paul's in 1921. The sudden cessation of school activ-
ities and disciplines left me inert. 'What on earth are we going
to do with her now?' were my parents' unspoken thoughts and
I was uncomfortably aware of them when they said, 'How
lovely to have you around, though have you any idea of what
you want to do – or be?' But no one had an answer. I had not
shown any marked attributes at school, beyond being 'bookish'
and getting a medal for drawing – the theme, I do not recall,
and I was not yet aware that my parents faced the first phases
of financial ruin. The investments they had made in Russia (on
the advice of The Traveller) had now vanished in the Communist
maw and the diminished capital upon which we were living

was the last remnant of those high-sounding Independent Means by which my mother had ensured the even tenor of my father's ways. We seldom spoke of The Traveller. It was evident not only that he had vanished, but that during the last years of the war – in Russia, no doubt – something terrible must have happened to him. We fell silent, each of us remembering him as each had separately known him. And then the unanswerable question would return and I wondered once again what was *I* to do about *Me*? Without him, any future blanked out.

Sometimes, my rattle-pate recognition of Russian objects – a Gardner bowl for example, or a rug that was Caucasian not Persian, as specified – intrigued my father who asked prodding questions all around. And then a battery of questions would engulf me: 'How did you come to know? Who put you up to all those answers?' It was when something came out of a sale room, or that I had admired, odiously knowledgeable. But I was not showing off; heterogeneous scraps of knowledge were from the cradle out spread around me, listening to my father as he arrived home triumphantly lumping along a roll of fine carpeting. 'Soap and water and *nothing* else,' he would roar as I worked gloatingly over the glowing flank with my mother's ivory nailbrush. 'That's no good, it's too bristly, it ruins the pile, just pat it with a damp cloth,' my father would say, leaving me with a fine piece of Aubusson perhaps, or a beautiful old Hamadan. So gradually my infant perceptions were strengthened as I grew, justified I might say, and my parents, recalling Dickens' Infant Phenomenon, referred to me as their infant *antiquaire*.

Those were happy times when, for a while, I forgot The Traveller's absence and gradually became myself, my own entity, with an overwhelming love of things – inanimate objects, a teacup, a Chinese vase, or a papier-mâché footstool,

all spoke or kept company with me; sometimes I was allowed to keep such treasure trove beside the whole world of Staffordshire figures and animals I cultivated. One particularly delicious pair of enormous black and white St Bernards each carried a royal infant sprawled across its back – the little Edward VII and his sister the future Empress of Germany – nearly as endearing as the dogs. I have them beside me now as I write, survivors like myself of much wear and tear, and wonderful quiet company.

☪

All around, there hung a curiously drab light. A sort of extinguished sunlight seemed to cloud most of England in those bleak post-war years of hardship, unemployment, disillusion and mourning. Young women, for whom there would never be husbands (the generation of likely fiancés having been wiped out in the war where losses were reckoned at about a million), now began to learn how to live on other terms, working in offices, or as shop assistants, or hairdressers, or dance-hostesses at one of those newly opened gigantic Palais de Dance, but gaiety remained rather forced, like the elaborate Victory Balls or Victory Parades, of which the Press made so much, but which deceived so few. It was a sombre time. Foredoomed endeavours proliferated: chicken farming and roadside tea shops with homemade cakes to tempt the few, new motorists. But food coupons and sugar rationing continued for some while, which was daunting, like the still darkened streetlighting. Wartime tensions lingered, producing few constructive peace plans. A lack of enthusiasm, an indifference even, seemed as if clamped down on an overtired, over-tried land, which had won the war and was now losing the peace.

My mother, shut away in the smaller quarters we now occupied, had discovered an escape hatch by which she sometimes indulged in a luxurious monologue recalling something of her youth. From her earliest childhood, or infancy, she had lived with her grandparents in Brighton, Tunbridge Wells – always out of London. She only rarely saw or visited her mother after her second marriage, to 'dear William' who bred a large, troublesome family.

My mother and her grandfather would take a daily airing in a carriage, bowling along the sea-front. Brighton, she maintained, was always sunny. Part of this essentially Victorian outing was reserved for a stop at Sweetings, the celebrated shellfish restaurant, where they would partake of half a dozen oysters and a glass of white wine, before returning home to the customary Victorian four-course luncheon. It was a programme which told of affluence and security; precisely what my mother wished for me. She also liked to tell me how my great-grandmother, having sewn black ribbons to her bonnet, had gone to see the Iron Duke's funeral procession from a house in the Strand and there met a handsome dark Scotsman – her husband-to-be – who lodged there and cajoled her to linger as the crowds dispersed. When questioned, my great-grandmother could never recall anything of the procession, but she recalled every detail of the room where she had met, and on sight loved, my great-grandfather. My mother, who had a penchant for the Iron Duke, would press for details of the procession, but it was always the same: 'I remember there was a Brussels carpet and dark green merino curtains edged with such a pretty fringe,' the old lady would say, dreamily, 'and the clock ticked so loudly, we hardly heard the tramp of feet below ... there was a big gilt looking-glass over the chimney piece and a marble bust of some Greek hero, not half so handsome as your grandfather was then ... I remember there was a little sofa covered in horsehair. Not a comfortable sofa,' she always added, at which point, my mother said, she invariably fell silent, no doubt recalling how little comfort had mattered to her, in love, in London, in 1852.

My mother seldom spoke of the past, or complained of the present, but I suppose she still secretly clung to some dream, now absurdly out of date and place, of a future where I would be launched on life like a delightful deb and soon married off – like pretty Miss So and So, only daughter of Lady Something or Lord Somebody or other whose photographs (smiling; one small string of pearls) regularly adorned the front page of *Country Life*. The inanity of this dream was only confided to me years later, when I had gone my own rackety way. I could never have fitted into that sort of niche, even if she had possessed the means to secure it for me.

I was quite unaware or indifferent to her care and returned to my old ways, playing the 'Magic of Magics' game, willing myself somewhere else; setting off on my bike to spend whole days in Richmond Park. Its beautiful stretches of ancient woodland and dells where the wild birds nested lent themselves to any amount of transformations: oak trees became the Cedars of Lebanon; a distant green rise led to a small wooden dacha where Aksakov's grandfather was sitting on the veranda beside an enormous hissing samovar and about to offer me a glass of tea – Russia attained! I would ride along the towpath from Kew to Richmond, on an unfrequented riverside path which Piggy and I had known well before the war, when we used to take Ollie to swim from that little beach in the curve in the river bank where her barking did not arouse the swans' fury. We were happy then; so long ago it seemed now, as I pedalled hot, out of breath and out of temper with my lot. What did I want?

I did not share my geo-romantic longings with Piggy; she was not tormented by the elusive Elsewhere. Her post-school days were not fraught with doubts. She too had left St Paul's in 1921, but for a niche already awaiting her. She was to train for some agricultural future, and in the meantime was lending a hand with her mother's vegetable and home produce venture, which prospered and became quite lucrative. Sometimes I worked beside her, collecting eggs from under fat hens, sorting potatoes, or tying up vegetables, a lovely job, yet I felt it could never be mine for long.

Local elections provided a mild diversion from daily dullness. People still believed in politicians, like a sort of Victorian hangover. Some well-known poet (Sir John Squire) suddenly stood as a Liberal candidate contesting a very stuffy Conservative, and

Piggy and I determined to further the poet's chances. After dark we made several stealthy expeditions, creeping round armed with pots of sticky paste, superimposing our candidate's poster on those of his rival, so that in the morning our man was found emblazoned on the front doors or garden walls of his rival's supporters. This most enjoyable and rather risky prank caused confusion and roars of anger all round. No one, not even our parents, suspected us of political activities until one day we were caught red-handed and a great deal of disagreeableness followed.

Apart from Piggy's family, I do not recall that we frequented any other neighbours. Not that my parents held apart, as superior persons, it was simply a question of different interests, or ways of living. But a little further down our quiet road there was one lively exception to the prevailing drifting sequence of time. Each morning, on the dot of eight, a remarkable figure was to be seen tearing along at a great pace to catch the 8.10 rattle-trap train to Waterloo. This was Bishop Montgomery, heading for Lambeth Palace, where he was engaged in ecclesiastical questions beside the Archbishop of Canterbury. His daily departure was something of a spectacle. He came charging past in full canonicals, a black cloak billowing round, his black-gaitered legs twinkling fast as he went, holding an overstuffed briefcase aloft in joyous greeting. Sometimes this was too much for the briefcase and it burst open, scattering administrative papers or drafts of sermons, perhaps. But the Bishop was a genial soul, his white-bearded, kindly face never clouded over. Mrs Montgomery was of more agitated clay. She too always appeared to be rushing about at top speed, dark unruly hair flying. There was something wild or gypsy-like about her; instinctively one looked for the caravan. There was a daughter, unhappily named Winsome, who was a little older than me, and a son called Brian, who was about my age. The three of us were sometimes packed off to gruesome sessions called *thés dansants*, organised for the benefit of the young, where we fox-trotted gloomily. The young Montgomerys occasionally spoke of older brothers in the Army, serving in faraway lands, and Brian longed to be old enough to join up and be with them. No crystal ball told us then that one day, one of those brothers would become the Field Marshal 'Monty' of El Alamein, as famous, in the Second World War, as Kitchener had been in the First.

# 10. Italy

ONE SOFT EVENING, smelling of spring and a countryside which our part of Old Chiswick still possessed, I returned home to find The Traveller installed on the sofa beside my mother, just as if he had never been away or caused us such anguish. I rushed towards him, knocking over the tea-tray, where, as always, relays of hoarded Lapsang had been brewing for his delectation. We were together again! That was *the* 'Magic of all Magics'. He was as elusive as ever about his doings, switching such talk to myself and how much I'd changed. 'Quite grown up – and d'you know you have become a very pretty Miss,' he said teasingly, at which my mother said, 'Trav'la! Please don't go putting ideas into her head.'

'Perhaps they're there already,' he replied, which seemed to nettle her, for she plunged into international politics; always a bait.

When, later, my father joined us, he still remained vague as to his long absence, but announced he was now settled in Paris – 'A huge apartment full of Russian stuff. Why don't you come over and have a holiday, it's terribly dingy here,' he added cruelly. No doubt the silence that followed reminded him of my father's built-in immobility and my mother's wifely submission. He shrugged and suggested I might enjoy it, anyhow. 'A sort of educational outing,' he suggested. 'I promise to take her around all the museums and monuments, churches, chapels and cemeteries too. You can't say no to that – she's absolutely rotting here,' he added mischievously. Perhaps this taunt struck home: suddenly everything fell into place. While my head was still swimming at the prospect, all was agreed, provided 'Miss Gabble', as my father called another of the governesses who never succeeded in teaching me to speak French, went along as a sort of chaperone. The convention still counted then, even in our relaxed household.

I have written of this fateful episode at length in *Journey into the Mind's Eye,* for it remains to me as an unfading image of perfect happiness, however deplorable it might appear to some. Seeing the way the men spoke to him, and the manner in which the women looked at him, I now became aware of him as a stranger – as a man. It was most disturbing. I believe that even then I had come to desire The Traveller as a woman desires a man and was instinctively aware that he would become my lover. It was as simple as that. Each of us must have recognised that decisive moment, when, according to ancient beliefs, the Fates change Horses.

Thanks to my chaperone's profound piety and her attraction to every denomination of Faith – churches, chapels, synagogues, mosques or temples – we contrived to spend many hours alone together; hours we spent exploring each other, or the many and various aspects of Paris. But abruptly, a peremptory-sounding telegram from my mother demanded my immediate return. There was no way of getting round that, so I packed gloomily. 'You must *never* tell, or you must tell *all* – though I don't really advise that,' said my lover. So I left, hugging the secret of our depraved behaviour.

☪

My mother welcomed me lovingly. 'I've got such a surprise for you,' she announced. 'It's all arranged, you're going to Italy with

Piggy.' Piggy's family had decided she too was due for a spell away from home, or the 'spuds', as they described her work in the vegetable garden, and she was to spend a few months in Florence where old friends of the family (always referred to as the Spinster Sisters) had opened a small establishment which took in a few young girls as boarders, to be 'finished' as the phrase went. This implied cultivating the arts assiduously and shed an undeniable lustre around each pupil's future.

When my mother heard of this, a curious change had come over her. It was as if all those years of acquiescence to my father's wishes had never been. Like my late educational stint in Paris, she stated flatly I would benefit from further travel. My poor deluded mother! Perhaps this was another step towards realising her secret *Country Life* dream of a deb's future for me. Nevertheless, by what means I shall never know – whether by dragging a cherished object from my father's dwindling collection of antiques, or selling a hoarded bit of jewellery – she found the very modest sum required for me to go to Florence with Piggy.

So, suddenly there we were, together as always, now installed in a villa, once part of an old convent, on one of the hills around Fiesole. The quarters chosen by the Spinster Sisters to establish their 'finishing school', as the *pensione* was grandiloquently described, were severely *cinquecento* and darkly inconvenient, with steep stone stairs, draughty corridors and narrow, deep-set windows which shut out much of the paling autumn sun, but were 'so good at keeping out the heat', we were told repeatedly. Autumn had come unexpectedly early that year; a chill wind brought gusts of autumn leaves from Vallombrosa, just as the poet wrote. It rattled the shutters remorselessly and roared down on to hearths where no logs yet burned. The Spinster Sisters' only concession to comfort was a small handful of charcoal sulking in the vast fireplaces of the parlour; they themselves had assumed a mottled mauveish-blue appearance and sniffed more than ever. '*Molto pericoloso*,' said the maids, as they thrust pans of glowing charcoal over our icy linen sheets, and we thought longingly of our lovely hot-water bottles, Boots' best, left at home when we set out for the sunny south. I have since discovered, after many sojourns in many climes, that civilised living, or rather, comfort, can be sharply divided between two emblems – the hot-water bottle and the ice-cube.

In this bleak setting, we struggled with the intricacies of Italian grammar taught by a sharp-nosed nun, or rattled down to the city in an extremely primitive tram in which we were at the mercy of every male passenger, who pinched us black-and-blue, the Italian way of appreciating our feminine curves. Once arrived, how many miles were we walked around by relays of elderly guides or retired British ex-governesses of remarkable stamina. Across the Ponte Vecchio to the Boboli gardens, with the Palazzo and its pictures, from the Pitti to the Uffizi, or the Duomo and back; coming and going between Medici princes, Botticelli's Venus, this fresco, that triptych and Della Robbia's cloying blue-and-white babies; the cultural haze only rarely dispelled by tea at one of the celebrated confectioners along the Tornabuoni.

I thought there was something strangely forbidding about Florence. To me it appeared almost hostile. A Dantesque gloom hung over the narrow streets that ran between towering walls which seemed to rise and gnaw at the skies above. The gigantic piazzas were edged with lugubrious arcades or loggias where dark-clad priests and nuns scuttled and bells tolled remorselessly above the clatter and hum of cafés where customers, both citizens and tourists, sat, curiously glum for the most part, as if crushed by the splendours of the gigantic pieces of statuary and historic architecture looming over them.

The little chattering street markets were better, that reverential spell broken by the shrill cries and intriguing local merchandise. The historic booths along the Ponte Vecchio, which specialised in fine jewels, corals, lace and such, smacked of frivolity, so we were never allowed to linger there. On our way across the Arno to some intellectual destination on the other side of the city, I sighted a Russian church, its gilded domes and a belfry as Slav as could be, but it remained an unachieved goal. Not *cinquecento* enough? I enquired bitterly of my smug cicerones.

The wooded hills above Fiesole were those traversed by the Medici princes, with their pages and palfreys, a glittering cavalcade about which we were lectured at the Uffizi. Sadly, our cultural horizons stopped short of any real acquaintance with the lovely, luminous Tuscan countryside. There were no expeditions to the outlying villages with their little chapels and shrines, surrounded by vineyards, olive groves and fields where the white oxen ploughed beside tall cypresses and slow-flowing streams; a landscape still identical to that of the Florentine Masters recorded in the pietàs and nativities. Such Illyrian distances were considered a waste of time, 'One whole day in search of a Giotto village? Rubbish!' and that was that.

The undercurrent of Approved Taste exasperated me most. It was 'correct' to admire *everything* for, of course, everything here was to be admired; no doubts or discussions ever sounded beneath the hosannahs. A chill air of complacency hung over us. English visitors felt safe in this well-behaved 'Abroad' where nothing nasty happened to foreigners – if you discounted pickpockets. It was safe to wander, safe to eat the food and safe to admire everything for anything historic was the epitome of good taste, like the Cotswolds, or the Rhine, or Notre-Dame. Florence had become the earnest tourist's Mecca, to which a pilgrimage was essential.

So, Piggy and I were now plodding on our pilgrimage, two silly flappers, as girls of our age were then dubbed. We knew nothing of the labyrinthine strands of social and intellectual life which coiled in and around Florence, an elusive world apart from tourists, and were quite unaware of remarkable figures such as Bernard Berenson at I Tatti, the Actons at La Pietra, the Sitwells at Monteguefoni; of the coteries of distinguished persons surrounding the matriarchal Janet Ross, who ruled from her Anglo-Italian family's hilltop castello nearby, or those international circles around the Huxleys (Aldous, then at the height of *Crome Yellow* fame, and his brother the naturalist). Nor did we realise that our nearest neighbour was a certain Miss Paget – referred to in hushed, tremulous tones – better known to her readers as Vernon Lee. This intimidating presence spoke a number of languages and had an elegance and profound scholarship which made all she wrote captivating. Her books on Italy, its countryside, its arts and history, were avidly read and were published in the famous small black-and-white Tauschnitz editions, available for travellers about Europe; they preceded Penguin paperbacks and I collected them assiduously. Vernon Lee had been born in Rome, the Rome of the Risorgimento, which seemed to add further lustre to her already laurel-crowned head. A far easier ambience floated around the baroque Villa Ombrellino on the hillside across the Arno, where Mrs Keppel, King Edward VII's last and most cherished charmer, lived in regal splendour. Her particular pew and prayer book were regarded as a powerful attraction at the English Church. No crystal ball told me then, that some thirty years later I would stay at l'Ombrellino as a guest of her daughter, Violet Trefusis, a flamboyant personality who maintained a sort of royal backwash of sumptuous souvenirs. She lived in a magnificent clutter of diamond-encrusted cigarette boxes heavy with the royal cypher, glittering bibelots, gold plate and lacquer and large sepia-tinted photographs of past royal house-parties standing in a rigid pyramid formation on the steps of a succession of splendid country seats, all sustained by a lavish Edwardian cuisine. The one distinguished individual we did occasionally encounter whilst going along the Lungarno was a wan figure, alone and palely loitering, who would exchange a word or two with our governess. This was Charles Scott Moncrieff, then engaged on his superb translations of Proust – perhaps *Les jeunes filles en fleur* – but he never had a word for us.

☾

One Florentine day remains unforgettably Slav. In the middle of a grammar lesson I was told that someone was waiting to see me in the salon. I went down and there was The Traveller, flanked by two young men. They seemed to turn upside down as I stared at them, slowly righting like the rest of the room which was whirling round giddily. I was speechless.

'Well here I am,' said The Traveller, 'and here are my sons. Aren't you going to say something?'

'I never knew you were married,' I heard myself say.

'I'm not. Whatever made you think I was?' he replied, adding, 'Well, not in your way anyhow. These two are bastards.'

The two young men, dark and handsome in a rather strange way, said nothing. The Traveller swept us off in a waiting *carozza*. We spent the rest of the day in a noisy trattoria, all together in an odd sort of harmony, though his sons spoke no English. I learned he had arrived in London – from where, as usual, he did not say – and hearing of my parents' disastrous state (about which he could do nothing although in part responsible) had decided to make a flying visit to Florence, 'To see you, Miss, my darling ... ' he said fondly.

The room began to go round again. Such happiness was short-lived, for he left the same night, giving me no exactitudes but promising to write; the usual vanishing trick, his special conjuror's magic. There was never any way out of the spell he cast.

Early in December during a pasta-laden luncheon at a grave-cold stone table in the old refectory, the marbelised Sisters abruptly announced that Piggy and I, as latecomers to the establishment, were to catch up on what the earlier pupils had already achieved and spend a week 'doing' Venice – Venice! 'City of all seductions, all loveliness ... ' In a mounting fever I recalled the exciting evenings of my early childhood when my mother showed me pictures of cities and ways of life far from our own; streets where elephants lumbered, deserts where no footprint fell, cities of spires, or domes; and seas where dolphins leapt. She had shown me many pictures of Venice, telling me it was like nowhere else – a *secret* city, difficult to describe, she said, and produced pictures of strange cloaked figures stepping into odd-shaped boats, wearing even stranger, rather frightening, beak-nosed masks. A *secret* city, she would say again, as we pored over paintings by Longhi or Carpaccio. My mother had never been to Venice herself, but she possessed a marvellous sense of place – of the *genius loci* – and its various forms of expression. Perhaps her wide range of reading had cultivated her subtle awareness of time and place.

A few days later Piggy and I set out for Venice in a state of euphoria. The governess chosen to escort us was quite unlike any of those scholastic teams which had conducted us about Florence with such remorseless zeal. Signora Morelli was a youngish widow, and although draped in mourning veils, was not lugubrious. This was her first visit to Venice too, we learned, as she offered us a pile of tourist brochures. We had plenty of time to study them, for our train dawdled, running later by the hour, something quite traditional in Italy at that time, so that when at last we emerged from the station of Santa Lucia – the end of the line – it was black night with drifts of snow speckling the dark hoods of the gondolas moored below the quay where we stood, shivering. A dim blur of lantern-light revealed a sweep of inky water, a dark emptiness. But where was Venice? The rattle and clamour of the station had died away and the stillness was absolute. Suddenly I had the odd impression that the emptiness before me was only some gigantic painted canvas, a sort of theatrical act drop which hung there awaiting its audience, before slowly rising to reveal a dazzling spectacle: Venice in all its splendour.

Everything I had ever read or heard or imagined of Venice was jumbled in my head: Venice was where the centuries overlapped, the city Carpaccio had painted, Canaletto too. Behind that act drop, Desdemona was clasped in the arms of her Moor and masked figures were playing for high stakes at the Ridotto, while, at this very minute, Casanova was making his escape from prison 'across the leads', just as he described in those *Memoirs* I was discouraged from reading.

While I pursued these agreeable fantasies, Signora Morelli was timidly trying to barter with a group of sullen gondoliers who were packing up to go home and demanding outrageous prices to take us to our *pensione* on the faraway Riva Schiavoni. No vaporettos were running so late, they told us with relish. They knew, and we knew, we were in no position to argue. It was December and in those days Venice was not geared for round-the-year waves of tourists. So, at last, Signora M. gulped at the price and we found ourselves crouched together, peering out from under the dark hood of a gondola.

Slowly, almost languorously, we lapped along that legendary

waterway, while Venice, like some fabulous frieze, unwound beside us: palazzo by palazzo, loggia by loggia, fretted windows and balconies pearled with snow slipped past, great doorways loomed over narrow alleyways, and mysterious little streams, or *rios*, seeped away deep into the heart of this fabled city – this dimension of legend.

It was a phantasmagoric journey. No windows lighted, no doors opened as we passed, no voice hailed us from bridge or landing stage. We too were phantoms in a spectral scene. The snow was thickening fast; where were we now? That great wall that loomed ahead, was it the Ca' Rezzonico, the palace where, according to The Traveller, Wagner posed and composed and, wearing a mauve satin negligée, wrote much of the *Tristan* score? But when I craned round to question our gondolier, he remained silent as if he were Charon conveying us across the Styx.

The spectral frieze continued to unwind beside us, until, slipping beneath a last bridge, the Rialto, had we known it, we saw with a sense of abandonment that the frieze was no longer there. We were in a widening space, our barque in open water passing the Piazza Ducale, and suddenly we were beside some slippery steps – the Riva Schiavoni, the Slavic shore – and the end of that hallucinatory voyage.

Later in my life I returned to Venice several times, by tourist steamer, by yacht, by plane, or approached it by land while staying in one of that opulent line of villas built by Palladio along the Brenta canal. But never again that first magic approach.

☪

Beside all the many adjectives applied to describe Venice, draughty should be included. Great gusts of chill wind shrieked round every campo and whined and flapped along the arcaded piazzas. There was no relief except relays of hot chocolate, a frivolously frothy broth, obtained either in fuggy cellar-like dives, or treat outings to the historic elegance of Floriani sophistications on the Piazza. Signora Morelli was truly imaginative about our sightseeing; high and low, great or small, she discovered Venice beside us, though the purse-strings were strained alarmingly.

Halfway through this ecstatic time, between day-long expeditions about this exotic yet arctic city of unheated churches and open vaporettos, Piggy and I developed chilblains, a thoroughly unromantic reminder of an English childhood. At last our tortured, swollen feet were such that we consulted a chemist in the Merceria. His dark little quarters were loaded with reassuring bottles and pill-boxes (love philtres and poisons, I was sure), but chilblains were a strictly Anglo-Saxon complaint. He shook his head, which was covered in a sort of velvet skull-cap.

'*Chilblainz? Chilliblini? Non so.*' He peered down at our swollen feet. '*Non è possibile,*' he groaned, so we hobbled away, ungainly but unbowed: Venice was worth every pang.

Returning to Florence was like being shot out of Eden. We said so loudly and were dismissed yet again as tiresome flappers. The Florentines, fervent Anglo-Saxons and trans-Atlantic enthusiasts remained in a state bordering on beatitude, so we fell back into our old routines which now seemed even more blighted. But we had been intoxicated by the mere act of *being* in Venice and its sensual allurements had taken hold, so we began to find the enthusiastic attention of some young officers at the Fortezza a solace. Soon we were pursued ardently by this dashing band, whose pale blue uniforms and high cavalry boots certainly had an air about them. Their wearers were handsome in a sloe-eyed, brilliantined way and we encouraged their advances.

In no time at all, a whole new vista of diversions opened before us – diversions and debauch it might be said. Our life in Florence took on a new colour. Admittedly, these glossy Valentinos were not as fascinating as The Traveller's sons, but it was fun when they followed our daily progress about the city, to the exasperation of our various tutors. Presently, they began to prowl around the gardens of the villa at night, no doubt led on by our puerile coquetteries. There were whispered exchanges and windows opened, leading with great daring to what Mrs Aphra Behn, the Restoration playwright, has described as 'the midnight's kind admittance'. But one dark, starless night, which promised well for this enterprise, all was discovered and outrage and scandal flamed around us. The Generalissimo commanding the Fortezza apparently shrugged and spoke of *giovanezzi*, but elsewhere what should have remained a storm in a Tornabuoni teacup became a witch's brew of malice. Piggy and I, and one other girl, were sent back to England – undesirable pupils for the Spinster Sisters' establishment.*

---

* Lesley fell pregnant by Aldo, her Italian paramour. 'I don't want to dwell on it,' she said with a closed, distant expression. She returned home from Italy and, at the insistence of her mother, did not abort the child, but lodged in Chinatown to see through the pregnancy in order to avoid bumping into friends. She was then sent to a clinic in the country masquerading as an art academy – 'a chaotic, unhealthy place' – to give birth. She read *The Memoirs of Casanova* while waiting – which annoyed her mother – and nearly died because of contracting puerperal or childbed fever, so took against the baby. For two years, the baby girl was cared for by a family of farmers who received a monthly allowance for the child's care. Lesley's mother eventually found a couple, through friends, looking for a child to adopt and give a good home to. When the couple, both lawyers, fetched 'their' daughter from the farming family,

Our return journey was disagreeable, in an overcrowded non-sleeper compartment, escorted by a po-faced ex-governess of German extraction. Still, at the last moment there had been a splash of fun caused by our admirers from the Fortezza who rushed along the platform, loading us with flowers and sticky sweets. We reached Paris early the next morning, with several hours to spare before catching the boat train for Le Havre. 'Zo! We go now to Notre-Dame and Louvre,' said our keeper. But we wanted none of that. We wanted the Galeries Lafayette, of which we had heard much from one of the more sophisticated girls at the *pensione*. We were not to be denied. Breaking down our keeper's resistance, she allowed herself to be stuffed into a taxi which sped us towards the much vaunted fleshpot heaven.

After our sombre war years at school in England and the restrained joys of Italy, the Galeries Lafayette's chi-chi glitter went to our heads. We whisked about like hysterical mice, soon losing sight of our keeper, as we tore up and down the giddy swirl of that central stairway; up and down, from one sumptuous display to the next, we pursued our reckless way, trying on hats, fingering artificial jewellery and gawping over rainbow ranges of make-up. Rouge! Mascara! Bottles and pots of goodness knows what! We were getting ourselves dabbed with perfume samples till we reeked and became light-headed. We had little money with which to indulge ourselves,

---

Lesley and her mother had to be present. The farmer's wife was in floods of tears and upset to see the little girl go; whereas Lesley was relieved since she could not cope with the idea of a child, financially or otherwise. Like many passionate women, she was not predominantly maternal. The informality and secrecy surrounding the adoption of Lesley's little girl were typical since, apart from the stigma surrounding illegitimacy, it pre-dated the Adoption Act passed in 1926 which introduced (and legalised) adoption procedures for the first time.

but Piggy purchased some unknown scent in a gilded bottle modelled on the Eiffel Tower, cradled in a blue velvet casket, while I acquired a sweeping scarlet feather fan, very tango-tango and quite unsuited to life at home. Perhaps I saw it as a banner of independence, a symbol of exotic living. There was no end to our bliss until our irate keeper and the boat train could no longer be denied and we sobered up on a nasty Channel crossing, realising life was real, life was earnest, just as everyone had always said.

## 11. Slade School of Art

THE YEAR 1919 was a turning point, a year of vast significance for post-war Britain and the woman's lot in particular. It was the year when women's legal emancipation first came about, the year when they were at last admitted to the universities – hitherto an all-male enclave. In that year women were admitted to practice at the Bar, bringing with them whole new concepts or interpretations of formerly wholly male rule. Lady Astor became the first woman MP amid howls of derision from certain diehards, while former Suffragettes felt their bitter battles had not been in vain. Yet the profound social and psychological changes brought about by the Matrimonial Causes Act (which gave women control over their own property) still hung fire until 1923. No wonder my mother seethed for women's independence – my own future freedoms in particular.

Of course neither Piggy nor I were aware of all this. We never even glanced at the newspapers and periodicals our parents combed. We were set on books, that vast expanse still to be broached. There were no paperbacks then; we bought off street barrows or from the cheaper shelves of any bookshop we discovered between Richmond and Old Chiswick, on our usual bike-round. Richmond was full of dark lanes and alleyways where there were inviting junk shops stocked high; all treasure troves. Here we overspent our pocket money or played around with credit, which was nerve-racking.

Sometimes I discovered something I thought might be rather special and traded it to another bookshop, making a few pence on the deal. Unconsciously I was acquiring a certain skill in wheeling and dealing which would have delighted my father had he known I was already following him towards collecting.

Peering into dusty little windows in which there were boxes of watches that would never tick again and muddles of cheap paste ornaments, I discovered the wonderful world of pinchbeck: that remarkable gold alloy with little gold in it, but a ravishing soft sheen. The old pieces, chatelaines, chains and brooches that were once valued through two centuries for their delicate workmanship, were now to be had for pence. So I began to look for pinchbeck in all its elegant variety. I had a clear field then, to obtain a number of such ignored treasures on pocket-money terms – snuff boxes, pins, brooches, fine shoe buckles, handsome bracelets – and I was to pursue this passion until, years hence, pinchbeck became a fashionable new cult and prices soared. Unconsciously, I was beginning to live out my father's inconsequential impulse to select, collect, and sell. Perhaps it would have been a better route to follow than that which my mother selected for me.

At home, the atmosphere was dank. My parents were in a state of indecision. Arguments raged. What to do with her now? They thought my drawings rather good, but would I really work and study? If they sent me to art classes, would I take things seriously, instead of idly drifting? 'Your last reports from Florence were disastrous. Nothing but frittering and flirting and avoiding lectures.' I was repeatedly asked: 'Do you ever think of your future?' Since all my desires were inextricably woven around The Traveller and Travel, I remained mute.

As our state of genteel poverty deepened, my mother began

to display a curious truculence. 'All that matters now is that Lesley is equipped to fend for herself – to be *independent*,' she would say bitterly, no doubt well aware how her own financial independence had seeped away, overcome by my father's inertia and obstinate refusal to accept partnership with any of the dealers and *antiquaires* who were anxious to obtain that hawk's eye which ranged so knowledgeably over the sale rooms and markets of a dishevelled post-war London. 'I'm not going to get tied up with any of that lot,' he would say, sinking back, a loner to the last.

Sometimes I caught sad snatches of talk, when my once softly loving mother rounded on my father for his inertia: 'You're just like Mr Micawber – always waiting for something to turn up! Well it won't if you don't go out and look for it,' she would say bitterly, as she burst into angry tears and then sob that she had not meant to be so cruel. At which he would shrug off a threatened scene and remind her how he had always insisted that he was not cut out for married life, let alone the family kind. Oh! Where were those two delightful people I remembered floating in their own remote airy soap-bubble; a laughing teasing pair who took me wandering about Old London, to picture galleries, and who read me beautiful poetry? I now began to see them as they had become: an odd couple, ill equipped to face the grim changes that stared them in the face, until, sunk in a sort of bewildered acceptance (or fatalism, had I known the word), they were swept along on a tide of disaster; a pair of puppet figures propped up, made credible somehow by my first bewildered efforts as a bread-winner. But again I am anticipating.

One day stung beyond endurance (was it that purchase of yet another walnut commode with chamfered panelling and drop-handles?), my mother took action. Armed with a port-folio of my sketches and some of my turgid illustrations to

Maurice Maeterlinck's *Pelleas and Melisande,* she bearded the formidable Professor Tonks of the Slade School of Art. The Slade possessed a special aura, setting it apart from any other art schools of the time, and might be described as the Eton among such establishments. My mother's temerity left me gaping. Nevertheless, she returned unscathed, and flushed with triumph, 'He was sweet,' she said dreamily – though sweet was not, I think, an adjective often applied to that severe figure. 'So kind, so nice,' she continued. 'He said you had real talent. He is going to accept you as one of his students. Now what do you say to that?' I was too stunned to reply.

A week or so later, I was enrolled at the Slade and found myself in a large classroom seated astride an odd-shaped wooden stool known as a donkey, for an easel was fixed in front, where the donkey's ears would have been. All around me were other students similarly seated, young men and women, making pencil drawings of the various surrounding plaster casts and statues. No one spoke; the air was heavy with concentration. Apprehensively, we awaited the arrival of one or other of the several professors who came round at regular intervals, to instruct, condemn, encourage, or weed out the failures. You had to work hard at the Slade; few concessions were made. At first, it seemed rather puzzling, sitting there scribbling away with a number of different pencils and being told to obtain the essential *line.* Line in its purity of vision was something Tonks held as the essence of draughtsmanship; to acquire an almost limpid line was the first principle of his teachings. This required extreme concentration, so we laboured on, longing for, yet dreading the Professor's visits. He appeared at unexpected times, a gaunt figure, a pale vision of power, white-haired, with piercing light blue eyes above a sky-blue bow tie. Some students were known to faint, or burst into tears, as he silently observed their efforts. Once, he stood for some time beside my easel and said, 'You have a seeing eye, cultivate it.' I did not know what he meant at the time, but looking back I see that it helped me greatly when I exchanged the paintbrush for the pen or pencil.

There were other less formidable teachers – Wilson Steer was one, a tweedy, bunchy man seeming to bring with him the rolling countryside and wide skies of his paintings. There were lesser, but severely strict, younger professors who also did the rounds. Those of us who passed the first days of tuition were soon working in the life classes, where it seemed much more difficult to find that essential line when confronted by gnarled or flaccid nudes. We were not spoiled, in the matter of models. Not for us the sleek inmates of the harem who had inspired Ingres, nor yet the pearly gold of Chassériau's muse. Perhaps all that could be ours when we had acquired mastery over The Line: I liked to think so. But we students were living in grim post-war times and my admiration for the old masters was considered romanticism – jejune.

My time at the Slade was in an intermediary period, post Carrington and Spencer and before the impudent gaiety and colour brought by Rex Whistler or Oliver Messel some years hence. The only real friend I made there was a large, warm, kindly girl, who became involved with Mark Gertler and was lost to me in the maw of high Bloomsbury.

☪

Each day, our classes over, we dispersed variously about the gloomy Bloomsbury streets. A clot of the more advanced students all rushed off to Charlotte Street where Stulik's restaurant was the headquarters of a group centred around Augustus John who was often there at that time, a rakish Bacchus with his harem of admirers pressed close, all attired in a kind of

uniform of loose, graceful garments, and noticeably unfet-
tered; with hair tumbling, and very free with their talk. There
were 'goings on', it was said with reverence, but I did not
really fit in, so dawdled away towards Waterloo Station, for I
was still kept on a string and expected home by seven, which
was ridiculous, but eloquent of my mother's views of the
Bloomsbury into which she had pitched me.

I don't think I felt lonely, or outcast, I was just on my own –
as I have been almost everywhere all my life. However, there
were a few delightful places where I would linger on the way
home. Harold Monro's Poetry Bookshop in Devonshire Street
was one and I often indulged in some of the sixpenny broad-
sheets he had launched: delightful versions of the old street
cries, ancient ditties, charming poems like 'O! blackbird, what
a boy you are! How you do go it! Blowing your bugle to that
one sweet star', or that pert ditty, 'O! Susan be kind to your
lover, but Susan be kinder to me' – such verses, with decor-
ation by Lovat Fraser or a Bewick print, were trophies I
brought home proudly and were at last discovered *en masse*
in *The Weekend Book*, a delightful salmagundi.

One magnet attraction which glittered through the generally
obfusc, overcast gloom of Bloomsbury was a small shop
known as Cameo Corner. Here were semi-precious stones,
pebbles and beads – above all beads of every kind and qual-
ity, real or false. They hung in long lines of temptation: amber,
from pale clouded yellow to flame orange, sulky amethysts,
jade, tourmalines, turquoises, all a-jumble. Beads were then the
height of fashion, worn in great swags, hanging to waist or
even knee level. During the next few months, penny by penny,
bead by bead, I achieved a splendid chain, choosing each bead
to represent one of my growing band of admirers, and I much
enjoyed 'telling my beads' to attentive listeners – which dis-
pleased my mother. She never knew that among these show-off

splendours I kept one apart, a glowing glass emerald – my Traveller – between two pseudo pearls, the black one for Kamran. I wonder what happened to that chain? It was quite large and lumpy, but it has vanished, leaving no trace.

☪

Early on, I had discovered the joys of acquiring books off street-market barrows, or combing through job-lots outside bookshops where sometimes a real treasure was to be found. For a few pence and a sharp eye my acquisitions were becoming quite a sizeable library, each volume a ticket to Elsewhere. I was forever asking for more shelves. My walls were becoming windows opening wide on to scenes, persons, incidents and histories of indescribable range. Elegant print spread across speckled pages which smelled deliciously musty. My parents often shared some curious haul I lugged back: German romantic poets; anything Russian of course; early children's books with curiously naive illustrations; French fairy tales; animal fantasies illustrated by Grandville, with elegant, whiskered, trousered dandy-cats; a German edition of *Shockheaded Peter* dated 1856 with crudely coloured illustrations; and beautifully bound odd volumes of the *Spectator* from the 1750s.

☪

As I became acclimatised to life at the Slade, I discovered that my earnest hours of concentration, like my Cinderella vanishing act, had intrigued a small set of Lotharios waiting to pounce. But I eyed them coldly. Silly boys and Anglo-Saxon ones at that, I thought, recalling Slav ardours. Such memories encased me, as pounce-proof as any of those iron chastity belts which gave mediaeval knights a sense of domestic security.

At the Slade there was, contrary to legend, a surprising undertow of stability, if not domesticity, quite apart from the pace maintained by the Fitzrovians, so named from the rather raffish Augustus John area around Fitzroy Square that they frequented. Quite a few students worked in dedicated calm. Others, less single-minded, but steady students, formed odd or even relationships, homo or hetero, while a few, myself included, appeared attached only to their respective donkeys, a relationship in itself. Certain of the more mature students were paired off in some acknowledged union and, having broken with the then still general habit of parental living, were plunged in precarious ways, sharing digs, or beds, when and where found. A few had the foresight or means to acquire an expiring post-war lease in some dingy quarter nearby where there were still old dwellings, redolent, in their noble decay, of a London of familial life. The students I knew took to living casually, paying on mysterious weekly cash terms. It was very, very perilous. A few courageously decamped to try some extended hinterland of allotments and a few forgotten, scattered army shelters. I recall a handful of such students who boldly ruralised, acquiring some crumbling cottage or lean-to shed in an indeterminate stretch of open fields where metroland ceased. It was to be another twenty years or so before aeroplanes roared overhead and up and down the great runways of Heath Row. Here, my fellow students improvised life in terms of primus stoves and no plumbing whatsoever, but a great deal of marshy space. Yet they dispensed a casual hospitality which I was sometimes allowed to accept; my mother, although still dubious of the benefits of such non-conformity, had finally resigned herself to the fact that life was never again to bear any resemblance to the world in which she had once felt at home – had trusted, alas!

Professor Tonks extolled 'the refinements of art' and was a great admirer of Sickert's work. He sometimes exhorted us to get out and about, to look at the world beyond the purity of Line. This applied especially to the more advanced students, embryo Duncan Grants or Stanley Spencers, and we stood in reverent silence before the former's extraordinary portrait of Lytton Strachey, a bearded figure enveloped in a large basket chair. Such sober if not sombre canvases were offset by the riotous cosiness of Spencer's country, where porkers were snouting above white fences on which gigantic sunflowers lolled. And there were many, many dismal but masterly renderings of the English scene – Nash's pale, chilly distances, or foggy copses and rain-bound, rain-rolling hills, from which historic turrets rose majestically, forever captured by a last testimony to an England that was receding, day by day, into that irrecoverable past. It had not yet become habitual to pursue the cult of brutality or new British ugliness for its own sake.

☾

Sometimes certain students were encouraged to go out and about and bring in sketches of streets, faces, scenes or some kind of incident encountered on our way, though this was not a regular part of the curriculum. On one such excursion, I had decided to try to net the charm of St James's Street, with its bow-fronted clubs and its few and exquisite shops, a hatter or a boot-maker. These almost sacrosanct establishments seemed to glow quietly; here was trade, but with some inward certainty of Noble Patronage – several bore the royal lion and unicorn which indicated this happy state. The distant perspective of St James's Palace with its stumpy towered gatehouses and strutting sentries offered a direct link to the nation's history. On this occasion (had I known it, of enormous import),

I had decided on a long view of the street as seen from across the road on the west side. There was little traffic: splendidly equipped tradesmen's vans, a discreet royal equipage, the to and fro of some ambassador and such scarcely broke the calm which reigned there and which in some strange way overcame the uproar of Piccadilly – the buses, the Ritz, the whole *va et vient* of London roaring by, two bows and three handshakes away. Men wore hats then and there was a subtle style in the manner in which their on-and-off greeting was performed. If, like myself, you cared where Lord Byron or another dashing figure of the past had lingered, bought his shirts, or dandy guardsmen had their side-whiskers trimmed before leaving for Napoleonic or Crimean battles, this part of London was a positive drug, shutting off any approaching threat of progress. A renowned, indeed historic, hatter could be found there, patronised by certain distinguished heads still demanding cocked or plumed hats, tricorns, bowlers, toppers and deer-stalkers. Thus my eye was always diverted from the direct view – forever swivelling towards historical or literary echoes: a rooftop or pilastered porch or marble stairway that was still undiluted history.

It so happened that as I was sketching furiously outside the ancient premises of the celebrated wine merchants Berry Bros, no other than Walter Berry himself became intrigued. He was a most charming, grey-haired man. Beside a small, inconspicuous window, the shop door opened on to one of the most fascinating, intimate interiors. There stood, or swayed, great man-sized scales where, for the last two centuries, topers and tasters could record indulgences. There, many a historic figure was listed by weight alone. The present proprietor, with whom I had the good fortune to become friends, took it upon himself to 'educate my palate'. By a series of lunches, Mr Berry set me straight about what wine went with what and the how, why and when of a proper approach to wine. So began a life-long love of red wine. But first, he insisted on a sort of Beginner's Class of white wines, never, never too sweet. There were some extra-curricular hours dawdling over Champagne, but I could never enjoy it – not even when it was pink, a last frivolity. Still, in a modest way, I was acquiring a palate – something Mr Berry ardently desired for me.

☪

Apart from Piggy's family, my parents remained steadfastly aloof from any neighbours and stayed tightly enclosed in their own shell. It seemed to me that they did not even look or dress like other people around. Men wore conventional dark suits, or blazers in the summer, and always hats – bowlers, Homburgs, panamas, straw boaters or caps. No one went hatless, except my father. He wore tweed suits, a Burberry for bad weather and his handmade boots from some temple in St James's – they were almost sacred objects, no one being allowed to dubbin them but himself. He was obstinate in retaining certain habits of his youth – nightshirts rather than pyjamas, for example. And when, years later, pyjamas were adopted by women, I saw his point – they were not really comfortable garments, with a cord fussing at the waist.

Sartorially my mother, too, continued in her own manner, favouring strictly tailored suits – grey, fawn, or dark blue – and fine lawn blouses trimmed with Irish crochet or Valenciennes lace, but nothing frilly, ever. Gloves were her fetish: they were of suede, usually hand-stitched; and skirts had to be lined with taffeta which rustled delightfully. In her early years of plenty she abided by many such rulings. Umbrellas were, of course, silk ones with elegant handles and of a graceful length, as were parasols. I don't recall any handbags in the early days except the small silver chain-mail ones. I don't know where handkerchiefs and those ubiquitous small leaflets called *papier poudré* were stowed, but Queen Mary, ever practical, was said to have insisted that minute pockets for a handkerchief were inserted in all she wore – even the State Robes.

And so, even though I grew up far away from Courts and Grands Couturiers, some of my mother's sartorial shibboleths lingered in my mind for ever more, though by the time I was of an age to benefit by them there was no money left, and I floundered in the new off-the-peg outfits of doubtful taste. I had early abandoned hats, which was considered odd, but I still clung to gloves. By the time I reached the Slade to study under Professor Tonks, I had become one of the bevy of girls swarming round Augustus John. We were all in the shapeless gypsy-like garments of his paintings with a faint echo of the pre-Raphaelites. Flowing skirts, shawls, both sexes in sombreros – you could be Victorian or gypsy so long as it was what was known as the Bloomsbury Look – anything but the tight, chic, basic twenties Charleston dancer's style of 'I Wish I Could Shimmy Like My Sister Kate'. We lounged passionately on creaking beds or divans piled high with cushions *à la* Bakst; there was much black and orange and tasselling.

☾

During my time at the Slade, a band of admirers circled waiting to leap, often escorting me to Waterloo by taxi to catch the last train home, in the hope of favours bestowed *en route*. If I was driven home it invariably ended in a fearful altercation on the back seat. One knocked me back on a sofa once and that was as far as it got. Piggy's brother was in the Navy and our mothers thought it would be such a lovely thing if Paul and I hit it off. He came occasionally and took me out in a punt. A nice man, a nice home and then probably a baby: the whole idea – my hair would stand on end! If the man, the home and the baby had been in a lean-to on the Steppes, of course, that might have been another matter. My mother began to ask questions when letters started arriving in envelopes. We had no telephone which exasperated Oliver Messel's older brother Linley, who I was walking out with, so I would use the telephone outside in the street, at tuppence a call.

Make-up was used lavishly; scarlet mouths were popular. My mother thought my complexion needed no gilding and used to lie in wait for me by the front door armed with a damp hand towel which she'd dash over my face to tone down

*Lesley Blanch in 1925.*

the more garish effects with which I began to experiment. Piggy was less adventurous and relied on the rather out-of-date *papier poudré* her mother used to combat the gloss. But she was growing up away from my efforts at sophistication and probably both looked and felt better as her unsophisticated self – although I was unsophisticated enough, for all my airs and graces. I was pretty in a sort of dated way, pink and white and curly, when taste was moving towards a more slinky, svelte look. So I experimented with a permanent wave for my disobliging locks. There were shortages of butter and sugar. Face cream was scarce so I nourished my face with lard and then washed it off; otherwise it went rancid and smelled. We didn't have hot water so I bathed at Piggy's house.

My mother had been quite well off, but the money trickled away gradually. The Fabergés The Traveller had given me were sold. I left the Slade in 1924: I had to earn my living double quick!

## 12. A London Life –
### Georgia de Chamberet

LESLEY HAD TO SUPPORT her parents who were sliding further into distressed gentility at a time of cataclysmic commotion marked by food shortages, strikes and worldwide economic depression. She picked a living as an illustrator for *Tatler* and Illustrated Newspapers Ltd (1928); from private commissions – such as *The Dialogues of Lucian*, privately printed in 1930 – and designing book jackets for T. S. Eliot at Faber & Faber: *a very grave, quiet, polite, nice man.* She also took on commissions to illustrate fine books – *Racecourse and Hunting Field: The Doncaster St Leger* was published by Constable in 1931. In the fifties, a limited edition of *Songs and Poems by John Dryden* from The Golden Cockerel Press was published with the credit, 'Drawings by Lavinia Blythe' (having reinvented herself, Lesley kept the door on her past firmly closed). Her favourite author-illustrators were Thackeray, Beatrix Potter and, much later, her friend Philippe Jullian.

*Sometimes advances were made, not then accepted, and I fled, my huge portfolio banging down the stairs after me and on to the next small, musty office. Covent Garden, Bloomsbury, the Adelphi ... dingy famous names and imprints, no mergers then. A vanished London. I was passed on to others; it was cosy in the tea, if not sympathy, sense of Rattigan's play – there was a genuine interest and wish to promote. A fellow or rival publisher*

*Illustration (Lavinia Blythe):* Songs and Poems by
John Dryden, *The Golden Cockerel Press, 1957.*

*would be called, using one of the old upright wall telephones,*
*'Are you free to see a girl who has got some quite good stuff for*
*jackets? I'll send her along.' And so it went; and kept us going –*
*somehow. They sent books for me to read and illustrate.*

Despite her efforts, Lesley still had no money and too many

admirers. She was dependent on men and had jewellery bought for her, was taken out to dinner and spilled soup down her dress purposely so her companion would buy her a new one, which she referred to as *polite prostitution*.

She frequented Elsa Lanchester's nightclub, the Cave of Harmony, in Charlotte Street, which was *popular with actors, artists and queers ... guests sat at tables and beer and hot-dogs were served as they watched cabaret turns of old Victorian songs and ballads.*

Other memories from Lesley's notes: she was sick in the lift coming down from the Gargoyle Club in Dean Street where *coveys of flappers danced until dawn ... Nancy Cunard was piquant, with her cropped golden hair and eyes rimmed with kohl, she had her own kind of wild style of dressing, decorated by African ornaments or bracelets up to her elbows, and she had African lovers ... Lunch alone with Lady Mountbatten at Buck House, her infatuation for the pianist Hutch was a hushed-up scandal ... Marie Stopes' excellent birth control clinics were reassuring ...* Noël Coward was a hit in his first play, *The Vortex, which had a drug theme and was outspoken ...* John Gay's *The Beggar's Opera* at the Lyric, Hammersmith, had been *totally forgotten over the previous two centuries, it was an important rediscovery, with its refreshing robust speech very different to those Shaftesbury Avenue 'anyone for tennis' productions. Nigel Playfair did Gay's play very simply: strumpets, trolls and doxies were considered outspoken and shocking. It triggered a revival of great plays.* Lesley loved the cinema: Wiene's *Cabinet of Dr Caligari*, Fritz Lang's *Metropolis*, Murnau's *Faust* based on *The Man Who Sold His Shadow* and Sergei Eisenstein's *Battleship Potemkin* made an impact.

☾⋆

Lesley collaborated with Theodore Komisarjevsky who pro-
duced sixteen operas in France, Italy and England in 1919–28,
with an interlude at the Theatre Guild in New York in
1922–23. A comedy by Henri Duvernois and Pascal Fortuny,
*Le Club des Deux Canards Mandarins*, was performed in
November 1923 at the smaller sister theatre, 'Le Studio', of the
Art Deco Théâtre des Champs Elysées in Paris. A photograph
of Lesley's costume sketch for 'Orchidée' features a belted
knee-length robe with striped pantaloons and underskirt – just
the kind of outfit she liked to wear. Diaghilev's Ballets Russes
turned many enthusiasts to Orientalism.

Komisarjevsky's reworking of classic texts and his per-
formances were provocative due to their techniques, content,
and the way taste and tradition were challenged. Ibsen's *The
Pretenders* was produced in Welsh in a vast marquee at
Holyhead in 1927. Lesley's portfolio contains original designs
for two of his productions at Stratford-upon-Avon. For *The
Merchant of Venice*, July 1932, there is scenery for Act 1,
along with costumes for a masquerader, a Venetian man, and
an extra. Komisarjevsky approached the play through the
characters. A fast-paced, carnivalesque version, the actors
moved like clockwork toys. The designs convey a blend of
periods and styles with elements of the *commedia dell'arte*.

*Macbeth* was performed in Spring 1933, after six days of
rehearsals, against metallic scenery and swirling light effects.
Komisarjevsky's interpretation of the play was as a psycho-
logical drama. Lesley's costume designs supplied a modern,
avant-garde twist, with Lady Macbeth wearing a crown cre-
ated from saucepan lids. Beneath the sketch for 'Macbeth +
household servant' are the words: 'The costume designs by
Mrs Lesley Blanch for Komisarjevsky's production of *Macbeth*
at the Memorial Theatre, Stratford on Avon. The costumes are
of no period and are designed to convey the warlike aspect of the

*Costume design by Lesley Blanch for Shylock in Komisarjevsky's* The Merchant of Venice, *1932.*

*Costume design by Lesley Blanch for two male characters, French Farce.*

play. Stylised steel helmets, heavy metal chains, and great epaulettes worn over heavily padded shoulders add to the sinister robot-like appearance of the players.'

Lesley designed the scenery and costumes for Cimarosa's *Giannina et Bernardone*. It was one of a trio of Théâtre Pigalle's 'Opéra-ballet de Michel Benois' May–June 1931 season. Her recently discovered portfolio contains original costume designs for thirteen characters – the priest was played by Thadée Slavinsky and Harold Turner played a servant; he went on to study with Marie Rambert. Modern British ballet's first male virtuoso, he partnered Tamara Karsavina in *Le Spectre de la Rose* in 1930.

☾

The terraced houses of Notting Hill were populated by poor white Londoners. Holland Park mansions with their succulent gardens gave way to tall, weather-beaten houses in long streets curving off Ladbroke Grove. Once the homes of well-to-do middle-class Victorians they were now overcrowded, squalid tenements. The area attracted a certain bohemianism. George Orwell stayed in cheap lodgings off Portobello Road in 1927 which would influence his memoir *Down and Out in Paris and London*, and the poet and patron of Modernism, Edith Sitwell, held a private salon at Pembridge Mansions, Moscow Road, in her 'dingy little flat in an unfashionable part of London' which attracted the major artists and writers of the day.

Marie (or 'Mim') Rambert married the playwright and drama critic Ashley Dukes in 1918. Rambert was inspired by the American-born dancer and choreographer Isadora Duncan. Her vision was that ballet should be less about technique and more about emotion and dramatic expression. *A Tragedy of Fashion, or The Scarlet Scissors*, a satire about a couturier who kills himself after the failure of his new collection, is recognised as being the first English ballet. It was performed by Rambert and her pupil Frederick Ashton at the Lyric, Hammersmith, in 1926.

With the flow of royalties from his plays – notably his West End success *Man With a Load of Mischief* – Dukes bought the freehold of a 'stone-built hall which had formerly been the toll-bar entry to London by the road from Oxford' in Ladbroke Road, behind Notting Hill Gate. He walled off two sections, for the ballet company at the back and the theatre at the front. The proscenium opening was tiny, and a flight of steps up the back of the stage led to the dressing room. When Harold Turner leapt from the steps in the revival of Mikhail Fokine's *Le Spectre de la Rose*, he had to land in the arms of three boys as there were no wings adjacent to the stage.

The Ballet Club opened first, on 15 February 1931. Lesley remembered the inaugural party at which *Freddie was offered up on stage as a swan, even though it was so small.* 'Mim Rambert's choreography,' he said, was 'too vigorous for him.' *Admirers liked my baroque curtain.* The company regularly performed on Sundays for nearly ten years, and also for short seasons in the West End and regional theatres. Initially, yearly subscriptions paid for the productions. The Mercury Theatre opened in 1933 with the play *Jupiter Translated* by W. J. Turner, after Molière's *Amphitryon*. Lesley designed the scenery and costumes, some of which featured in the Theatre Art International Exhibition at New York's Museum of Modern Art (16 January to 26 February, 1934). Also in her portfolio are original costume sketches for Ashley Dukes's play *A Woman of this World* – a new version of Henry Becque's comedy *La Parisienne*. Clotilde was 'a woman with the morals of the cat and the manners of a highly cultivated kitten', which is evoked by the design.

In 1934, Lesley travelled with Mim Rambert to Leningrad and Moscow on a trip organised by the British Drama League. They remained lifelong friends.

☾⋆

The Traveller advised Lesley: 'Marry first for love – get it out of your system – next for money, get that into your pocket, and then marry for pleasure, which has nothing whatever to do with love or money.' Lesley married advertising agent Robert Alan Wimberley Bicknell in 1930, for love of a house: 3 The Paragon, Petersham Road, Richmond: *epoch William & Mary, overlooking the Thames. A small garden ended with a fig tree and a gate on to the towpath and the river. Wisteria trailed round the iron balconies of my river home. It was paradise ... lost by my fault and gained by that too.*

He had left his wife for Lesley, but their relationship was short-lived. *It was a lovely room with its big bow windows curving out over the river, that soft flowing grey tide overhung by the skies, now a moody misted surface barely moving, it seemed, then a swift flow, splashed with light, sparkling as it passed, a thousand little glittering reflections dappling the walls of my bedroom, shimmering over the satiny billows of the eiderdown.*

*Such was the bedroom in the house which he obtained for me and which not unnaturally he wished to share with me. But I did not like the ding dong rhythm of the matrimonial bed; perhaps it was due to having enjoyed so many French eighteenth-century paintings of* la vie galante *or the paintings of Lancret or Boucher. Echoes of Fragonard's* La Chemise enlevée, *a postcard of which The Traveller had once sent me, lingered and pronounced for an alcove rather than a double bed: an alcove discreetly curtained and tumbled sheets which*

*seemed to me far more conducive to the emotions. In any case
the river flowed past, indifferent to the dramas along its banks,
while the beautiful room rang with angry exchanges, recrim-
inations and outbursts of fury when I dawdled and doted over
that little chocolate dog, Mooney, who became for me a
symbol of love and tenderness. He was a little mongrel from
Battersea, the lost dog's last refuge before annihilation. There
was nothing lap-dog about him, though he was not too big to
climb up whenever he could. He was sturdy, stumpy, on short-
ish legs, and a touch of spaniel gave him those melting
milk-chocolate coloured eyes and nose and drooping ears. He
was loyal, loving and brave and for twelve years we were
together. I can not write of him now, after half a century, with-
out tears splashing the page.*

*So it was, perhaps, his constant presence in the lovely river-
room that increased the hostile atmosphere composed of
frustration, jealousy and accusations, to a moment when I
emptied a pot of new green paint for the balcony railings over
my husband's head. Or was it in part the colour I had chosen
for the walls? I was quite inexperienced in the matter of dec-
oration and had chosen the wrong yellow: one awoke as if in
an omelette, to a heaving bilious yellow. Shafts of sun reflect-
ing from the river lessened its brightness. No doubt there were
other causes, many others, which presently decided him to
depart in a dudgeon. He withdrew from the scene with that
rather pompous dignity which offended men generally assume:
a pity, for it only lessens any possibility of reconciliation. Thus,
I found myself in possession of the lovely house by the river,
alone in the bilious yellow bedroom, which now seemed less
bilious, for there was the jaunty presence of my little chocolate
dog lolling beside me, but soon squirming and wagging his tail
to indicate it was walkie-time in paradise. Our daily ritual was
to stroll along the towpath outside the garden gate beside the*

*fig tree that shaded a little rickety summer-house overhanging the wall.*

☾

Martha and Walter Blanch were in financial dire straits and his health was deteriorating. They moved in to The Paragon. Lesley's father died in November 1933, aged seventy-three. Her mother had to take in lodgers. At some point between 1936 and 1938, one of them was the occultist, mystic and sorcerer Aleister Crowley, who claimed to be the Beast from the Book of Revelation. Lesley would come home to find strange markings and insignia all over the kitchen floor. Apparently he adored Martha, and enjoyed nothing better than talk, tea and crumpets. Lesley's mother also created floral displays for Constance Spry's shop window in London's West End, and gave the florist ideas.

Lesley worked hard to support her adored mother whom she referred to as 'The Begum' (a woman of high rank in certain Moslem countries). She did a brief stint as a copywriter in an advertising office and designed a poster for London Transport in 1933: *it was a great moment for advertising firms, it was the beginning.* However, she abandoned stage design and illustration in 1935, to join British *Vogue*'s features department – becoming features editor in 1937 and was *instructed to write on everything but fashion and beauty: theatre, films, books, people.*

Audrey Withers, editor of *Vogue* from 1940 to 1960, was one of the most influential women in the country during the War. She edited by day and by night was a volunteer fire-service driver, wearing a gas mask as she drove senior officers. She cycled to work at her offices at No. 1 New Bond Street which were anything but glamorous. At the sound of the air-raid sirens, she and her skeleton staff would head for the basement shelter five floors down, although they later gave this up and continued working at their desks. She brought in new contributors, including Bertrand Russell, Simone de Beauvoir, Anne Scott-James and Elizabeth David.

Lesley's pieces for 'Our Lives from Day to Day' and 'Spotlight' have a sharp, spirited flavour – she wrote about cultural goings-on around town and *le gratin versus café society: rich Americans, idle aristocrats, film and theatre celebrities, gigolos and hangers-on.* Advice was given to keep up the morale and enliven women's daily lives. She developed *a new kind of caricature-portrait.* Lesley would interview her sitters and *ask questions about the sort of things they liked – their hobbies, passions, and the routine that made up their daily lives – then go away, returning later with something so full of detail that you can look at it for a long time without seeing everything I have put in.* She continued to draw these throughout her life and sent them to friends as Christmas cards.

The photographer, illustrator and designer Cecil Beaton was from a middle-class suburban background like Lesley: they both excelled at 'self-creation' and playing with image, each in their own way. They shared a passion for the eighteenth century and rococo romanticism – the glorious opposite of prim, gothic Victoriana. His Georgian Arcadia at Ashcombe was a triumph of individuality and sylvan beauty.

Lesley told Beaton's biographer, Hugo Vickers, that when she first met Beaton at *Vogue* she was rather frightened of him. Had she had the confidence, they could have been friends, but it had to wait until later. She was devoted to him, and said that *there was much more to him than people realised. They saw the tinsel image and they looked no further. Underneath there was great understanding.* Lesley often re-jacketed books with photos or illustrations of her own: her copy of Melnikov-Petcherski's *Dans les Forêts* published by Gallimard in 1957 has a handwritten note tucked inside: *photograph on the cover given me by Cecil Beaton, on his return from Russia, 1938.* Cecil Beaton's *Time Exposure* with a commentary and captions by Peter Quennell, published in 1941, is inscribed: 'To Lesley Blanch – an issue of *Vogue* is not *Vogue* without her article – and she has been very kind in her articles to: Cecil Beaton, with many thanks CB.'

☪

Lesley's 1929 edition of *Harriette Wilson's Memoirs of Herself and Others*, with a preface by James Laver, tells a story on the first prelim page: *my old copy was lost in the fire bombs at Albany G1. This edition kept me company all through the war, both at Richmond and St Leonard's Terrace. Dear, saucy Harriette, how many nights of bombing in 1943–44 did she prove good company. The long introduction to the new edition I did in 195– has vanished. The Folio Society did a cut version, later ... I forget when, I think it was about the best thing I did. Oh well, it's all pork and greens as HW would have said.*

*Part Two*

# SCENES FROM THE HOME FRONT

Lesley Blanch Gary

# 13. Vogue Remembered

I WAS PITCHED into working for British *Vogue* without the slightest apprenticeship, in 1935, when Mrs Alison Settle was at the helm. I was always thinking about Pushkin and earning a precarious living painting and drawing. It turned out that I expressed myself better in writing. A frivolous piece I had written called *Anti-Beige, A Plea for the Scarlet Woman*, published in *Harper's Bazaar*, roused *Vogue*, its rival publication, and I found myself installed with a desk and secretary in Mayfair. My first day was marred by arriving without hat or gloves, both considered *de rigueur* then. I felt like a timid novice creeping about a glittering table consecrated to chic. The social editor, a glossy American, asked me to write captions about Ascot. I did not know what a caption was, but did my best. He returned my copy with a note saying: 'It's fine but you've left a couple of widows to be lifted.' It took the rest of the morning to discover that 'widow' meant a word left by itself at the end of a line, which was both ugly and wasteful. All kinds of technicalities lay in wait for me and had to be mastered quickly, as *Vogue* came out fortnightly at that time. The focus was on Gracious Living which I referred to as 'Good Gracious Living'. It consisted of giving a great deal of attention to the trimmings of life – the right restaurants, the clever little wines, the emotional cheeses – while keeping these subservient to fashion and social life.

In 1937, Betty Penrose, the editor and a brilliant delegator, gave me the Features section. Anne Scott-James was the Beauty Editor then and beautiful she was. I was instructed to write on everything but fashion and beauty – theatre, films, books, people. So I broke away from what I called the *Voguey-Poguey* pattern which took an excessively social or *mondain* view of the rich texture of London life, featuring a great many people from *Debrett's*. British *Vogue*'s younger readers (pre-Sloane Rangers) were women of a particularly vapid kind, who did not have the imagination to take one step outside the prescribed chaperoned social rounds that in the summer boiled up to The Season, which revolved around being presented at Court, or being seen in the enclosure at Ascot, at the right 'first nights', or dancing at certain nightclubs. Some debs did charity work of a polite order now and again. I used to think the Social Editor looked tormented sometimes, rounding up Debrett. When it got near press day large jars of aspirin were opened and people scooped them up in handfuls although I rarely needed them since I'd probably been interviewing someone over lunch and high living had stunned me.

The typical *Vogue* reader was difficult to define; women throughout Britain fastened on to it and the fashion and beauty pages were superb. People bought *Vogue* to see how they ought to look, what to wear. We collaborated with both the French and the American editions and relentlessly pursued possibilities and personalities in the worlds of high fashion and entertainment. Special Features had been pallid when I arrived, so I shook up the way in which new books or art galleries and new painters were written up. Since I wasn't at all concerned with fashion I didn't have to worry about my pages being elegant or think about what were the stylish things to do, see, read, or feel. I used to plunge into personal interests because I have always felt you should write about what you feel most strongly. There was always a severe struggle with one's professional conscience not to go overboard about one's more unbridled passions – Russian music and films, Naive-style painters (not fashionable then), or the Byronic myth of the glowing Orient. When I started doing 'Spotlight' the people in the theatre and cinema were very responsive and understood my wish not to be dominated by chic alone. They realised I saw things from a different viewpoint from that commonly thought of as *Vogue*'s. I covered the less-visited museums like Dulwich, with its superb collection, and the beautiful Horniman toy museum in Whitechapel, or broke new ground by devoting space to British cinema as Elstree film studios were flourishing. I would tell readers about the old music halls which still thrived in remote parts of London and put on first-class entertainment, or Ludwig Bemelmans whose children's book *Madeline* made him famous. With a great deal of first-rate talent on hand, I wrote about a flow of theatrical troupes from other countries, like the Habima with its expressionistic Polish-Russian productions straight from the Warsaw Ghetto; eye-openers from the opera and ballet; or artists like Tchelitchew or Gertler (rather pointedly I did not dwell on the Royal Academy). I remember writing about the Pollock family, pure Cruikshank, who still painted the Penny Plain and Twopence Coloured Prints by hand; and Paul Draper tap-dancing to Bach (considered very new) at a nightclub. I was kept busy and brought some colour and international panache to my pages. I wrote about Chagall; the Lunts from New York playing one of Noël Coward's languid bitter-sharp couples; or Noël himself performing in one of his plays with Gertrude Lawrence; and Sacha Guitry from Paris and his then wife, the irresistible Yvonne Printemps, in one of his sly comedies of infidelity, *very* French; Katina Paxinou playing in Ibsen; Elia Kazan; stage designers; opera singers; all the Ballet personalities. The Blum and de Basil ballets, and the first great mainspring of British ballet – Marie Rambert's school, and the Ballet Rambert; Topolski just over from Poland and his first stage set; *Great Expectations*, the play, long before the film, with a likely-looking newcomer, Alec Guinness, as Herbert; Peter Ustinov as a schoolboy coming to my house to read me his first play and playing all the parts through three acts while food cooled.

I talent-spotted and worked remorselessly to open new vistas to my readers, urging them to try out the cheap steamers that plied between Westminster and Southend, where there was a wonderful eel restaurant, much appreciated by the then celebrated critic James Agate, whose recommendation might possibly persuade them to go far off their usual 'beat'. I'd suggest they get lost in the maze at Hampton Court, or discover the royal wax effigies in Westminster Abbey, quite unlike those at Madame Tussaud's. These kinds of stories would be mixed with other commissions. As I found my line and developed it, I nevertheless respected the original tradition which gave *Vogue* such special character. The people I profiled – writers, actors, directors, a chef, a woman pilot (then very new), vaudeville comedian Sid Field who was to become famous – all seemed happy with how I presented them, not that I eulogised them particularly. Noël Coward could always be relied on for his own 'talent to amuse'.

I used to have to make snap decisions, often a month or so before a show opened, in order to beat the technical problems of printing so far ahead – which meant judging at rehearsals, crystal-gazing, really; and going to smell out talent in the provinces. Fortunately my judgements were often justified by subsequent success. But it was nerve-racking. People who were written about and photographed were usually quite pleased with the results. I remember Rebecca West coming reluctantly to the studios and later saying that the whole feature was exactly how she had wanted it to be.

I even urged my readers to enjoy the slapstick antics of all-in wrestling as performed in the very out-of-town rings, a sport which was quite unknown to most people in the gilded confines of *Vogue* and offered very good entertainment. A kind of arranged romp, all-in wrestling had nothing of the illustrious background of boxing, but was like a morality play of good man versus bad man. The most outrageous costumes and musclemen were to be found in those celebrated rings such as the one used by boxers in Blackfriars, or the more lowly ones deep in the East End. Once I went down to see some trial bouts in Mile End Road. I was watching very attentively so as to not miss any spectacular turns, as I intended to do a splendid write-up, when suddenly a hulk rushed towards me, carrying his struggling opponent whom he threw over the ropes in my direction, shouting, 'You want 'im, you can 'ave 'im, lady!' All-in wrestling was certainly entertainment of a very new kind for those of my readers who still went about wearing hats and gloves and lunched together in the tea-room restraints of Knightsbridge. In short I tried to stir up my readers to discover fresh diversions.

My days were very varied. Sometimes having taken some visiting American film star out to lunch at the Ivy, I would rush back to correct some proofs, before having tea with Ivy Compton Burnett; one of those famous special tea parties which were part of London literary life. At other times I stayed all day in the studios where Cecil Beaton would be photographing the people about whom I was going to write. I remember one evening in particular, when the last sitting was reserved for Mrs Asquith, or the Countess of Oxford as she became, who was a formidable figure. On arrival she was asked to put on a black evening dress selected by the fashion editor. It was icy cold weather and when she took off her coat and blouse she revealed extremely thick white woollen underwear. 'I am not going to take it off,' she stated, eyeing the dress with slim shoulder straps and a very low *décolletage* warily. The studio assistant, a nice but perpetually agitated lady, began to fret. Mrs Asquith was firm, 'You can pin it on, but I'm certainly not going to undress.' I broke the news to Cecil who laughed uproariously. In some miraculous way, he persuaded her to put out one skinny bare arm and the rest of the dress was pinned round her. She was photographed sideways on and no one was any the wiser.

I frequently went to film shoots and plays, and remember Vivien Leigh's first performance at Ashley Dukes's little ballet theatre in Notting Hill Gate in his production of *The Mask of Virtue*, a dramatic version of an eighteenth-century tale by Diderot. On the first night a few rather unwilling critics had been persuaded to attend and one and all were completely bowled over by the exquisite beauty of this ravishing young creature. She was an overnight sensation. I saw her often after that, for she was immediately snapped up by the cinema. Vivien was quite worldly and ambitious, and was already married to a young lawyer. She had one strange obstinacy, which threw film directors and dress designers into fits. She thought her gracious swan neck too long – she had quite a fixation about it – and always tried to shorten it by wearing a black velvet ribbon tied up high. Those were very early days in her career and I came to know her better later, though I was not in Hollywood when *Gone with the Wind* was being made by George Cukor, putting her on the world's cinematic map for ever more. George was known as a woman's director as he always got wonderful performances out of his actresses. As shooting began and a few scenes had been done with Olivia de Havilland and Vivien, a fearful inter-directorial-managerial drama boiled up in the MGM studios, and George withdrew from the picture, right in the middle of shooting the grim scenes of the wounded and dying after the battle of Atlanta. Olivia and Vivien had no confidence in the new director and would rush to George's house at night to get his advice on how to play their scenes in the next day's shoot. This was a well-kept secret at the time, although the ladies eventually acquired confidence in their new director.

The social pages used to be very amusing when Cecil Beaton brought back photographs taken over a weekend at his country house. They were in the nature of a fabulous, fashionable private joke, giving the reader the feeling of peeping through the keyhole which readers always liked. But there aren't any keyholes to peep through now, everything is wide open, and indeed, that Gracious Living atmosphere which *Vogue* hankered after has completely gone. People used to come in with fascinating stories about life on Daisy Fellowes' yacht off Corfu, or in Johnny McMullin's caravan at Salzburg, and it seemed exotic – but now everybody goes further and further, summer clothes are photographed in Peru or India and there's a kind of inverted exoticism about going to Butlins.

*Vogue* has always been elegant and nothing will ever stop an elegant woman looking elegant in any idiom. But once it would have been a different imposition of elegance. We have seen the annihilation of formal elegance which is why the Queen has a special grace as the last figure of true formality. I was never much of a one for the Crown, but when I see a picture of her in full rig, I look at it with relish. She has an archaic quality, is almost a heraldic figure, like her grandmother. Were she to move towards mere fashion she would appear conventional rather than symbolic. I have always detested conventions, although I greatly respect traditions, being both iconoclastic and traditional.

I never did find out what *Vogue* is for – I was always too busy earning a living to think about its precise function. I suppose *Vogue*'s object is to show the best, and it has certainly recorded the shifting social scene and captured the *look* of each decade. But I don't know that it has always captured the *spirit*. It always had impeccable taste about fashion.

The man who could have run *Vogue* single-handed was Cecil Beaton. He was a superb photographer, wrote and drew beautifully and had all the right contacts. He was profoundly professional too. There were other photographers, but he had an all-round talent and approach and was everything *Vogue* wanted, being the perfect balance of Inside *Vogue* and Outside World. I seem to remember he used to drive up to the office with a Negro chauffeur and chinchilla rug. He was a barometer, the first to understand new trends, and had a wonderful sense of humour. I enjoyed seeing his photographs 'before and after'. He'd redraw on the proofs or yell, 'Slice the hips, that sag must go,' and the retouchers worked overtime, so that his subjects would ring up and say, 'The most divine picture, I want twelve more prints.'

Why did I leave? Because in 1944 I was offered a job writing about the cinema, which I love, for *The Leader*. And then I suddenly felt domestic and married again. I met Romain Gary at a party, was sent the manuscript of his first novel *Education Européenne* and thought: 'Lord, another manuscript,' sighed, read it, and found it wonderful. It later won the Prix des Critiques. He came to the studios and I had him photographed for 'Spotlight'. A year later, in April 1945, we were married. Living in London during the Blitz, three flats were shattered from under me. By the end of it I wanted a change.

# 14. 'Spotlight': Writing from the Vogue Years

## THE YEARS BETWEEN

On 28 June 1919, in the Hall of Mirrors at the Palace of Versailles, the last signatory flourished his name on to the historic document. The Peace Treaty was signed. Victor and vanquished dispersed, ruminating severally. It must never happen again – peace, it's wonderful – or little man, what next? What indeed. It was peace, but not plenty. All over Europe the people muttered, the rulers mumbled. Nothing was clear. Slackened war tension brought no constructive peace plans. Darkened streets, food coupons and sugar rationing continued for many months – for years, in some cases. There were unofficial Victory balls – raffish, hysterical affairs – and official stop-watched Victory Parades, with bunting'd grandstands in the Mall (the last echoes of jingoism surviving among civilian spectators alone), and in July 1919 a huge Victory Parade with King George V and Queen Mary taking the salute outside the Palace. Beside them stood Queen Alexandra, in a flowery toque and violet dotted veil, a figure from another age – another England: the solid unassailable England of the Crimean, Zulu and Boer Wars. Now she was watching yet another England forming: a country which had won the war, but was to lose the peace. For all the blood, mud and high endeavours of the battle, it was not the war, but the peace which turned us sour.

Disarmament brought disillusion, unemployment, war debts, peace profiteers. Shell-shocked wrecks. War widows struggling to bring up their children. Temporary gentlemen tramping the streets in search of a job. Surplus women feeling cheated, and hurling all their forces into a career. The new poor starting brave but doomed ventures such as tea shops or chicken farms. Bewilderment, incompetence. A tragic and cynical realisation that peace problems could be shrugged away for the time being anyhow.

Against this background, the Americanisation of Britain began. All things American were sought after. Chewing gum. Cocktails. The short stories of O. Henry. Ragtime. Negro music. American slang. 'Oh Boy! It's cute!' we cried, and wished that we could shimmy like our sister Kate. Stomping along, we black-bottomed our way into the Jazz tingle of the early twenties while bishops denounced us, egged on by Fleet Street, now fully awake to pepped-up Yankee press methods.

The legal emancipation of women proceeded slowly, but surely. Post-war girls found their pre-war domestic niche cramping. Lady Astor was the first woman MP in 1919, and the same year women were admitted to the Universities, the Bar and many other professions. But the profound social and psychological changes produced by the Matrimonial Causes Act did not occur till 1923.

Fashion moved as slowly towards that sartorial freedom enjoyed by the tubular, crop-headed, uncorseted dryad of the careless middle twenties. In spite of the rigours of war work, most women of the immediate post-war years were still spanking fine females, ponderously corseted, lushly coiffured, with sturdy black stockings (silk was reserved for best), massive millinery, and modest lingerie. They had tousled eyebrows, bright expressions and no make-up. They looked over-weighted, overheated and overfed. And indeed, by our latter-day standards they were.

Meantime, peace gathered momentum. German commercial travellers reappeared, and were not discouraged. The Bolshevik menace, however, was dwelt upon with unctuous vigour. Melba sang. Massine and Cecchetti danced for Diaghilev. Lenglen played tennis. Chaplin capered. Mary Pickford was the world's sweetheart. Darling Ellen Terry, now a very old lady, spoke well of the talents of her young relative John Gielgud. The doctrines of Freud and Jung began to take effect. 'Wishful thinking' explained much. Sex, and variations on its theme, abounded. Orientalism was the rage. We played Mahjong wearing exotic lamé lounging pyjamas and waving long ciga-rette holders. We collected jade; talked Tutankhamen. Amateur pianists still whacked out the *Indian Love Lyrics*. We discussed the bitterness of the Georgian poets; the mystery of Lawrence of Arabia; the chunked hunks of Epstein genius; and the beauty of Lady Diana Manners who had just married Mr Alfred Duff Cooper.

In 1923 motor cars were still regarded as capricious toys for the well-to-do. The BBC had just begun to broadcast, with amateur charm, from Savoy Hill. We listened-in through unbecoming, uncomfortable earphones. Beige was the rage: so were Chanel's knitted dresses. These were by no means as revealing as the present-day sweaters. They hung like sacks, and could have aroused no misgivings among such sticklers as the Hays office censors, who have just cracked down on what they describe as 'sweater shots' of Hollywood glamour girls.

In 1924 the Bright Young Things were in full shriek, gate-crashing along from one bottle party to the next. Skirts were above the knee; waists almost below. In the race for pleasure condensation was all. We lived in flats (or at nightclubs), wore rayon, ate from tins, dieted, read Huxley and the Sitwells as short cuts to culture, were Eton-cropped, drove in baby cars such as the Austin Seven, and refused to be amused by the Wembley Exhibition, which was a dismal failure, in spite of the royal family's indefatigable efforts. The Prince of Wales was rendered, life size, in Empire butter: Queen Mary tore round and round on the giant racer.

Shaw's *St Joan* vied with exotic importations sponsored by C. B. Cochran such as the Guitrys, Pitoeffs, Duse, and the Habima Theatre. Noël Coward sprang into fame with *The Vortex*. Nigel Playfair's Hammersmith production of *The Beggar's Opera* was the first of a long line of stylised revivals, and ran for three years. Lovat Fraser's genius blazed out, uncorrupted by considerations of chic or box office, to become both. Hogarthian bawdry became quite a cult, pleasing gallery and stalls alike. The poxy doxy aspects of the eighteenth century were 'definitely' more fun than the dainty *dix-huitièmes* of former years.

In 1925, Queen Alexandra's snowy funeral snapped a last link with the elegant Edwardian era. In 1926, the General Strike was ruthlessly suppressed. There were troops in Hyde Park, and those who lent the Government a hand (the attitude was semi-sporting – Government versus the rest) were much lauded for their endurance, on all-day shifts at canteens, or conveying foodstuffs. (No shadow of future fire-fighting units, grim decontamination or rescue squad work had yet fallen on our fool's paradise.)

Marie Stopes was winning her crusade for Birth Control, though the principle of quality over quantity was contested every inch of the way. To an older, blinkered generation, there was now no getting away from sex. It was forever rearing its ugly head. And although *Lady Chatterley's Lover* was banned, it got round that women, as well as men, now knew what they wanted. Tallulah Bankhead was just then entering on her days of fan-fame. Maugham wrote *Our Betters*; Coward came back with *Fallen Angels*; and Arlen wrote *The Green Hat*.

Intellectuals took refuge in films. The founding of the Film Society in 1926 established the serious cinema. Those were the days. Great days, with Sunday showings of fantastic German pictures, *Caligari* and *The Student of Prague*; realistic, idealistic Russian pictures, *The General Line*, *Potemkin* and *The Mother*. Diaghilev gave us *Le Pas d'Acier*, with constructivist sets and Prokofiev music. There was Chekhov at Barnes.

At the turn of the decade, the pace quickens. Holiday horizons widen. Sun worshippers crowd the beaches of the Riviera and the Lido, discover Dalmatia and Greece. Cecil Beaton, who caricatures and photographs *le monde où l'on s'amuse*, writes of Antibes, 'the stockingless Eden'. We sit on high stools, at bars, in beach pyjamas. Maquillage is fast and furious. Toenails as well as fingernails are richly crimsoned. We are brittle-slim and bronze-brown. Crooning and cruising, it's just heaven and too, too divine. Cole Porter sings 'Let's Do It, Let's Do It Now'. Lots of us take his advice. Amy Johnson's epic flight to Australia makes headlines. Christopher Wood's suicide awakes us to his neglected genius. Nudism is a cult and a joke. Mickey Mouse is the Panda of these days – everybody's poppet. Civil aviation expands. Dunne experiments with time, but most of us live in the present. Cloche hats still extinguish such great beauties as Lady Ashley and the Gellibrand. Diamond bracelets double and treble on some arms, and are vulgarly known as service stripes.

Talkies get under way. Garbo survives them. Transatlantic contrapuntal ecstasies enthral. There's religion in rhythm, swing the treacly Negro voices: perhaps so. 'For God's sake don't let us mix politics with religion,' cries Sir William Joynson-Hicks in 1931, aptly summing up the general attitude towards civic responsibilities. But after the Hunger March to demand the abolition of the Means Test had been dispersed by batons, a social conscience began to take vague shape, and most of the younger intellectuals inclined sharply to the Left. Still, nothing constructive was done.

Syrie Maugham and a bucket of whitewash transformed interior decoration. Salzburg fostered the love of Baroque. Shell-Mex advertising and Underground posters brought art to the hoardings. Rex Whistler was perfecting his delicious draughtsmanship.

Connoisseurs collected Fortnum & Mason's delicious catalogues as well as specialised groceries. Constance Spry's Flower Decorations were brilliantly successful. Junk fiends combed the Caledonian market. Simple pleasures pleased sophisticates. Pub-crawlers played darts and were politely tolerated by the Public Bar. Both sexes now wore the pants. Bridge boomed, so did dirt-track racing and 'going to the dogs'. A swimming pool in the garden and a projection room in the house made country life much more 'amusing'.

Swing was taken *au grand sérieux* and jam sessions abounded. Little, cheap Soho restaurants flourished. London was loosening up, becoming continentalised. Debunking dawned, and the larger lunacy set in. Thurber, the Marx brothers, the Crazy Gang – you were funny that way, or you just weren't. In 1934 de Basil's Ballets Russes found an enraptured public. Massine's new symphonic ballets aroused a storm of controversy, and Arnold Haskell coined a fresh word, *balletomania*. 'Integrity' was a popular but misused word. Surrealism appalled or entranced. England led the world in art-dealing, and Sickert and Graham Sutherland showed our range and versatility. Penguins changed the face of reading matter, and bolstered up the wilting cause of Adult Education, as well as giving us thrillers, classics and politics, for a sixpence a time.

In 1935, the Jubilee sealed the love and appreciation felt by the whole nation towards their good King and Queen. In 1936 there were three kings in one year. The Abdication came as a shock and a loss. The Church cast the first stone and was later reported to be grieved and alarmed at the lack of response to a nationwide religious drive. Neo-Victorianism was in full flutter by Coronation year. Tiny hats perched coquettishly, waists were corseted, busts encouraged, and women rediscovered femininity; promiscuity was *vieux jeux*, and prettily pink and white young matrons pushed pramloads of perfectly spaced little pledges. It was all much too good to last.

By now, English women were fashion-conscious to a remarkable degree. They had noted, successively, the elegance of both the Royal Duchesses, the chic and grooming of Mrs Simpson and the beauty and charm of Queen Elizabeth. The establishment and growth of an English *haute couture*, mass-produced, well-designed, low-priced clothes, and a scientific approach to beauty culture, fostered by Hollywood standards, were spreading a nationwide cult of perfection. Fashion attained a classic form. It was practical by day, romantic by night. Figures were a streamlined normal. Make-up was based on health. Macabre effects were gone, though an almost decadent standard of Graeco-Roman luxury was sought after. Parties became more and more extravagant; the German Embassy gave some of the best. It was 'madly chic' to fly to Paris for lunch, or a fitting. There were fabulous fancy-dress parties such as Cecil Beaton's Fête Champêtre, the Georgian ball at Osterley Park, Lady Mendl's Circus party at Versailles, and the Directoire Ball at the Palais Royal. Their Majesties visited Paris amid official splendours, and, from under a fluffy parasol, the Queen won all hearts, both there and in Canada, and in the States. An apotheosis of pre-war magnificence was reached by the French President's return visit with a Gala night at Covent Garden, ablaze with tiaras, orders and decorations. But the party was nearly over. The Spanish war drew to a tragic close. We had had our warning of the shape of things to come, but we were all doing the Lambeth Walk and reading *Gone with the Wind*, and saying things were 'tops', 'the end', or 'not my cup of tea'. Munich broke over our defenceless dunderheads like a clap of thunder, and split the country asunder. Appeasement or war? It was the parting of the ways. The shamefaced arguments continued for more than a year. Solidarity was only achieved by the agonies of Dunkirk – the leadership of Churchill.

## A Babel of Tongues

The clatter and chatter of London life persists, though many Londoners are dispersed. Even if engulfed in darkness, those who remain are not entombed in silence. Where once a babel of tongues rattled on, inconsequentially, scandalously, platitudinously, on the Ballet, on debs, on new hair-dos, Schiaparelli, the World's Fair, new faces, new places – the same babel persists, as inconsequential, as scandalous, as full of platitudes as ever. But the subject matter has changed, overnight, with our lives. Last May, in our London Season issue, I wrote, 'Imagine how bewildering a cross-section of London chatter would sound to a listener-in: imagine the BBC technicians wiring various vantage points within the prescribed social area to hear something of this sort ...' and such and such followed, a spate of that chic gibberish which passes for conversation. But now, I think the casual listener-in would hear something of this sort ... Since he joined

the Ministry of Information he won't even say when ...
Darling, not one of them was house-trained, and they all came
out in spots ... Matron glared at my nails ... After all, look
what Chamberlain's done for us ... I'm trying to get *Grapes
of Wrath* in braille to read in the train ... Ethel's child is in the
Contamination Squad ... My husband always says that when
the Russian Steam Roller meets the British Lion the German
Eagle will be up the Pole ... I quite thought she was a sand-
bag ... Let's face it, my sweet, the trenches aren't my cup of
tea ... James, put the gas-masks in the back ... What, *more*
precautions? ... After the blackout I lost count ...
Commandant calls it standing at ease ... I dare say *The Times*
did deny it, but all the same, I know for a fact there were
eight of them, covered in swastikas ... I haven't the heart to
do my eyebrows now ... Baby's teething, so we never heard
the sirens ... Oh! Cecil will never be beaten ... They say she
was cashiered for giggling in the ranks ... Well, *he* calls it
amusing the troops ... It read so strangely: 'Contaminated
Women this way' ... Warden positively slapped baby's hands
away from the rattle ... Our garden looks like a devastated
area since they arrived. You can thank your stars you live in
a danger zone ... The Divisional Sergeant uses a waterproof
foundation ... She's landed with a bed-sitter ... I'm funny that
way – if I'm upset I scream and scream and scream – doctor
says it's good for me ... Even her hair is khaki now ... Do you
wear it over or under your gas-mask? ... We cancelled our
standing order for lilies ... The night cook was out, he got at
his iron ration ... Poor lamb, her money was in neon-lights ...
The only excuse for their beds is that they're bombproof ...
Thank Heaven I'm C.3 ... I never can remember which is the
gent, Goebbels or Goering ... Granny's been impossible since
she got her stripe ... Their shelter wouldn't even keep out
leaflets ... One or two lumps a week? ... Maddening woman:

she kept saying, 'A direct hit just *isn't* me' ... I said, I should think it would be you all over ...

## LIVING THE SHELTERED LIFE

London, with red, white and blue circles under its eyes, carries on. Arguments on the for and against of taking cover continue: each side glows with a happy conviction of right – one lot have been foolhardy, the others obedient – or one lot have been brave, the others lazy, according to how you look at it. Vegetable window-boxes thrive; parsley and herbs being less light-obscuring than cabbages. Wedding cakes assume a surrealistic aspect, for, since sugar-rationing, their icing façades have been replaced by satin covers, elaborately trimmed with lace frills, hand-painted bouquets, scrolls of silk cord, and embroidered in suitable felicitous phrases. What a chance for hard-hit milliners to launch forth into new extravaganzas. The balance of trade could, of course, be stabilised by confectioners designing our hats. I think a bun beret by, say, Gunters, would be both becoming and practical. Caught in some bleak public shelter, during a long-lasting raid, how cosy, how reassuring to know that one's hat was as sustaining as elegant.

A propos millinery, snoods have taken a turn for the military. Last year they adorned the back of every woman's head. This year, the Home Guard cover their faces with them, by way of camouflage, and drape them across their tin hats, with leaves and twigs added to taste, as worn at the training school at Osterley Park.

Meanwhile, a general atmosphere of Crazy-Week-cum-polyglot-topsy-turvydom continues. Dog-lovers now walk their darlings up and down, cautiously, never too far from the home covers, lest sirens sound, while the remaining urban

babies are trundled further afield, boldly, in hard-boiled calm.
Kay Hammond says her children are such tough little guys
that they become threatening and abusive if they don't hear at
least two or three good, shrill siren blasts each day – pre-
blitzkrieg London proved altogether too placid, after bucolic
air-battles; 'Mummie, *don't* sing lullabies, I can't hear the
sirens,' said another tough tot. Staid elderly matrons turn red-
hot-mommas and crowd Fortnum and Mason, ordering
champagne cocktails as pick-ups instead of their usual coffee-
and-cake elevenses. The more sedate, Anglo-Saxon residential
districts, such as Kensington and Bayswater, are assuming the
aspect of some Mediterranean port, with lines of washing fes-
tooning the balconies, and swarthy, chattering Gibraltar
refugees lolling over every other window-sill. Lemons are
becoming as exotic and rare as caviar. Guests are now as
apologetic over taking sugar as if it were cocaine. Camp beds
and deck chairs are at a premium; camp-equipment and picnic
departments are doing the roaring trade denied them in hap-
pier holiday seasons. Simple pleasures count more and more.
An undisturbed night's rest now has all the delights of a
month's holiday. Almost all day and all night alarms spent
anywhere, in any shelter, produce the strangest friendships –
which are maintained, matily. 'Père Louis' in Greek Street, the
newest, best of the smaller restaurants, proves that the finest
French cuisine can flourish inexpensively, and under a Cockney
*patron*. (Though what with his regional dishes, his *piroshki*,
vodka, lyrical curries and legendary hors d'oeuvre, an entirely
international tone prevails.)

At the Dorchester, business booms, especially in the base-
ment, where everyone spends the alert being shampooed and
set and manicured and massaged, and foam bathed and
Turkish bathed. Perhaps all this indicates a return to real cave-
dwelling, and adjectives such as *deep-dug, embowelled,*

*abysmal* will become house agents' synonyms for desirability. Already, troglodytic conditions seem normal; many people have moved into their basements for the winter, and are planning sort of dormitory-bunk-house sleeping accommodation. Moving with the times, the Building Centre shows a commendable, if cynical sense of realism, and sponsors lectures on *Housing Single Women*, and exhibitions such as the Town Planning Institute's *If London Began Again*.

Some shops, such as John Lewis, carry on with fittings, in their shelters. Dickins and Jones have canteen refreshments for bomb-bound customers. Austin Reed's supply books and magazines. At Harvey Nichols you can have a permanent wave by way of distraction. Sampling the shelters and swopping experiences is still a good game. Subterranean restaurants such as Lansdowne House, Czardas, Boulestin and Hatchetts are always crowded out, but then Arthur Young's swing band (at Hatchetts) could pack an attic at Croydon. At Grosvenor House, the new deep-shelter restaurant defies even sirens. It's left to the band to play All clear, fitting the phrase to various tunes. Cinemas now flash *All clear! All clear!* across the screen, regardless of the picture. It looked wonderful scrawled across Lillian Russell's 1880 bust, the other night.

The Players' Club top-floor entertainment prides itself on being able to transfer to the cellars and continue the show in something under six minutes. The Savoy Theatre ought to be a cosy, sit-tight spot to be caught out in except that, oddly enough, as I write this, nothing is on there, except all-day rehearsals of the new Hulbert–Courtneidge musical, *After the Rain*, which is due to open in London in November at the Palace. This has all the ingredients for the success of *Under Your Hat*. Practically the same cast, practically the same plot. But then why not? Musical comedies, like tragedies, or tailored clothes, should follow a strictly classical form. Except that the usual South of France second act is now tactfully transferred to South America, and lovely, gay, tinkling Leonora Corbett is a British Secret Service Agent instead of an international spy, it's said to be gag for gag the same boisterous fun.

The Gate Theatre has closed down temporarily, but what with Cocteau at the Arts, with an Oliver Messel décor; and Conrad at the enterprising Neighbourhood Theatre, with Jean Forbes-Robertson in Thomas Browne's play *Tomorrow*, based on Conrad's strange and terrible story; and a new Fred Ashton ballet to open the Autumn season at the Wells, the highbrows are well set up. Lowbrows, or nobrows, can glut themselves on Flanagan and Allen being crazier than ever, at the Palladium, and Max Miller being cheekier and chappier at the Holborn. And everyone will enjoy Cochran's own play about Marie Lloyd.

Film fans, waiting impatiently for Chaplin's *Dictator* film, due here in November, can split their sides at the Academy's banned French film *Amok* which is likely to rival *Young England*'s perverse success: it is riotously funny, what with its 1932 fashions, its strong sexy theme, panting passions and faultless evening dress in jungle swamps – and a comico-horrifico ending to shame *Sweeney Todd*.

But perhaps the best entertainment of all comes from those impromptu, after-the-show turns which enliven audiences caught at theatres or concerts. The public has seized its chance, and those who have always cherished secret longings to perform now bring their music, their top hat and rabbit, or whatever parlour trick they favour, like Edwardian guests, hoping to be asked to shine ... But there go those sirens again! One way and another there's not a dull minute ... *It's getting ever so exciting ... I do hope our side wins*, as the fifth columnist said ambiguously.

*Editorial Note.* We are not prophets. When this was written, the theatres were open. As we go to press, they are shut. We hope, and expect, that by the time you read this they will be open again. But we ask your indulgence if some of our statements are inaccurate; these are unpredictable times.

## To Have or to Hold

Unaccustomed as I am to writing upon any subject with deep feeling (I leave that to the Fashion Staff), the raging question of letting one's treasures brave the bombs is one upon which I can be both eloquent and emotional. I risked my most precious possessions, and lost them. Even so, I would rather have had them round me, to enjoy, during these disturbing times, than had them stacked away, serving an indefinite sentence in a repository, while I pined in bleak impersonal insecurity, my eyes as well as my belly rationed. Surely it is setting a disproportionate value upon things, to evacuate them, carefully, expensively, while we remain to take it. When I see people living in denuded rooms, against the happy day when they can be reunited to their belongings, I feel the worship of Lares and Penates has gone too far. *Lay not up for yourselves treasures*, says the Bible, topical as ever.

But national treasures are another matter. They should, of course, be protected. Of that there can be no two minds. The controversy begins, surely, over what constitutes private property or public treasures. Many of the statelier homes of England have been split asunder by such differences of opinion. Diehards in possession have stoutly refused to admit the likelihood of bombs on property which they and their families have owned for centuries. Their frantic heirs could not convince them, and were – alas! – sometimes accused of being grasping, or alarmist. Certain private collections, such as that of Bridgewater House with its dazzlingly restored Titians, are very properly regarded by their owners in the nature of a national trust, and guarded accordingly. The core of the controversy is the question of taste. Who shall say that this is better than that? To the football enthusiast, I dare say a Tottenham Hotspur boot is as worthy of preservation as that lock of Keats's hair which Mr Beverley Nichols prized, and, if I remember rightly, lost.

To store, or not to store – the controversy continues. Whether to stake all or pay all, for storage costs are mounting exorbitantly. Whether to board some treasures out with friends, or to disperse them widely, like the Wyndham Birch collection. Whether to remove to the country, if your way of life permits this agreeable solution, and then surround yourself with every sort of valuable, as Lord Berners has done at Oxford, imposing his own individual oddity, elegance and culture upon the more austere and academic surroundings. Whether to rely on luck, remembering Sir Kenneth Clark, who kept all his treasures in London until after the first big raids, and decided to remove them just in time, for the next night his house received two direct hits. (Even so two Cézannes and a Renoir still adorn the walls of his office at the Ministry of Information.) Whether to be more chary, remembering Harriet Cohen's deplorable loss of all her rare musical MSS; or Virginia Woolf's treasure house, for, when it perished, the rare Bell murals were lost with it; or Mrs Derek Fitzgerald who pined for her Sassoon family treasures, prudently stored, and had them fetched back, only to lose everything, a few days later; or the Duc d'Aremberg, who as Belgium fell, put his fabulous pictures, Rembrandts, Rubens, and the like, into vans which were to convey them to safety, but which have never been heard of again, vanishing, magically, from the Flanders plains. Whether to make for the soulless, reinforced concrete charms of some big hotel and be stoical about the impersonality, or whether to retain a few personal treasures.

At the Dorchester, Sir Victor Cazalet has installed some of his modern pictures, while Lady Diana Duff-Cooper has whittled down her treasures to three – a picture of her son, a pair of candlesticks, and portrait of her mother, the late Duchess of Rutland, drawn by Queen Victoria. Which reminds me that Pamela Stanley, who played that august lady Victoria Regina, clutches a favourite piece of *blanc de chine*, taking it from place to place, devotionally; while at the Savoy, Lady Oxford proclaims her dearest treasure is an antique jewelled Portuguese crucifix which she always wears.

Most people compromise. Cecil Beaton has sent his Dalis and his effulgent cut-velvet curtains to the country, but still uses Talleyrand's desk. At Wilton, which has been taken over by the authorities, Lady Pembroke has retreated to two or three rooms, massed with her favourite possessions. Before his Welsh home became a hospital, Sir Michael Duff had all the mahogany doors removed, foreseeing scars which would be left by tray-laden probationers kicking their way in and out. The present Lord Nelson still uses his ancestor's desk, but as it is in the country, even so national a treasure may be enjoyed with little risk.

It must be admitted that some good can even come out of the evil of air raids. Sentimentality apart, some things are better bombed. Just as certain slum areas should never have been built, or lived in, so some rich, dominating, selfish establishments are better over and done with. Things can be as tyrannous as people. Some possessions possess to the exclusion of all else. Some houses have got out of hand and overfull: their fall has liberated the crushed owners to start life afresh, unfettered, from a new suitcase. Then, too, the destructive force of bombing can produce new creative beauty, as in the case of Rex Whistler. Although his studio has been bombed, Mr Whistler, who is now in the Welsh Guards, has the creative exuberance of the true artist, and is at work elaborately decorating the walls of the mess, thinking it well worth while to embellish even so impermanent a place as an army billet.

And again, it must be admitted that nothing short of high explosives could have changed some of those prejudices to which many of us are slaves. Just as many evacuee children have learned to know and love the country, so some of us, by losing one set of possessions, gain other, newer interests. A friend of mine who had a lifelong collection of classical records, and who had always refused to countenance jazz, was at last persuaded to buy a contemporaneously hot number. He returned home with his purchase, to find that his music room had received a direct hit. His symphonies were dust; his quartets were ashes. He was left standing on the pavement, clutching the foundation-disc of his new collection, 'Beat me, Daddy, eight to the Bar'.

And so it goes – to lay up your treasures against a happier day, or to enjoy them now; lock things in strongboxes, or sleep with them under your pillow – to have or to hold? The debate continues, with nothing sure.


## WAR ON WINTER

Cold? Yes, we know what cold means, in this 'temperate' zone of ours. Not the deadly, dramatic cold of other countries. Not the menacing sledgehammer cold of Berlin. Not the shrieking cold of Italy, with the *tramontana* knifing down the narrow streets. Not the steely, vital cold of Paris, with its comforting whiffs of coffee and *tripes à la mode*. Not the livid cold of North Africa, nor the starry breathless glitter of mountain cold in Switzerland, Austria, the High Tatras. Not the vast snowy silences of Russia, nor the icy animation of Breughel's Lowlands.

No. Here in England cold means something different. Our cold is a damp cold; a dank cold. The cold of seeping damp walls; of acid east winds; of bilious bleary fogs; of sullen dark dawns; of unheated houses; of draughts and banging doors, and chilblains. Of gooseflesh and snuffles. Of straggling bathrooms with mediaeval plumbing. Of tepid radiators goggling windily. Of the constant fretting rattle of a loose window-frame. Of smoking coal fires. Our cold is undramatic and unbecoming. It is accumulative, gripping, griping – hateful. It turns us into shuddering nip-nosed miseries.

We cannot help being born to a climatic martyrdom, but need we embrace our cross? Our passive acceptance is not so much an example of tough endurance as a survival of puritanism; a perpetual manifestation of that spirit which mortifies the flesh and finds virtue in discomfort. How else explain the positively voluptuous abandon with which we give ourselves into annual icy thrall? We seem becalmed, or rather benumbed into living as for an eternal midsummer: which is at once an impractical, unhealthy and inaccurate notion. Here in England, furs are for the rich. Central heating for the few. Thin shoes and sheer stockings for the fashionable. Cold baths for the brave. Chiffon underwear for the fair (and brave). And bad colds for most.

It has taken a decade of cheap travel and the movies (for all our achievements as explorers and colonisers bore no fruit in this respect) before we became nationally aware of the efficient and agreeable methods of warming up employed by other countries. For all their variable climates, the wigwam, the dacha and the palazzo are better equipped to withstand the cold than any ordinary British home, where uncased pipes burst, while plumbers shrug. Our insular conservatism hedged us icily, for centuries, until, a few years back, we began to grab at such comforts as fur-lined over-boots, igloo-like padded topcoats, ankle socks, fur hoods and mitts, covered-up wool evening dresses, bright-coloured wool stockings, portable electric fires, and all the many devices that combat cold.

This winter will be long, dark, hard and damp. Our diet does not increase our resistance. The strain of war inclines us to feel cold more easily. It is an hour the colder and darker when we wake. The coal shortage threatens. We cannot load ourselves with extra woollies, for coupons cramp. But we can refuse to remain passive, shuddering martyrs, while forethought, energy and ingenuity can achieve so much towards cosying up this winter of our discontent.

There are various basic principles of warmth for both people and houses, certain rules, experiments, gestures, tricks and foibles which are listed on the following pages. Study them with zeal – with martyr's zeal, in view of what lies before you if you neglect to face up to the problems. And do not be misled by those who would tell you that consideration of comfort is out of place, today. No one goes hungry if they can help it: then why endure unnecessary cold? Warmth directly affects health, temper, nerves, efficiency and morale. Ask any old soldier. Warmth is much more than mere comfort – not that comfort is ever mere.

## BLITZED BRITAIN

Blitzed Britain, now more red than white – and not at all blue – settles into its staid Behemoth-like lumber towards total war effort, and faces this third war winter with equanimity. Three winters of war: first the Bore war, then the Blitz war; and now? Only one thing is sure, Londoners still jolly themselves along with most of their customary diversions. The Sickert show at the National Gallery is always packed. The concert halls are stormed. Cinemas are full from noon onwards. An avid public queues for theatres, and falls on each new batch of books. Publishers could sell their limited stocks over and over again, but the paper shortage menaces this inescapably. Yet Chatto & Windus have brought out a twelve-volume edition of Proust, which sells riotously and, remarkably, is most demanded by the Forces. There is an enchanting mixture of photographs, notes, and sketches, called *Polish Panorama*, by Lewitt-Him; *Valse des Fleurs*, Sacheverell Sitwell's essay in the nostalgic; while Faber announces a collection of Augustus John drawings, soon.

This is the heyday of the journalists and war correspondents, and commentators. Thanks to the radio and films, they become as familiar as politicians, and nearly as powerful. Quentin Reynolds, Raymond Gram Swing, Dorothy Thompson, J. B. Priestley, Ralph Ingersoll, Ben Robertson, Virginia Cowles, and many more. And we, their readers, their listeners, enjoy the rare sensation of seeing the daily pattern of our lives simultaneously perspective into drama and history. Which is heartening. Among the spate, I recommend *Vogue* readers to *Looking for Trouble*, Miss Cowles's lively chronicle of Europe under fire. And if it seems to some that the author appears at times to be a self-appointed press agent for our oligarchic system – well, there are others who feel its continuance today needs some explaining.

Andrew Shirley's book on Richard Parkes Bonington is admirable. Bonington was much neglected: soon dead; sooner forgotten. His recognition came in retrospect, and now there are few collections without some aspects of his variable genius. He is the romantic narrative painter. The exquisitely easy land-scapist. The draughtsman who sketched oriental *houris* with all the voluptuous vitality of Liotard or Guys – the incisive portraitist whose Ingres-like jockey is one of the great portraits of the world. That so meticulous and partial a biographer as Mr Shirley should omit the National Portrait Gallery's self-portrait is a sad oversight. This sketch is, I fancy, wonderfully expressive of the gangly *Quartier-Latin* boy who was also the genius of English watercolours.

In the theatre, much is mooted, but little settled, as this goes to press. Vivien Leigh returns to the stage in *The Doctor's Dilemma*. Ivor Novello is launching another musical on the Berkeley Square lines, an 'I have been here before' experiment with time, calculated to give J. W. Dunne to think furiously. Beatrice Lillie may appear in *Don't, Mr Disraeli*. Lady Eleanor Smith has written a play about the cataclysmic Caroline Lamb, while Lord Vansittart has just completed one on Lord Melbourne. C. B. Cochran (who ought to be created Minister of Entertainment) is toying with the idea of producing Enid Bagnold's magnificent play *Lottie Dundas*, and has himself written a play about dear, blowsy, rowdy, brassy Marie Lloyd, the rampagious ducksie who will live forever in the red-plush annals of the music hall. Peter Ustinov (of Limpopoland and the Players), whose own play *The House of Regrets* is now being fought for by Broadway and Hollywood, produced *Squaring the Circle*, and cherishes a visionary scheme for a London reper-tory theatre, a sort of *Compagnie des Quinze–Commedia dell'arte–*Habima set-up.

As to films, any day now we are promised *Citizen Kane*. Orson Welles wrote, directed, and plays the title role of this controversial record-breaker. Welles is the white-headed boy, or the anathema, of Hollywood; his Martian hoax-broadcast had all America in palpitation; he is said to be walking out with Dolores del Rio, to be the genius of the age, or a fraud. Anyhow, he's 'noos'.

Meantime, British cameras keep turning the picture. *Pitt* is in full swing at Shepherd's Bush, with Carol Reed directing, Cecil Beaton designing, Robert Donat playing Pitt, and Robert Morley as Fox. At Denham, Robert Helpmann is making his first film, playing a Dutch Quisling, in a Michael Powell picture. At Denham, too, *Hatter's Castle* is being cut and polished. This is fine, melodramatic material, with Robert Newton ranting and raging as Mad Hatter Brodie, and that lively and subtle, serious creature Deborah Kerr as Mary. Her Sal, in *Love on the Dole*, was brilliantly done. She is unlike any other cinema star today. She is emotional, but not intense, limpid rather than luscious; calculatedly thoughtful, but not calculating; *not* just another blonde.

## NOËL COWARD'S NEW MEDIUM

Noël Coward has a hair-trigger sense of both his medium and the mood of the moment, while at the same time remaining violently and unassailably himself. He can be at once creative and reflective; the Pierrot of the Minute and yet the dramatist who is also moralist and recorder. As surely, but not nearly so slowly as Ibsen, he points the moral and adorns the tale.

He has become the major British theatrical phenomenon of this age. Not so much because of his long list of brilliantly successful entertainments, his dazzling versatility as actor, playwright, author, musician and producer; but rather that through two – and into the third – successive and widely differing decades he, above and before everyone else, first sensed the idiom of each era. He has gauged the changing tempo with barometric accuracy and been successively eloquent of the twenties, the thirties, and now the early forties. *The Vortex*; *Dance, Dance, Dance Little Lady*; *Bitter Sweet*; *Private Lives*; *Cavalcade* – they told their tale: it was the nation's tale of disillusion, raffish, brittle gaiety, escapism, nostalgia and a slowly gathering momentum of national unity.

And with the forties smashing all hell loose, Coward has turned to a new medium – the cinema. This is his first film, excepting for a memorable appearance in, and as, *The Scoundrel*, made in America. I was fortunate in being able to see a very advanced preview of the film. It was a rough cut, some scenes still missing, the soundtrack erratic and no music dubbed in; yet even so, I saw clearly that once again, just as Coward epitomised the twenties and thirties, so now he speaks for the forties. His film is a wonderful and moving conception, or rather a reflection, of all that is greatest in the British spirit at war. Significantly, he has contrived to catch a vast issue behind the smaller personal ones. He stresses that intangible, yet steely-strong quality of spiritual values which is so apparent among naval personnel. To approach so vast, so concrete a subject as the Navy and to extract that one essential quality of reverential service, while avoiding any least suspicion of mawkish morality, is a unique achievement.

*In Which We Serve* has been made at Denham Studios, under the aegis of Two Cities Corporation, and is largely a one-man show. Coward wrote the script, co-directed the picture with David Lean (who is considered the best cutter in Britain), wrote the music, played a leading role and was generally responsible for all the complicated negotiations of finance and casting known as producing. It is the story of a destroyer and the men who serve in her. Coward plays the Captain, Celia Johnson his wife. The Petty Officer engineer is played by Bernard Miles; his wife by Joyce Carey, Lilian

Braithwaite's daughter. John Mills, lately invalided out of the Army, plays Shorty, the rating, with Kay Walsh (who is married to David Lean) as Freda, his bride. These characters and their lives and thoughts revolve in a complicated, contrapuntal form around the picture's focal point – the destroyer.

Apart from the overwhelming sincerity of this film, its most notable feature is its conscious, but never self-conscious use of stylisation and rhythm; the balance between imaginative treatment and realistic subject. From the first, Coward worked on the script in conference with his co-director David Lean and the cameraman Ronnie Neame. This has produced a wonderfully smooth sense of unity in the conception and execution of each of the episodes, which are linked by theme music and by a series of ripple-dissolves, or shots of water rippling, breaking, dashing and sweeping across the screen just as it breaks across the exhausted, wounded, desperate survivors clinging to the Carley float, watching their ship keel over, their shipmates drowning, themselves harassed by machine-gun fire and lessening man by man, as the Messerschmitts swoop. This terrible and truthful sequence recurs throughout the film, as we follow in a series of flashbacks the various scenes remembered by the wounded men.

'God bless the ship, and all who sail in her.' We hear the moving toast made by the Captain's wife to her rival, the destroyer (how well, how warmly, Celia Johnson plays this), and we flash back to all the artless merry festivity of a family Christmas, as we see the waters close over that same ship; the bullets which spatter round the Carley float and menace the helpless men turn into the patter of rice, thrown at Shorty's wedding. We see his life at Plymouth, his raucous, jolly Mum, his pretty, inarticulately happy little bride; and so the rhythm of flashbacks is continued, as the threefold story develops. The ship – the men – their past, their people – the ship – the men –

their past – their present. It is terrible and true. A documentary as well as a drama. Nothing is overdrawn. It is the life and death of such men and their hopes and fears and struggles shown with all the texture of life: comedy beside tragedy; inanities, petty annoyances and great moments; the sublime beside the ridiculous.

I'm afraid this picture will be called a naval epic. I hope not, for the phrase brings back awkward memories of all the other pictures so grandiloquently described: patchworks of studio shots and newsreel veracities jumbled insensibly, with Army, Navy and Air Force personnel looking like Tyrone Power and Errol Flynn – or could it be the other way about? At any rate, no star system has been allowed to prevail in this film. There were no concessions to the ogre Box-office. Casting was made with suitability as the sole criterion. It was a profound relief to such a carping hawk-eye as myself not to spot a chain of famous faces thinly disguised by Max Factor; to lie back, as it were, upon the bosom of Mr Coward's artistic integrity and to know that never, never, would Veronica Lake pop up out of the conning tower, no matter how tough things become.

In this picture, as in so many from the British Studios, there is a magnificently high standard of acting. The sense of timing, of subtlety and restraint, is admirable. Coward plays with a burning reality and a sort of humility which is eloquent of that reverential, almost religiously ritualistic approach which he brings to the subject. Even in the lighter scenes, where the famous nonchalant, clipped Coward manner is glimpsed, his sincerity is such that you feel that it is the Captain speaking like Coward, not the other way about. He found the film-actor's technique uphill work. Those darting gestures, the monkey grimaces, so eloquent, so individual across the foot-lights, were fatally animated before the camera. They had an organ-grinderesque vivacity unsuited to the silent Navy. But

Coward's unsparing self-discipline surmounted the difficulties and his performance is deeply moving.

Then, too, the casting of the women has been perfectly in key with all the rest of the film. They are, before all else, real women. Women who do not maintain an even perfection; who can be lovely and desirable, but also wispy and tired and look their worst as well as their best. Take for example the scene where Shorty's little wife Freda is pregnant. There is no doubt about it. She pads along, heavily, pathetically, proudly, her smock unmistakably bulged. There is none of that nonsensical wasp-waisted grace that Hollywood so immaculately conceives.

Kay Walsh's playing of this scene is outstanding. We see her knitting, as the little house cracks and trembles during a blitz. She conveys that stony, abstracted, elemental calm peculiar to such women in such moments. Here is an actress who is not afraid to show thought and emotion, who puts the characteristics of the part before glamour or self-advancement and has no cheap tricks of stardom.

Much credit for the reality and accuracy of the film must be handed to Mrs Gladys Calthrop who continues, in the studios as in the theatre, to act as artistic director and supervisor or, to my mind, interpreter of all Coward's work. No detail is too insignificant for her attention: the frantic felt hat of the Petty Officer's wife – frantic in an entirely unsensational, but acutely observed manner; the pattern of the kitchen lino; the Victorian tin hip-bath among the ruins, characteristically as solid and unassailably British as the men and women buried beneath those same ruins.

During the six months or more of filming, Noël Coward was living near Denham. He, the Leans, various members of the unit and Mrs Calthrop took houses nearby. Mrs Calthrop, who is a Commandant in the MTC, was released to work on the picture. This tireless and enigmatic woman was usually the first on the set, the last to leave. Each morning, on the dot of 8.15, she would arrive, with Coward, to view the previous day's rushes.

Coward set a strict standard of efficiency, punctuality and courtesy. When he was satisfied, he never failed to thank his company with warm, unstinted praise. Work began at 8.15 each day and continued undisturbed by any of that social chitchat and dalliance which so often disrupts the work of less distinguished artists. There was, however, one notable disruption, one historic break in the routine. Their Majesties and the Princesses visited the set with Lord Louis Mountbatten, who is a close friend of Coward's. In a blaze of flashlights, naval uniform, gold lace, salutes and handshakes, the life-sized model of the destroyer was shown to Royalty, who climbed around, spoke to actors, supers, studio technicians and naval experts, waxing more and more enthusiastic as the film's ideology was explained and candid cameras cranked, for an unofficial studio record.

Coward and Mrs Calthrop always lunched in his dressing room, on a snack hotted up by 'Smasher', his faithful dresser. Sometimes, when delegating a technical sequence to David Lean, he would remove from the set to play six-pack bezique, his passion of the moment. If, in the shooting, a scene needed any script alterations, he would sit down there and then, on the set, or anywhere else, and rewrite, try out, discuss, rewrite again and again, if necessary, with that lightning speed and perfect discipline which has made him so fine a person to work with and for. Among the studio technicians it is thought that a new, vital, creative force has now come into British pictures, and that this small, independent unit which Coward has formed will be an outstanding influence.

The unit starts next on *This Happy Breed*, adapted from his play of that name, and for which Hollywood bid heavily, but was snubbed away. Coward himself, however, says he cannot be kept any longer from the greasepaint, the lodgings, the backchat, squalor and rigours of a touring company. So while David Lean directs the picture, Coward is taking the play, and two or three more, out on the road for a six months' tour of the provinces where, he maintains, the finest audiences are now to be found. I do not think the cinema has won him over for keeps, which is the cinema's loss, but I do know that the making of his first film and the manner in which his team has co-operated and interpreted his work, has determined him to continue making his own pictures, here, in his own manner, with this same unit, thus contributing to that in which he believes so firmly – the future of the British film industry.

## THE TRUE STORY OF LILI MARLENE

Every war, and indeed most of the epic moments in time are commemorated musically and come to be remembered most widely through some simple song. The Norsemen warriors had their Sagas. The Crusaders their Troubadours. '*Malbrouck s'en va-t-en guerre*,' sang generation after generation, their music merging with 'Lilliburlero', the *Marseillaise* and such meretricious yet moving ditties as 'Tipperary', or 'Keep the Home Fires Burning'. Each is eloquent of its period. All the chivalresque glory of the Holy wars is in '*O Richard, O mon roi!*'. All the simple tough-gutted Cockney idealism of the 1914–18 struggle is sounded in 'Tipperary'.

But this war failed to strike a note of any consequence, in spite of every effort to plug 'Roll out the Barrel'. Then, suddenly, 'Lili Marlene' swept across Europe to North Africa, was sung by the Germans, by the Eighth Army, by the Americans, by the Italians, even; each country stringing its own words to the tiddly-um-tum tune, till it has become the No. 1 song of the war – the song that will go down in history, not only by virtue of its popularity, but because, too, its strange, haunting history has been recorded, or documented, in a film made by Humphrey Jennings for the Crown Film Unit.

You will be seeing the film soon. But here I'm not concerned with a critical analysis of the picture, as such. This is when, for once, I am more intent on matter than manner. But although all Humphrey Jennings' work as a director is distinguished (for example *The Silent Village* and *Fires Were Started*), it is, to me, the story behind *The True Story of Lili Marlene* which makes the film the most significant of all our war films to date, whoever plays in it, however it is made.

Humphrey Jennings not only directed, but devised and wrote the script. He was first intrigued by some casual reference, probably in a war correspondent's dispatch (or perhaps by John Steinbeck), to the strange popularity of the song. He began to think, to make enquiries; he questioned refugees and soldiers; he traced the song back to the last war, which was its inspiration, and ran it to earth among a collection of minor poems called *Die Kleine Hafen-Orgel* – the Little Dockside Barrel Organ.

He began to research feverishly. He knew he was on to something remarkable: something which had that indefinable quality we call glamour, and which is sometimes allied to fact, and captures the imagination, and intrigues all who encounter it. It's hard to define. The battle of the River Plate had this quality. So had Marie Antoinette's life and death: but the subject is too controversial, too personal to continue. Back to Lili Marlene.

It all began in Hamburg in 1923, in the disillusioned days still shadowed by the last war, when Hans Leip, a minor poet-painter, published *Die Kleine Hafen-Orgel*. The verses are eloquent of the melancholic period – they are bittersweet, second-rate and haunting. One is all about a girl called Lili Marlene, who loved a soldier – the girl who always loves the soldier – the blonde, shabby little girl who is always hanging around the barracks, waiting for the soldier to join her. Only she's a true-love, not just a skirt. The soldier pines for her. She embodies all his dreams. *So we shall meet again beside the lamp-post ... As once, Lili Marlene, as once ...* Yes, it's all there. Nostalgia, frustration, true love, hope: the sentiments as eternal, for every war, for each soldier and his girl.

No one took much notice of the song, until some time in this war a Swedish cabaret singer called Lale Andersen sang it huskily at some dingy Berlin nightclub. Even then it didn't mean much, although its catchy tango-rhythm tune was written by Norbert Schultze, one of Dr Goebbels' Tin Pan Alley boys. A few records were made and that, it seemed, was that.

But when the German troops marched into what the Luftwaffe had left of Belgrade, they set up their usual radio station, the Deutscher Soldatensender programme for their forces. At the close of the first night's transmission some of the records were mislaid, and instead of the usual fadeout to martial music, the only substitute that could be found were some unknown vocals. One was shoved on at random and out floated the husky tones of Lale Andersen, singing 'Lili Marlene'.

It was a smash hit. Requests for more poured in. Goebbels was swamped in demands for Lale Andersen programmes. Thus it became the regular fadeout signature tune of the Deutscher Soldatensender. For five hundred consecutive nights, the song went out over the air. The Nazis ate it up. They listened to it everywhere. In Africa, Russia, France – even in the U-boats, at sea. And in Germany its popularity was put to

propaganda purposes. There were Lili Marlene War Relief
Concerts, Lili Marlene Milk Bars, Crèches, and all else. Frau
Goering, the ex-actress Emmy Sonnemann, put it over in a big
way at the Kroll Opera House, and high Party officials were
enchanted, and forgot to crave for Wagner. Lale Andersen
toured occupied Europe singing it to the stormtroopers. She
even sang it from the Belgrade radio station which first
launched it.

And while the Afrika Korps tuned in, so did the Eighth
Army across the desert. They, too, liked the catchy tune as they
battled in our favour and the long lines of prisoners stumped
into the prisoner camps. 'Lili Marlene' was heard on both
sides of the fence. It became the Eighth Army's battle trophy.
The song went with them, on into Sicily as a real battle song:
it cheered the landings and the weary mountain marches. Its
various wordings, comic, pathetic, bawdy, topical, were col-
lected eagerly. It was a smash hit all right.

And then, abruptly, 'Lili Marlene' was finished – for the
Germans, that is. With the catastrophic defeat of von Paulus
at Stalingrad in 1943, came Dr Goebbels' decree banning all
entertainment for those days. The spell was broken. For the
first time in seven months no Nazi stormtrooper was lulled to
sleep by the familiar strains. Three days later came the report
that the idol had feet of clay – was not worth missing, was
better forgotten. Lale Andersen, it was said, was now in a con-
centration camp. It was better so. After all, she'd been caught
writing home to Sweden in a most indiscreet way: 'All I want
to do is to get out of this miserable country.' Yes, better for-
gotten. A less critical soprano, Maria von der Schmitzen, put
over a new number, 'Everything will blow over, everything will
pass'.

But not Lili Marlene. She reappeared, dinning in German
ears again, in a most unexpected way. The BBC were sending

out the song, this time with yet another set of words, in their transmission to Germany. The words were biting, cynical, and rang uncomfortably true. Goebbels was hoist with his own petard. The German people began to put their own words to it, something like this:

> *Hitler, Goering, Goebbels*
> *should all be sent away.*
> *Cart them off to Siberia*
> *Then we'll have peace at home.*
> *They'll never get to Moscow,*
> *They'll perish getting there,*
> *As once, Napoleon,*
> *As once, Napoleon …*

The topical versions sent out by the BBC were sung by Lucie Mannheim, the famous German actress, now a naturalised British subject, who, with her husband, the actor Marius Goring, does a considerable amount of such work.

The film was made in the economic, unspectacular, telling manner peculiar to the Crown Film Unit. By economic I don't mean cheap. They always know just what they want, and how to get it with the least possible artifice. They know that to 'present' cinematically is often to distort. They prefer to be as factual as possible. Truth speaks louder than fiction in their case. The reconstruction necessary in *Lili Marlene* was as documented as possible. Whenever possible, the actual people or the nearest prototypes have been used. Pat Hughes, who plays Lale Andersen, is in real life a cabaret singer – but not a star. Hans Leip is played by Jennings, who is himself a painter and writer. Eighth Army men are played by Eighth Army men. Lucie Mannheim appears as herself in the BBC sequence, and so forth.

Some of the most interesting sequences were taken down at the docks, among the mean streets and aromatically named wharves where all the spices of Arabia used to be unloaded. The area has been much bombed. Rattle-tiled roofs abound. Shattered windows are boarded up, though the graceful beauty of the old church spire is untouched, just as when it was the centre of a prosperous eighteenth-century merchants' quarter. The lilac and elderberry bushes still tangle across the deserted, disrupted graveyard. The Thames still laps up against the famous Wapping Old Stairs, and the children still come pelting down Tench Street to see the cameras grind, to trip up on the electrician's cables and to harass the Unit at work. The great gates into a section of the docks were chosen to represent the Hamburg barracks. A few Gothic-script notices, a striped sentry box, the German Eagle on the iron-spiked gates, and the atmosphere was established.

I watched the Unit working. For once, the order was reversed. For once a camera crew waited, not for the sun to come out, but for it to go in: for that nostalgic, atmospheric moment of dreary half-light with scudding clouds across the fading sky. For wet streets, to reflect the one poor lamp-post's glow, under which stands the symbolic figure of Lili Marlene, always watching for the barrack doors to open.

There was a buffeting high wind that October evening, and as soon as the big fire hoses had flooded the street convincingly (not forgetting to souse the sentry's helmet) there would be the usual minor delay in focus, or lights, and the gale had dried everything up. It would have been a washerwoman's dream. And it was a very odd sight, between takes, to see the local kids back-chatting with the authentic-looking German sentries, and joined perhaps by the special dockyard Army Security Guards and a policeman or two, in a mélange of improbabilities.

The film spreads over Hamburg, the Balkan radio station, the North African Campaign, Berlin, Lale Andersen's life, the BBC propaganda programmes, to finish on a prophetic and inspiring note. Just how would be telling, so that's all of my true story of *The True Story of Lili Marlene*.

## SOME OF ALL THE RUSSIAS

Now that propagandists are busy hammering the sickle home and Russia has become the vogue, I want to make it very clear that I have long been an ardent Russophile, so that anything I may write here is the outcome of many years of cumulative admiration and is in the nature of a humble tribute to some aspects of their national genius.

I am often asked upon what precise aspects of Russian life and thought I base my enthusiasm. Whether it is theoretical or practical. Whether my admiration is a retrospective one, full of nostalgia for the old régime, the exotic architecture, colour and music of this most Westerly of the Eastern races; or whether I am won by the clean sweep of the Soviets, however violently achieved, their new horizons, visionary concepts and vigorous actions. But surely, the two are indivisible? The one is the logical outcome of the other. Each is a manifestation of the Russian character, each an aspect of 'all the Russias' over which the Tsar ruled; 'all the Russias' which are now the USSR.

The sound of Pushkin and Kryllov lives on in the present-day Moscow Children's Theatre, which is so enchantingly gay and so far removed from that bleakness which, we were so often told, prevailed everywhere. The martyrs of Siberia, the warriors of Borodino and all the heroic madness of the Dekabrist Rising live on in the epic battle which rages today.

'Holy Russia' did not perish with the old régime. The phrase is no leftover ecclesiastical tag, relic of devout days now vanished. It is eloquent of all that mystical veneration and love which, basically, all Russians feel for their country above party politics and all else. There are few Russian émigrés today who do not feel the Soviet struggle to be theirs, too. There are few who would not put aside old and terrible personal memories, and having lost their Russia to another Russia, yet go into battle side by side against the common foe. 'Holy Russia'; 'Mother Moscow'; it is for these the Russians fight today.

Gogol wrote of his country in these terms: 'Ah! the troika, the bird-troika! ... Is it not thus, like the bold troika which cannot be overtaken, that you are dashing along O, Russia, my country? The roads smoke beneath you, the bridges thunder ... Ah! horses, horses! Russian horses! What horses you are! Does the whirlwind sit upon your manes? O Russia, where are you speeding? Reply! But she replies not. The horse-bells break into a wondrous sound: the shattered air becomes a tempest and the thunder growls. Russia flies past everything else upon earth and other peoples, kingdoms and empires gaze askance as they stand aside to make way for her.' Thus wrote Gogol: beautifully and lovingly.

Here on the western edge of Europe, we still know little of the country which sprawls across Europe and Asia to merge with China. It is associated vaguely with samovars, the ballet, past splendours and present squalors. A decade or so of smug yet titillating moral condemnation stressed the ruthless quality of their experiments, while dismissing the idealism actuating many of the more uncomfortable social changes.

Culture, it was said, perished with the noblesse. But how to define culture, precisely? There are so many forms. There is the cuisine of the French; the toleration and kindness of the English; the plumbing of the Americans; and the last war, as well as this one, has familiarised us with German *Kultur*. The lavish sophistication of Fabergé's jewelled oddmedods is probably the most perfect expression of that form of culture which the October revolution sought to destroy. And as a future citizen of this brave new world for which we are fighting, I prefer the later forms of Russian culture, which are first based on a new way of life and yet which have, as their background and birthright, so many splendid and cherished expressions of artistic culture. It was Lenin who said, 'The people's culture is not something that springs from nowhere, nor is it an invention of those who call themselves specialists in proletarian culture. That is nonsense. The people's culture must be the logical development of those funds of knowledge which humanity has worked out ... '

It is generally supposed that Russian culture, as we interpret it, began with Turgenev's wan gentry and ended with Diaghilev's eclectic urbanities. Russian music, it was conceded, was tuneful and soulful, but in rather bad style. It bore an unmistakably unreserved quality of emotion and had, like Chaliapin's voice, that smoky, warm, centrifugal force which is so essentially national, so strange, and intensely foreign to the British. Their art, beyond some ballet décor, was practically unknown, and for the most summed up as craft (Palekh boxes and embroidered blouses). Nothing was known here of such painters as Levitzy, Kiprensky or Brullov; and today, almost as little is known of fine contemporary graphic artists such as Tchekonin, Kravchenko, Pimenov and Brodzky. Even their abundant and delightful children's book illustrations are comparatively unsung. France was more knowledgeably appreciative, thanks, in the first place, to the Exhibition of Russian Historical Art which Diaghilev organised in Paris in 1906, and which was followed by the series of Russian concerts, and later still by the ballet which was London's first introduction to these glories. It is strange to reflect how Diaghilev is remembered as the embodiment of pre-war and post-war culture in Europe – yet, somehow, apart from Russia. But he was ever an impassioned nationalist, as well as a unique connoisseur. In all the trajectory of his life he never lost his unbounded admiration for Russian art. Had he lived he would, I think, have returned there for many more new sources of inspiration.

Most visitors to the USSR, I have observed, spend much time visiting the magnificent collection of modern French art in the Tretiakov Gallery, or patter reverently along the mileage of the Hermitage, to worship before the great masters, ignoring whole schools of Russian painting. When I was there, about ten years ago, I found it enormously interesting to trace the repercussions of Western Art, movement by movement, over the past 200 years, usually reflected a little later, a little more emphasised, or Slavicised, in the process. This time lag does not, I think, denote any derivative weakness, but rather marks Russian remoteness and the strong, even violently personal flavour which they impart to everything they create or absorb.

Bigger, brighter, better, worse – there are no half measures; no compromise. They are excessive. The scale of Leningrad, with its vast pillared and porticoed classicism, putting Carlton House Terrace in a nutshell. The colour of Moscow: with its Asiatic huddle of onion domes, striped, starred, gilded. The *dix-huitième* elegance of the palace at Tsarskoe Selo, with its rococo gold-and-white panelling, suddenly transfixed, or as it were impaled on a stab of sharp, purely Russian colour – a streak of scarlet or deep blue, incongruous, yet fitting. Both the building and the destruction of the Dnieperstroi dam are manifestations of their character. People who say that the scorched earth policy comes easily to those who have nothing to lose should remember the flames of 1812. Under quite another régime, the same fervency prevailed. Catherine Wilmot, in her famous letters from Russia, in 1805, typifies this quality with wit and observation. She writes of the peasants: 'At the rising and setting of the sun, and on other occasions, they begin to cross themselves, but so *obstreperously* that the operation does not finish under a quarter of an hour. They bow their heads down almost to the ground and then not only *recover* their balance but throw themselves proportionally back again, crossing themselves at arms' length!' Yes, they are an excessive people, and, as our own Oscar Wilde says, nothing succeeds like excess.

Theatrically and cinematically, their genius is recognised. They have always loved and supported the drama, and it has always been one of their most vital and significant forms of culture. Where first the fabulously wealthy nobles, such as Count Sheremtiev, ran their own private theatres with serf players and musicians, this was developed by merchant millionaires such as Mamontov, the Maecenas of Chaliapin. Now the State plays a similarly benevolent role, subsidising every kind of theatre: the Gypsy Theatre, the Jewish Theatre, the Red Army Theatre, the Children's Theatre, and countless national theatres such as the Ukrainian, Tadjikistan or Buriat-Mongolian Theatre which recently brought its new opera *Bair* to the Moscow Theatre Festival. Nor are these subsidised productions used only for propaganda. Looking over old programmes, I find many aspects of civilisation: Goethe, Offenbach, O'Neill, Shaw, Shakespeare, Carlo Gozzi, Racine, Ibsen, Dickens, D'Annunzio, Crommelynck, Mickiewicz, Euripides.

The grandeur of the Russian literary panorama is recognised: though here, perhaps, its full range is not gauged. (German and French translations have always covered wider fields.) Lermontov and Leskov are almost unknown. So are the slow, rich, earthy family chronicles of Aksakov. And Goncharov's classic tragicomedy of inertia, *Oblomov*. (What are you doing? Nothing. And what is he doing? He is helping me.) And Herzen's extraordinarily interesting *Memoirs*, with his heroic idealism and his fantastic family life, exiled in Turin, in Putney. Or Dostoevsky's visionary vindication of so many Soviet principles, written prophetically, in 1881, and to be found in his *Pages from the Journal of an Author*.

But it is perhaps in their humour that we know least of Russia, which is strange, since we share the same brand. Not gross, like the German; not *fine*, like the French, but a mixture of Falstaffian, smack-bottom belly-laughs – that robust, self-send-up quality apparent in Zoshchenko's short stories – and that capering, inexplicable fantastic craziness found in Lear or Lewis Carroll, and in such stories as *The Nose*, by Gogol.

Many of our airmen back on leave from Russia spoke with surprise and delight of this shared sense of fun overruling the barriers of language. Which augurs well for the future.

# 15. Russia: Landscape of the Heart

A tattered blue volume carried me to Bakhchysarai, where the celebrated 'Fountain of Tears' recalls a Tartar Khan's unrequited love for his beautiful Christian captive and inspired Pushkin's romantic poem of that name. Perhaps it was due to those exceptional travellers whom as a child I had followed from the armchair, that when at last I began to travel for real, I discovered no flesh-and-blood companion could compare with the company I had kept between the covers of a book. Going alone seemed best. Thus, when I went to Russia, I sought the background of Tolstoy's novels, the Moscow of the young Herzen, or many other fascinating characters of Slav literature who had become my friends.

☪

I first went to Moscow and Leningrad in 1932 because of my interest in Pushkin. Stalin was starting his purges and there were few tourists. As I spoke a little Russian the authorities didn't bother with me much. I wasn't aware of the persecutions, but one saw it was a grim and harsh life all round. There were still children hunting in packs, the *Bezprezoni*, looking for food. There were still droshkies, and I would take one and go to museums or the *traktirs* – cafés.

It was not until this first big voyage that I felt something of that strangeness, that rising sense of excitement and adventure which travel must always mean to me; and which earlier and later mild holidays about Europe never produced. My brief expeditions to the USSR were considered rather dashing at the time but were generally frowned upon since few people saw any reason to go there, then. But the land I was determined to find had very little to do with reality and was in fact as remotely romantic as my childish view of the Taklamakan Desert which I had so often set out to cross on my magic bike. My Russia was derived from an almost exclusive diet of nineteenth-century Russian writers and painters – Pushkin and Lermontov, the paintings of Antonio Veneziano, or the images of peasant lore in popular culture – all of which had formed a rich amalgam of fantasy, a Slavic haze, in which I strayed happily.

I had acquired a smattering of the language so I could move around with a surprising amount of freedom, eluding the as yet not very organised eye of the travel bureau. I would squeeze myself on to a rare local train or bus where the public clung maggot-like along the sides, enabling me to reach an outlying point of interest I had read about in my edition of Murray's *Guidebook for Russia* 1893 – a derelict convent or chapel, perhaps, where a few ancient believers might have survived and I would be able to listen to their quavering melodies – Dmitry Bortniansky's liturgical chants maybe – and I would imagine Pushkin listening by my side. During these journeys I was still referring to a most treasured possession: Murray's 1860 *Guidebook for Moscow*. I usually had it beside me at home as I read about Russia, so that I could read about certain places mentioned. And so, in Russia at that time, as in all my later journeys there from Siberia to the Caucasus, I felt myself to be oddly at home although truly abroad.

My conception of Russia was derived from an almost exclusive reading of nineteenth-century Russian writers in all their variety: sombre, fantastic, fatalistic, historic, mystic, rustic or even photographic for there is enormous local colour to be derived from early amateur photographs of landscapes that are now factory sites, or industrial wastelands. Early books on Russia provided almost too much local colour: a strong pigment in which to wallow. Going about Leningrad as it was when I first knew it, I saw everything from this blinkered point of view. The Moika Canal was only of interest because the house where Pushkin died was beside it. The Nevsky Prospect I saw only as the place where Gogol had encountered his own nose out for a stroll. I haggled at the Intourist Bureau (only recently installed and apt to be vague) for some clearly unobtainable permit such as for a visit to Ufa: a remote province where I chose to believe I would find the home of Sergei Aksakov's childhood with his grandfather and samovar installed on the wooden veranda one early summer dawn. And so I saw far less of the red or grey which was in fact the local colour around me in Russia then, except for saluting the cruiser *Aurore* which was moored arrogantly below the blank windows of the Winter Palace; and attending a first performance of Shostakovich's opera *Lady Macbeth of Mtsensk* (Leskov's grim tale read in translation was already part of my local colour). I recognised the composer from his photos on the stairs and introduced myself. He invited me to a party in the Green Room after the performance. There was a samovar and cakes, and several of the performers, and people I didn't know, who were all very welcoming.

I was still relying on the magic bike to show me only what I wanted to see; the whole still tinged by a range of past colours. Perhaps it is not a bad way to have travelled. In contradiction to Dr Johnson, I was regulating reality by imagination.

I was looking for the sort of villages where the Golovlyov family might have lived, while regretting that I was not going to be allowed to visit the old house on Zainulla Rasulev Street where, surely, I would find Aksakov's grandfather, the old settler and patriarch, 'acting in accordance with the spirit of his age while reasoning in a fashion of his own'.

Nineteenth-century provincial Russia was a vanished land, but I still could travel there with Tolstoy, or Leskov, or Lermontov if I felt romantic and wished to conjure his Caucasus. And of course I do. On the several occasions that I contrived to reach the Caucasus many years later it was Lermontov's stories and those of Bestuzhev-Marlinsky that fired me to go there; it was they who had assuaged my eternal thirst for travel. It is by the literature, the legends, the music of a land or a landscape that we can most fully appreciate the journeys we come to make later. This is not preconceived travel, nor is it acquired knowledge, but rather, the acquisition of a certain awareness of what will be encountered – nothing very precise, for that would smack of the guide book which must never be allowed except with reference to railway timetables and such.

Perhaps the fact that I could muster a few phrases in Russian or that my pocket was stuffed with Volume I of Alexander Herzen's *My Past and My Thoughts* inclined the authorities to indulgence with regards to my unauthorised escapades about the city. But they were adamant when I said I wanted to visit Ufa, to pay homage.

I was soaked in local colour: the pillared country houses where Turgenev's gentry languished, Gorky's dark underworld, the province of Leskov's tales like the glowing countryside of Aksakov's childhood, not to speak of Tolstoy's immense vistas. This was the land, the atmosphere I sought: that of Holy Russia, Mother Russia, White Russia, All the Russias of tradition,

and even Red Russia whose guest I was, since I was an entirely
non-political animal in those days. I caught snatches of my
Russia as I was plunged in emotion standing before the house
where Pushkin died or getting wedged in a bus that bounced
down Nevsky Prospect, recalling the coachman's song of that
name with which a Russian friend used to regale me when
he was drunk. Such were my Russian days, a series of magical
voyages into private realms, where I could tread fancy
free.

## 'SWEET CHANCE THAT LED MY STEPS ABROAD ...'

My real travels only began for me in all their dazzling pleni-
tude in 1946 when I left England to join my husband Romain
Gary in the Balkans where he was in the French Diplomatic
Service. All kinds of travel restrictions had been applied during
the Second World War and lingered on to frustrate the would-
be voyager. Many people had come to share my childish
longing for other scenes and skies. I was even told that what
I had written acquired a forbidden, or hallucinatory, flavour
for the frustrated stay-at-homes who had only lately emerged
from the stress and trauma of those grim war years, when
England was a beleaguered fortress, its inhabitants severely
rationed and under constant attack. When at last peace was
declared in 1945, most British citizens found themselves
almost as cribbed and confined, still rationed, still yearning for
the inaccessible 'Abroad'.

It was my singular good fortune during those post-war
years of British deprivation to be travelling a great deal and in
an unrestricted manner. The posts to which my husband was
assigned would become for me so many launching pads from
which I leapt towards those faraway lands I had always

craved – Turkey, the Sahara, Guatemala and the Caucasus were all discovered then – always travelling, always seeking that fugitive strain. Indeed, I took to addressing my husband as 'Chance' in reference to the poet William Henry Davies' beautiful lines, 'Sweet chance that led my steps abroad ...'

Turkey, which in time grew to be my most loved 'Abroad', was then beyond my limited means, although travel was cheap enough at that time for those who accepted the rough and tumble of the now vanished Third Class. Even so, Turkey seemed out of reach and I returned to reading and re-reading Pierre Loti's haunting and beautiful descriptions of the Sublime Porte, biding my time, consoled by less exotic expeditions within easier European horizons.

America was a never-never land, attained by expensive and lengthy crossings on one of the big liners refurbished after years of disuse or war service. Atlantic flights were just getting under way again, long costly flights that had to come down to refuel *en route*. Jet flights were unheard of then; jumbo jets quite unimaginable. Yet presently the word 'jet' passed into the language, synonymous for luxury and chic, and the privileged few who 'jetted' were referred to by the media as 'the jet set', soon to have their very own ailment: jet-lag.

While those post-war years of restriction were frustrating so many would-be travellers, and I had escaped, a whole new and revolutionary concept of travel was taking place. A vast international network of big business became aware of the financial benefits to be obtained from an interlocking system of tourism on a mammoth scale. Suddenly, everywhere was accessible to everyone and a rush of nations began sweeping across the globe: the West going East and the East coming West – a ceaseless, seasonless tide. The age of charter flights and package holidays had begun. Giant hotels rose where coral atolls had been, and mileage became the new status symbol. The realities of mass tourism have overrun the globe, overwhelming its multifarious flavours and traditions and destroying forever those romantic images, or illusions, of remote lands which we once sought and which could, often, still be found.

☾

'A boudoir in the Steppes' is how Isfahan was described to me by André Malraux when I told him I planned to visit Russia again. Malraux loomed over the world of French culture, famed for his extraordinary life of adventure and learning. His writings and pronouncements were never questioned even when as Minister of Arts he commissioned Chagall to paint the ceiling of Paris Opera House – a choice which was a triumph of audacity.

☾

I might be said to have touched a certain reality on my last visit to Russia when, on my way to Siberia in the mid-sixties, I spent a whole wet day in Moscow visiting the house in the city where Tolstoy lived much of the time and which was less known or visited than his famous estate at Yasnaya Polyana. Imagination would not have to be regulated here in this small square solid stone house in a side street. It had not been turned into an obvious shrine, but was left exactly as it had been when the family lived there. The largish yard and garden had stables where no doubt his favourite grey was kept. The moment I crossed the threshold I was struck by the powerful atmosphere which seemed to promise that the great man must be somewhere near; a life-sized black bear stood at the foot of the stairs, his paws clutching a tray on which lay a series of slightly yellowed visiting cards inscribed with names known to those familiar with Tolstoy's life. I was the only visitor that day, so the spell I felt around me was never broken as I wandered from room to room. There was the long dinner table, chairs ranged round where Tolstoy ate his porridgy mush, and the Countess contrived an excellent menu for her family and friends and the inevitable hangers on. There was the awful bedroom with a prim white quilt on the bed to which the lusty giant continued to inveigle his reluctant wife, late into his seventies. There was the sad little nursery with the toys and cot of the little lost tots whom they mourned so bitterly. In the salon the grand piano at which a family friend who taught music to the younger children performed Beethoven's Kreutzer Sonata; it was to have such a dramatic effect on Tolstoy that the Countess received the novella about marriage, divorce and love which he wrote as a result as a personal outrage. Upstairs there was a little room apart – Tolstoy's study where he could get away from family life and write. It was not a dark room, although the windows looked out on a yard and some trees, but it seemed dark to me: the furniture was dark and heavy, upholstered in black leather, the shelves were dark, the books were bound darkly, the whole effect was one of gloom. But just outside the door on the landing a dwarf-sized staircase led to a cupboard which was stacked with large jars of that delicious green pickle so dear to the Russian heart and stomach. Tolstoy had a particular weakness for these pickles and would break off in mid-work to enjoy a few bites from time to time. While fearing the effects any injudicious indulgence of such pickles might have on him, the Countess had nevertheless always maintained that a good supply should be at hand. In their zeal for authenticity, the museum curators had decided to keep the pickle cupboard going. When I was there, the curator in charge was a charming woman called Mme Cutuza. I asked her if she was descended from the great Field Marshal – she was and seemed both intrigued and pleased that I knew his place in Russian history. She told me that Tolstoy had wanted to write a precursor to *War and Peace* about the Decembrist revolt, but he had been dissuaded from this project by meetings with some of the Dekabristi exiles themselves. They had insisted that no one who had not been one of their band could ever truly understand their motives and sufferings.

In the fifties, after Stalin's death, I went back and travelled in the Caucasus. Things were easier there, and under Khrushchev too, just as everything changed with Gorbachev.

*Part Three*

# SCENES FROM A
# MARRIAGE

*Joyeux Noël from Lesley and Romain Gary*

# 16. Romain: A Private View

AUTHOR'S NOTE – LESLEY BLANCH

I always knew I had married an extraordinary man, one who over the years became something of a legend. But lately, judging by the number of letters I receive asking for my memories of him, or my opinion on this or that thesis or doctorate, and all else concentrating on Romain's origins or 'lost identity', I see that my ex-husband has become a cult figure no less. These massively scientific documents and analyses leave me cold. I am more interested in the letters of young enthusiastic readers, a whole new generation hungry for every detail I can give them of a man whose writings seem to speak to them particularly.

Perhaps I should try to put down some of the various aspects of the man I knew so well, and recall a few incidents, *les petits décors de la vie,* those smaller details that lie behind the sweep of a whole life, eighteen years of which we spent together.

To capture Romain – the Romain I knew before and behind the headlines – is to net a shifting image. In those years he lived in a state of perpetual transition – now you see him, now you don't! The many Romains I knew form, dissolve, and re-form before me as I write. I seem to hear him laughing; the old sardonic chuckle, 'You're nuts! But if you want to, why not?'

*Garavan, 1997*

## FIRST MEETING, LONDON

At first sight, I thought he resembled a bear lumbering about on its hind legs – a clumsy brown bear, rather untidily buttoned into the dark blue battledress of a Lieutenant in the Lorraine Squadron of General de Gaulle's Free French Forces.

Our meeting took place in London in 1944 during that time of extreme tension when the Buzz bombing was almost without respite, and there was a simmering air of apprehension as the Allies riposted with a series of low-level attacks over occupied France, preparatory to the decisive landings of June 1944.

Romain Gari de Kacew, as he was then known, was temporarily grounded from flying operations as a result of severe wounds received earlier, and was attached to General de Gaulle's headquarters in Kensington. I was told he had fought *une belle guerre* – as if any *guerre* could be *belle* – was something of a hero, and had won the coveted Croix de la Libération.

This intriguing figure had, like myself, joined a party given by one of the many Free French then in London. He was standing rather apart from the rest, and now subsided to the floor in a lounging sprawl, where he set about demolishing a bowl of olives – then an exotic rarity – spitting the stones round him while maintaining an air of melancholy detachment.

Our hostess firmly removed what remained of the olives and beneath the rather strident rattle of French conversation I caught low, growling sounds of protest. It was that deep, centrifugal sound – so unmistakably the sound of a Russian voice. So the bear was a Russian bear to boot.

Since everything Russian always affected me, drew me, as I

have recounted in *Journey into the Mind's Eye*, I found myself impelled towards this Bruin figure. We were introduced, but while we were exchanging those stealthy glancing appraisals which seal or shatter a first meeting, I was aware of his curious resemblance to portraits of Nicolai Gogol, the great nineteenth-century Russian novelist. I told him so and he seemed startled.

'What you know of Gogol?' he asked aggressively. I replied that *Dead Souls* was one of my *livres de chevet* or bedside reading.

'You are reading in translation? So you don't know anything about him at all,' he answered rudely in the imperfect English he then spoke. Nettled, I replied in my best *pidgin* Russian – '*Pravda, no ya durachka, i vash yazik mnogo trudneye.*' (True, but your language is very hard for someone as stupid as I.)

He burst out laughing, a delightful, childish laugh revealing short, rather uneven teeth, or so they would appear by present-day standards of artful dentistry. Later I learned he had been wounded in the jaw by flying shrapnel, which gave him a slightly puckered or crooked smile, at times almost a mirthless snarl. But it only strengthened that animal attraction he possessed. It was something which I and a number of other women found irresistible.

By now the nightly ritual of bombardment had become too heavy for us to remain where we were, on the top floor of an already once hit building, and the party decided to move on to an underground nightclub with a riotous reputation and black-market liquor (which had no appeal for Romain as he seldom touched alcohol in any form). In this febrile atmosphere our acquaintance ripened rapidly. We danced and I discovered this bear was still the dancing bear of tradition. It continued to lumber, but how engagingly! Such was my first meeting with the man who was to become known as the writer Romain Gary.

He was born Kacew. Gari de Kacew was his *nom de guerre,* a name he adopted while serving with the Free French Forces and by which he was known among them. It was a measure often taken then to avoid retaliation on families remaining in France under the Occupation. In Russian the word *gari* means burn – in the imperative sense – burn! Gari not only became his *nom de plume* but later the name he made legally his own. He dropped the aristocratic French *de,* which seems to have been merely a bit of show off, and now spelled Gari with a 'y' which I thought took away any last vestige of the exoticism his personality demanded.

When the enthusiastic younger readers of today ask me what Romain looked like in those earliest days, I realise there are few people left who can conjure up the pre-legendary figure who was to live through so many transformations and be recorded by so many cameras.

That of Lee Miller was one of the first. She and I worked together on various assignments for the Ministry of Information and I persuaded her to photograph him for an article I had written on his first book, *Education Européenne.* This was about to be published by the Cresset Press in an English translation, as *The Forest of Anger,* which, curiously, preceded the French edition, owing to the fact that no regular contact with France or Paris editors was yet re-established; but as soon as it was, this book won the Prix des Critiques, and the cameras started to focus on him.

What, then, did this unknown young author look like in 1944? He was tall, about six foot, and being rather thickly built looked less so. His long, sallow, doom-laden face was lightened by those heavy-lidded oriental, or rather Asiatic eyes. They were of a most startling light blue, the kind I have seen among the Kurdish tribes. His lank hair was that dense black which resembles the plumage of certain birds ('Birds of ill-omen I suppose?' he said when I told him). He wore it parted in the middle and it fell down straight on each side of his face in a manner which seemed to defy military regulation. If I remember rightly he was beginning to cultivate that slight line of moustache which recalled a tango tea-dance seducer of the 1920s.

And he had the strangest hands. They didn't seem to belong to the rest of him, so that I came to regard them as separate entities. They were nothing like those long sensitive hands associated with artists or musicians. They were not the hands of a man, nor yet the hands of a woman. They seemed curiously androgynous, small, soft and short-fingered. They were hands which, confronted by any practical demands, flapped helplessly like fins attached to his wrists. They were hands likely to drop anything he was given to hold, car keys, a coffee cup, or all else.

But when it came to holding a pen, those same ineffectual-looking hands assumed a life of their own, gouging out words hurled on to the page, stabbing fiercely, piercing the paper, raging along, no hesitations, a furiously scrawled barely-legible lava-flow.

☪

In those early days together, when he was recounting his youthful life in Nice, the almost mythical figure of Ilona was soon made known to me. She threaded through his recollections, a chimeric, romantic figure of lost love, all beauty, all desire.

Coming down to facts, of which there were few, I gathered Ilona was Hungarian, of Jewish origin, and rather older than

Romain. She occupied a room at the *Pension Mimosa* which his mother, Nina Kacew, ran with such dauntless courage. Ilona appeared to be surrounded by an aura of fragility and was mostly confined to her bed, where Romain joined her whenever possible. Together they knew timeless hours of bliss.

I never learned anything of her background, or why she languished in Nice. She was just Ilona, with huge grey eyes, gazing mistily from the pillow.

'Didn't she ever get up, or go out?' I enquired and was told she occasionally attended some special concert, conveyed by expensive taxis. 'Although,' Romain would add indulgently, 'there were perfectly good buses,' and he would dwell on her elegance and the sheer silk stockings she wore.

This was, of course, a dagger to my heart, for at that moment of clothing coupons and scarcities, I, like every other English woman, wore ill-fitting cottony stockings described by the Ministry of Supplies as 'serviceable'. Nylons only came our way after the American Forces arrived, and they sometimes obtained our favours by dangling these treasures before us.

Towards the end of the war, Romain began trying to trace Ilona, but she had vanished. 'If ever she is found, of course she will have to live with us,' Romain announced. 'Of course,' I replied soothingly. At that moment in the first flush of our relationship I would have welcomed Lady Macbeth or any other uneasy addition to our household without a qualm.

Only years later did news of Ilona reach us. She was believed to be married to a diplomat living in some faraway post. I never knew if Romain succeeded in contacting her, but much later he told me she had gone out of her mind and was dying of cancer, cared for in a convent. For Romain, I think she remained the love of his life – the embodiment of unattainable, abiding longing, something his nature demanded.

A chaos of contradictions remain round Romain's early years of poverty and humiliation. They were the years he has described in *Promise at Dawn*. Yet there still remain dark voids deepened by his determination to conceal as much as he revealed. He loved to deny, invent, hint, or, in the midst of some enthralling piece of self-revelation, vanish as in a streak of lightning. When I first knew him I took everything he said as gospel and so became puzzled when carefully collected fragments did not fit.

But then Romain was always the stuff of legend; they grew round him, mushrooming up overnight. Often when he fostered them himself they became even more picturesque than the truth; but what was that, I sometimes wondered? Which was the real Romain among so many? I have been told that on one occasion, being asked who he would like to be if he were not Romain Gary, he replied, 'Romain Gary' – a riposte typical of his dark humour.

☾⋆

Moscow is held to have been the place of his birth – Pushkin's 'golden-headed Moscow' which he said should be the birthplace of every poet. But on some of the papers he showed me at the time of our marriage, it said he was born in Wilno, Lithuanian-Polish Wilno, at that moment still part of the Russian Empire. Later he told me he was born 'somewhere in Russia', his manner as casual as my question. I do not believe he ever knew precisely where, as he never knew for certain who was his father.

Like a glittering Harlequin figure, many coloured fragments of truth and fiction shimmered around him. He had been born in an Emir's palace in Samarkand; a Polish prince had fathered him; he was the son of Ivan Mosjoukine. His likeness to this celebrated film actor of pre-Revolutionary Russia was certainly striking; although it became a well-established legend in Nice, Romain would never confirm or deny this fascinating parentage.

Sometimes a snatch of something that sounded convincing would emerge from a casual conversation. One raw January day I was complaining of the cold. Romain would have none of it, 'Cold? You don't know what cold means. Try Poland in January,' he said, and went on, 'I remember they dressed me in a very short fur coat – my legs were always bare – just socks.' When I questioned this extraordinary costume, he laughed and said, 'Well it was like that. They thought it looked elegant – "Frenchified". There were always bits of fur all over the place. They were furriers.'

'They', I gathered, were the family with whom he and his mother were then living; perhaps the Jewish family of the man whom he vaguely believed his mother had married. He always referred to Leon Kacew, that shadowy figure, in terms almost as shadowy. 'I do not know if he was my father,' he told me, 'all I know is that he disappeared into the gas ovens of Treblinka and from that moment he *was* my father.'

Moscow and Mosjoukine remained glittering bait to dangle, yet it seems strange that between mother and son, this indissolubly linked pair, there never came a moment of truth. Did his ambiguous reserve defend his mother's way of life as a beautiful small-time actress in the provinces? Did she, too, embroider cold facts to warm their loneliness? Did some shadow of doubt always remain between them? So it seems, or so he would have it appear, for her sake or his own.

Yet somewhere, someone will always question or try to analyse him scientifically and pin down his ancestors, illegitimacy, religion and race; Russia, Poland, Mosjoukine, the Talmud. On they go, forever digging away after a myth.

Romain presented himself as he chose, myth or truth merging. Let us leave him to his legend.

Long years ahead, mystification would reach its *apogée* in *l'affaire Ajar* which he confided to me at rare intervals as it developed. When he telephoned and recounted these tidbits he would sometimes begin to laugh uncontrollably – that old, delightful laugh of pure malicious enjoyment – and I could visualise him rubbing his hands together in the way he did when relishing some scandal, or a disaster affecting 'them' or 'that lot' as he had come to dismiss a large portion of the Parisian world. 'You will see – just wait,' he would say and rang off before I could ask for more. Mystifications until the end; even to the bitter end of that imbroglio.

## LIFE IN LONDON, MARRIAGE

In the little eighteenth-century house I had leased in Chelsea during the war, I had not been able to do more than install a few necessities. Before moving there I had been bombed out of two other places and lost a lot of cherished belongings. However, 32 St Leonard's Terrace became a centre for my friends and a home for Romain. In a sense it was his *repos du guerrier*.

There were very many people of interest coming and going through London at that time, people from all the Allied nations, Czechs, Norwegians, Americans, Dutch, Belgians and Poles; among the latter Feliks Topolski, the dazzling draughtsman, who made a sketch of Romain for us. He had become one of the official War Artists recording various battlefronts and the fearful destruction of London during the Blitz.

I don't remember how we managed on our minuscule weekly rations, but we did; they were much enlivened by the *gros rouge* which Romain used to bring in from the *popotte* at the Free French Headquarters. We had no carpets and clattered about noisily. The kitchen was fitfully equipped, but the plumbing worked and Romain achieved what he then considered the sum of total bliss: lolling endlessly in a hot bath, planning some new book, scrawling notes for it across the tiled wall and using my few remaining lipsticks to do so.

The bedroom was the only room we attempted to furnish. A large gold bed presided; it was a lovely eighteenth-century ruin, but still elegant. There was also a beautiful Italian baroque table, marble-topped and splendidly carved, though now rather chipped. I had salvaged it from the last debacle; such flamboyant gold-leaf was infinitely reassuring in the dark days. On the chimney piece I had placed a small, naive early Staffordshire china rabbit which had been in my nursery. Romain, who at all hours was likely to be stretched languidly on the bed (still with his shoes on), would contemplate this rabbit with a sort of incredulous attention, 'You say it was in your nursery – and your mother had it in hers – *quelle continuité*!' Such 'continuity' was something he had never known and could barely comprehend.

We were very happy in that little house. When it was bombed and half one wall fell away while we were having our breakfast in bed, we continued to live there behind the lean-to emergency repairs which the Government undertook in the case of war damage.

My English friends became Romain's too. They doted on 'Lesley's Frog',* as they dubbed him. He enjoyed the easy friendship they offered like the comfort of their still cosy houses. Hideous blackout curtains, boarded windows and

---

* Frog being a popular nickname for a Frenchman – cosy rather than derogatory.

tarpaulined roofs told of bomb-damage, but so long as a roof held, life below went on agreeably.

Charming rooms, so English in their special careless mixture of family furniture, flowery chintzes and dogs in their baskets; there was little enough to eat, but usually served on lovely old china. This was an atmosphere Romain had never before encountered and it enchanted him. In Nice he had known hotel rooms, or the houses of a few Niçois families. At that time, I think, the French interior did not interpret comfort in a casual manner. Formality and the Louis XVI style were not relaxing, but brooked no argument as to their superiority.

☪

In my childhood I had always heard and read much poetry; Pope's majesty, Byron's magic, or Blake's holy music were all part of the daily language of my old home, so that when I quoted such immortal lines as:

> *But at my back I always hear*
> *Time's wingèd chariot hurrying near*

Romain was spellbound and wanted more. Thereafter, I fed him book after book and he read avidly. His remarkable gift for languages and his acute ear at once understood and was nourished on such fare.

When he was writing *The Colours of the Day* and outlining its theme for me (love and fulfilment ceding to honour), I reminded him of the Richard Lovelace poem *To Lucasta on going to the Wars*:

> *I could not love thee Dear so much*
> *Loved I not Honour more.*

'Lovelace? But he says it all!' Romain was urgent and imperious, 'Get me everything he's written. I want it now.' Fortunately, an anthology of English poetry was among the few books I always kept beside me and for some days Romain was immured with the Immortals, feasting on Donne, Marvell, Coleridge, or the Border Ballads which he told me recalled the early Russian bards, or those Cossack songs with which his mother used to sing him to sleep.

*The Colours of the Day*, that most beautiful, poetic title, derives from his war years when air crews were briefed for operations and 'Colours of the Day' was a code phrase by which certain instructions or lighting signals were known.

Although Romain invariably presented a façade of gloom he could at times be roaringly funny. The reader must take my word for it. Such snatches as he vouchsafed became cherished memories to those who encountered them. But his wit, or barbed repartee, was often a calculated attack, deadly in its effect; sometimes a gross broadside, launched to shock and shatter.

He also possessed a hidden, almost childlike sense of humour which enjoyed such innocent enchantments as Babar, or the Beatrix Potter animal stories – Mrs Tabitha Twitchit and her obstreperous kittens; the Flopsy Bunnies; or Mrs Tiggy-Winkle the Hedgehog hostess, amused him by their sly characterisation. I think he enjoyed the onomatopoeic appeal of their names particularly and we would compare them with some of Gogol's wilder flights – Bobchinsky and Dobchinsky – Dickens' Chuzzlewit or Squeers, and Hoffman's Dappertutto.

He first encountered these Beatrix Potter tales while the V2s rained down their nightly destruction, and such reading matter, alternating with John Donne's Poems and Harriette Wilson's titillating *Memoirs*, were advancing his English at a great pace, as well as having a remarkably soothing effect. Ever after, in moments of stress, he would call for Mrs Tiggy-Winkle, as for an aspirin.

C*

Romain's health was always a matter of intense anxiety to him. It bordered on hypochondria. This was at odd variance with the stoic manner in which he had faced battle, death and wounds during the war. A fatalism upheld him, then. 'Whatever happened I knew I would survive,' he told me and added the strangest rider, 'Besides, I hate myself so much, I accept pain.' This cryptic utterance remained unexplained, though Freud would have made something out of it, no doubt.

But to return to the plainer sailing of minor ailments: small accidents could work him into frenzies. A nail run into his foot, when jogging, produced visions of blood poisoning, lock-jaw, gangrene and amputation even. However, the pains incurred by injudicious eating, acute indigestion and liver trouble, though duly noted and dramatised (low moans, belching and a hand clapped to the spleen), did not appear to count as a threat to life.

Sometimes it seemed as if he regarded his life as a sacred trust, something quite above mere egomania; rather, something which at all costs must be preserved until it had fulfilled its purpose. Which was to write, to write all that inner doppel-gänger master had decreed and achieve all that his mother had decreed for him too, social status – money – glory; but first the writing. Nothing must threaten that. People, or events, or the intrusion of daily life were all enemies blocking the way to the ultimate goal of fame.

Once a truly sinister danger loomed menacingly. We were in Paris at the time, on leave from the French Legation in Sofia, when a telegram informed us that a cat belonging to one of the Legation staff had developed rabies and had been destroyed. Had we been in close contact with the cat we were advised to take precautionary measures.

Now although neither of us had even seen the cat, this piece of information threw Romain into an agony of apprehension. I remember sitting up all night in our hotel room (somewhere off the Avenue de l'Opéra, so well do I recall the occasion), while he contorted and contracted his body in spasms of imaginative hydrophobia, foreseeing the ghastly end and making sure I understood it too.

Finally, when even the assurances of Dr Agid, his oldest, dearest friend, ever our prop and stay, had failed to calm him, the doctor had to conduct him, quivering, to the Pasteur Institute, to undergo the painful series of injections usually reserved for those who were at such risk.

☪

We sometimes went down to Richmond to see my mother; they had a great liking for each other. I had kept a room there, still much as it had been since long before the war. This was more of what Romain called *continuité* and I called roots. I did not realise at the time how much he had observed of that room as he wandered round it, taking everything in with a sort of restless fascination, pulling out my collection of *éditions d'art* from their shelves (and not replacing them), folding and unfolding an eighteenth-century screen stuck with rare Russian playing cards, moving about with an almost childish air of greed. He loved that room in its mixture of centuries and moods, and I was to discover how much, years later.

He had been particularly amused by my collection of early photographs and prints, *cartes de visite* and such, over which

I then painted the heads of my adored cats and dogs. Thus a daguerreotype of, say, the Prince Impérial would now appear to be a spaniel, its paws and tail emerging furrily from the baby prince's original outfit. A group of what must first have been some affectionate Victorian family, I had transformed into a gathering of my living pets: two cats, a mongrel dog, a guinea pig and a hedgehog.

The incongruity and drollery of this pastime of mine was something Romain particularly enjoyed. Just how well he remembered it I could not then guess. But one day many years hence when we were in Los Angeles and he was writing *Lady L*, he handed me some pages to look through and I was astonished to find my room faithfully recorded down to its last gros-point cushion, ikon or *narghilyé* and, furthermore, a description of Lady L seated there painting one of my sentimental transformations. 'How could you have possibly remembered everything and recorded it like that?' I asked. 'Immortalised it,' he replied with an air of finality.

But there was this difference. In the book, Sir Percy sniffed censoriously at the gold bed, deplored this and that hint of *galanterie*. Romain had not appeared to remark any undue eroticism in the atmosphere. I think he took it as he found it, a lovely large, rather disordered, colourful room crammed with books, pictures, ikons, musical scores and a whole jungle of plants. He seems to have forgotten to mention them. A pity, for they were a curious mixture: rare and ordinary, geraniums and daturas.

While we were in Chelsea we had adopted a ginger kitten. We called it Mortimer and Romain, who had never known the ordinary child's nursery and nursery pets, was enchanted with the little creature's antics. One sad day Mortimer met his end under the wheel of an army lorry. We buried him in the garden and mourned him. To my surprise Romain suggested I should make one of my transformation portraits of Mortimer and in due course a suitable early Victorian child's photograph was transposed to Mortimer's whiskered face; his feet now appeared to be shod in the child's high button boots and I added his bushy tail sweeping out from under the frills of a plushy skirt such as Victorian boys then wore. This souvenir followed us on our travels. I have it still and was touched when on one of my rare visits to Romain in his Paris apartment he asked after it.

Sentimental rubbish, I hear you say, and no doubt it appears so to some, yet it serves to show a certain unsuspected aspect of Romain's character and so has a place here. As I have said, this is a *chronique*.

C⋆

We got married on 4 April 1945. A few days before the wedding, I returned home rather depressed by a film on rebuilding London's ruins which I was reviewing for the Ministry of Information to send to America. I found Romain looking particularly disturbed. 'There is something I have to tell you,' he said gloomily. I steeled myself for the worst. 'I think you ought to know – I'm Jewish,' he said.

I don't remember my reply as his announcement did not seem of much consequence to me at the time. In my family I cannot recall ever hearing disparaging remarks or indeed any remarks whatever made regarding the Jewish race or religion. But Romain had spoken with a curious mixture of defiance and discomfort, while I was not yet aware of just how heavy a load a Jewish heritage could seem, how it could close round with stifling tentacles of emotion and even shame. I recall him sitting there in one of what I called his 'disaster poses', head in hands.

'Well I thought you ought to know,' he repeated lamely. Suddenly he looked amused. 'So you'll be my Goy wife,' he said, and with that the matter was closed.

As our wedding day loomed closer it seemed an unwelcome interruption to the agreeably free way we were living. Romain developed a streaming head cold and took to his bed (a psychosomatic manifestation of delaying tactics no doubt). Carrying invalid delicacies up two flights of stairs was making me a little testy, but he showed no signs of recovery and continued to stream. 'If I don't feel better on Tuesday I shan't come to the ceremony,' he announced thickly. To which I replied, 'Oh do try, darling, it won't be the same thing without you,' and burst out laughing at my own quip. But the invalid was not amused. This was no laughing matter.

When two days later we were married at the Register Office I thought it all rather an anti-climax – smug and conventional too, like the rings we exchanged. I suggested he should wear his in one ear, pirate-fashion; it would have suited his exotic appearance. But I was ahead of my time – men did not indulge in such fantasies then.

☾

At the end of the war, when Romain relinquished his uniform for civilian clothing he seemed bewildered, bereft, as if a supporting limb was amputated. This uniform stood for all that was dearest to him, and for many years a battered old cap accompanied us everywhere, fetish-like, on our emplacements, symbol of those marvellous years of battle and comradeship.

Another lesser battle was now faced – that of civilian clothing. The population of England had become accustomed to the strict limitations of clothing coupons and Romain on leaving the service was entitled to some sort of grant, I suppose from

French headquarters – in any case, something designed to set him up comfortably if not in style.

But style it had to be for he had an innate sense of masculine elegance. He had always admired the lean long-legged Englishmen, their impeccably cut suits, the well-polished surface of their shoes, their immaculate shirts and lack of any ornament except a signet ring.

Such style was the product and tradition of Savile Row, so to Savile Row we went, poring over swatches of Irish homespun, Scottish tweeds and bales of wonderful cloth which certain tailors could still reveal. Alas! With all the skills these gentlemen commanded, they could not give Romain that long-legged pared-down elegance he craved. He was of another race – another world and build – and there was nothing to be done about it. I remember how we stood aghast before the tailor's mirror. Had he chosen the wrong material? Was this really the head cutter who stood beside us? Could nothing be done? The shears were poised on the second suit before he was persuaded to choose something darker, less bouncily tweedy, something more akin to the sober darkness of his uniform. But he never got it really right till a Greek tailor was found in Paris who understood Continental, as opposed to English bone structure, and was able to present Romain in that suave manner favoured by the diplomats, among whom his lot was to be cast for some years.

☪

I write of over fifty years ago – today other standards prevail. Formality is interpreted in the most casual terms. However, I remember a time in the late sixties (we were divorced by then) when Romain was constantly represented in the press wearing the most spectacular outfits – enormous capes, sombreros, ponchos, shubas and all else, a sort of sartorial revenge for the years of diplomatic conformity. Driving along Boulevard St Germain, I would sometimes glimpse him on the terrace at Brasserie Lipp, ensconced there in brooding majesty and in what appeared to be fancy dress. He had become one of the features of the Rive Gauche, like Sartre and Simone de Beauvoir had been, across the way at Les Deux Magots. Was this something which perhaps gratified his eternal craving for dramatic effects – for *théâtre*? One Romain playing another for the space of a *Pernod à l'eau*?

Like the actor he was at heart, he responded to whatever clothes he wore. In the conventional suit of a diplomat he seemed cribbed, diminished; but once into something macho – a wild check shirt or a rough sheepskin jacket – he swaggered, becoming a figure of adventure; one of his own characters perhaps, or some composite author-adventurer, a Kessel–de Monfreid figure; their books had been a strong influence in his youth.

It was in uniform I always thought he seemed to be most truly himself; and when on the occasion of General de Gaulle's death he appeared at Colombey-les-deux-Eglises grizzled and ravaged, standing among those others who had been beside the General in those fateful years, he wore again that cherished uniform and the decoration he prized above all the rest: La Croix de la Libération.

I have often thought that the General, whom Romain revered and loved profoundly, came to represent the father he had never known; a presence or symbol of all in which he wanted to believe, a figure that had never failed him, the embodiment of liberty, of *La France libre*.

Was he vain? But of course. How could he have been otherwise, nourished on his mother's adoring admiration. He was a *beau ténébreux* and something of a dandy. He always found it impossible to pass a looking glass without giving it a lingering glance. There was one photograph of him, taken I think by Horst, which we both liked particularly: it had caught something of his graver self below all the poses. There was nothing in the least self-conscious in the way he would study it admiringly. He seemed completely detached: 'It is a face of incredible beauty,' he once remarked when he and I and our close friend the painter Eden Box were sorting through a pile marked for publicity. The remark was made with perfect detachment, Romain contemplating one of his many selves. And how many there were! Some were detestable. I lost count alternately loving and not loving them.

## WE LEAVE LONDON FOR PARIS

In the autumn of 1945 we left England for France and folded up the little house in Chelsea regretfully. It had been very snug there in spite of the bombing and we had never lacked for fuel. In Paris it was appallingly cold and extremely uncomfortable. Since most houses were unheated, hot water was almost unheard of. Owing to Romain's Free French background we were billeted at the Bristol, a still luxurious hotel in the rue St Honoré. French friends envied us and, in particular, the almost legendary comfort of hot baths. The only trouble was that no one ever knew the exact moment at which the hot water would run and we scarcely dared to go out in case we missed this treat. At night we went to bed leaving the hot tap turned on, and if in the middle of the night a sudden gush of water wakened us, we would fling ourselves out of bed and leap into the bath, which made for rather disorganised sleeping.

At this moment – a crucial one – Romain's future hung in the balance. His brilliant war record, his Gaullist and

Liberation affiliations had to be acknowledged. A decree had lately been passed by which the *Carrière* formed a *Cadre Complémentaire* and the Quai d'Orsay (the French Ministry of Foreign Affairs) admitted certain 'Outsiders' to their closed ranks.* Romain was listed as *Secrétaire d'Ambassade Deuxième Classe*; a modest beginning, but one which could lead him anywhere. He would have liked to become a *conseiller culturel* at some embassy where he might further 'the interest and the glories' of a rather tarnished France. But this project did not materialise. Some more rigid members of the *Carrière* considered him too young, too much of a gypsy perhaps, and in spite of the support of André Malraux who was then Minister of Information, he waited some time for a post.

While waiting for the official wheels to turn we continued to dawdle about Paris. Romain developed a hunger for the atmosphere of the studios where a circle of newer artists worked. Long evenings would be spent trudging along the icy ill-lit streets and interminable boulevards. Public transport was scarce, very few people had cars then, and we had no money for taxis, which were rare.

Romain never seemed very sure of his way about the city and had absolutely no sense of direction. He also appeared to have no visual memory of any street or house as he walked on his way. I soon found that if he was left alone he generally missed the simplest rendezvous, and would be found later pursuing some eccentric route or walking in a circle, which seemed odd for the pilot or navigator he had been.

On these nightly expeditions to remote studios, we would

---

* The Quai d'Orsay was a blend of the old aristocracy and newer upper-middle-class representatives from the world of finance–big business, the majority of whom came from the Ecole libre des sciences politiques. From the 1930s onwards reforms were made to open it up.

grope across inky courtyards waking irascible concierges, toiling up endless spiral staircases to attics which were either cold as the grave or overheated to an apoplectic degree by iron stoves which roared and fumed. Then we settled down to *séances* which would last into the small hours. Canvas after canvas would be held up for our inspection, or we would pore over enormous portfolios of sketches until every adjective, exclamation or observation was exhausted.

To Romain this was the purest enjoyment. He did not even recoil from those long stumbling walks through the dark empty streets returning to our hotel. To him, I think it all represented some kind of apotheosised city – 'Paris, France' as a foreign visitor might have put it – and at that moment Romain, the Niçois Russian, still remained something of a foreigner there.

☪

There were times when, for all the adoration and longing with which Romain recalled his mother, he would suddenly attack or denounce her in a bewildering way. It was as if his nervous system snapped suddenly under the strain of such overpowering love. I had been speaking of my own mother and the exasperation I sometimes felt when trying to cope with her problems from afar.

'Your mother! You can think yourself lucky not to have had a Jewish-Russian mother! They smother you! They eat you up alive! My God, if you only knew!' and then he would begin to tell of his struggles as a boy, trying to free himself from her loving tyranny, even to *feel* free, but that could never be achieved, such were the ties that bound them one to the other. The anguish of this lost love was a hunger never to be assuaged. As he himself has written: it was too early, too rich a feast. Any love that came later was just cold cuts.

On an occasion which I remember still with a sense of bewilderment, almost of shock, he furiously denounced her for the manner in which she had filled out his application form to obtain French nationality. 'Jewish! She put it down in black and white! Religion Jewish! Didn't she know what she was doing? Didn't she realise what her precious French felt about Jews? It would have been quite simple to have put Orthodox. Now I'm stuck with it, it's on all my papers, there's no getting away from it.'

This tirade had occurred very soon after he had entered the Foreign Service and was apprehensive of the reaction among his colleagues at the Quai d'Orsay, some of whom were reputed to retain strong sympathies with the former Vichy régime. That he, a scarred, bemedalled *Compagnon de la Libération*, should be even aware of these lesser beings amazed me. I wanted to kill them for their power to affect him.

It was only after many years that Romain came to count among his closest friends one or two members of that eclectic institution.

☾

Such rare tirades attacking his mother were of course followed by moods of abject contrition, expressed in terms of high drama, head in hands, groaning, inconsolable, and determined to be so. This I called 'gnawing his Cross' and the phrase became part of our private language. Exasperated and exhausted by such dramatic intensities I sometimes sought to snap him out of it by unkind remarks such as, 'Do get away from that wailing wall,' or, 'Can we bring the curtain down now?'

Looking back I know I was harsh. I could offer him all the sympathy of my heart, but I could not endure the histrionics that were Romain's daily fare.

'That pessimist husband of yours – is there nothing he enjoys?' I was sometimes annoyingly asked. Of course there were a few things which lightened the gloom, as I have mentioned earlier. The theatre in all its forms was one and it remained a passion. The cinema, with rather more reserve, ran it close. Certain ballets enchanted. Opera never, the exception being almost all Russian operas and Kurt Weill's *Threepenny Opera* which exercised a peculiar fascination over him. As I have remarked earlier, those years I spent with Romain were years of transition. His tastes were forming and re-forming and his later awareness and enjoyment of music was then in a very embryonic state. But he responded instantly, almost violently, to paintings of every kind and age: Cranach, Chardin, Klee. Just as art galleries drew him magnetically, so he sedulously avoided museums or concerts, where he fidgeted painfully.

There were exceptions. Occasionally, in a mood of joint melancholy we would go to some Russian Orthodox church, and, standing in the shadowy depths, Romain's long ikon-face merging with those of the painted saints around, we listened to the beautiful ancient chants and were transported. Then Romain, lately become so resolutely French, returned briefly to some Slavic limboland of jumbled, remote ancestry where I, so yearningly Slav, joined him. And later emerging into the dark streets we would eat *pirogi* or pickled cucumbers at some small bistro that called itself a *traktir*.

I never remember him speaking of the equally beautiful singing of cantors in the synagogues; his upbringing had been strictly non-denominational and as long as I knew him he never attended any kind of religious services as such. Although he told me his mother had, in moments of crisis, occasionally hurried him to the Russian Cathedral in Nice for a blessing – thus leaving nothing to chance.

Food had been one of his few genuine pleasures, an abiding one, before, when in Hollywood, he began diets that were torture to keep his figure (baked apples and black coffee), to say nothing of the frantic antics imposed as a slimming technique in the celebrated gymnasium of Mr Joe Pilates, of New York. Before, he had been greedy in a jolly way, the way of a bon vivant rather than that of a true gourmet. Confronted by some favourite dish such as *gefüllte* fish or blini, he lost control.

I early discovered that Romain heartily enjoyed predicting disasters; not only those on a world scale, but ones likely to occur to those around him, and he was positively crestfallen if nothing bad befell. A friend undergoing some trifling operation was in Romain's view already laid out in his coffin; on learning of this friend's quick recovery he still clutched at gloom, remarking, 'The surgeons have probably rushed the job and left some scissors or something inside him, and now he'll have a relapse – you'll see.'

On one long journey – to where I forget – our train stopped at Milan and was put into a siding for a few hours before proceeding on its way. I had been told of a wonderful flea market just outside the station and decided to rush for it. Romain stayed stretched out on his bunk merely remarking that I would only get lost and the train would probably leave without me. And so it very nearly did. As I returned and raced shrieking and panting to where the train had been when I left it, I saw it some way off, in another part of the shunting yards. It appeared to be slowly pulling out. Stumbling and frantic I managed to get near enough to see Romain leaning far out of the carriage window, his face for once positively radiant as he watched his predicted disaster coming true. Somehow I scrambled into the last carriage and on joining him found he had returned to his bunk and was lying with his face to the wall; there must be no happy endings.

Human relationships (sex apart) were likely to threaten or impinge on that secret dimension into which he retreated. Even the fraternal comradeship he always looked for among men could be too demanding. His inner life became a kind of morbid duo Romain was conducting with the other Romain, who knew that to seek or even admit happiness in ordinary terms was something this doppelgänger inner self could not allow. There were all the miseries of the world waiting to be recalled or anticipated – to be welcomed perhaps?

Efforts to rally his spirits were most likely to succeed if I harped back to one of those episodes he liked to recall, tales of derring-do and high romance.

'Come on Glum,' I would say (I often called him Glumtie or Cupid or Tumbletoes if he were extra clumsy), or whatever name applied to him at that moment. 'Tell me about the time you fought a duel with Ali Khan over that lovely Russian girl in Damascus,' at which the cloud might lift and, shaking it off like a dog emerging from the water, he would launch into one of his shimmering monologues.

Romain's view on love and sex – they were mostly separated – was always clearly defined. Early on in our relationship, he had dwelt at length on the desperate attraction he felt for very young girls.

'How young?' I asked. 'Oh, fifteen or so,' he replied. Nabokov had not then written *Lolita*, but the Lolita syndrome was well established in Romain's psyche.

'My ideal,' he continued with a most disarming frankness, 'would be to have a very pretty young daughter whom I could … make love to! Are you shocked?' he asked solicitously. No. I wasn't shocked. I don't know why not. The theme of incest runs through much of history and literature and is not necessarily always the kind in which the Sunday papers revel. Some of the classics admit emotion.

Today, remembering this strange conversation, I see that, in a sense, Romain was to achieve his dream when later he chose to marry a beautiful and very young woman whom, he was fond of insisting, he often regarded as his daughter.

## SOFIA: BALKAN DIPLOMATIC LIFE

During this time of waiting I returned to London to set my affairs in order and be ready to join Romain wherever he might be sent. I prayed it would be somewhere of a wild or exotic nature. I always craved for far horizons, though Romain had had more than enough of them. When he telephoned to say we were to leave for Bulgaria, I was delighted.

Bulgaria had unwisely collaborated with Hitler and now, at the end of war, it was occupied by Allied Military Forces – the American forces alongside the Russian and British, while the French were represented by a Diplomatic Mission. Although I knew he would mind quitting the Paris he had only begun to savour, he too seemed intrigued by the notion of plunging into Balkan life. Romain was appointed First Secretary to the French Legation in Sofia and left Paris in the spring of 1946.

I was instructed to join him as soon as possible and hurried back to Paris to obtain an *Ordre de Mission*, without which permit no international journeys could then be undertaken. The direct overland route, Paris–Istanbul, was not then in use. I travelled circuitously, by a Romanian ship, which at one point had served as a Russian army hospital boat. We sailed from Marseilles by way of the Levantine coast to Turkey, dawdling delightfully. From Istanbul, after more dawdling, I reached Sofia on a local bug-infested train.

It is generally forgotten today how long certain wartime restrictions lingered: through the fifties, and in certain cases left thwarting traces well into the sixties. Currency regulations were rigid and squirming efforts at evasion were sternly checked. Visas presented unending problems for the would-be traveller, along with the complication of moving about a shattered post-war Europe. Railways that once criss-crossed the Continent now ran fitfully, if at all. Many ports remained blocked with war debris and drifting mines were a menace on high seas and beaches alike.

It took time to travel and the time it took was not grudged, for every aspect of the journey seemed as important as the arrival. Each stage was an integral part of the whole. Not many people today can remember, or imagine, the almost stately traditionalism of travel in those years just after the war. Hanging out of the window, or just standing in the corridor watching the changing landscape as we rumbled along, was one of the special joys of travelling on a branch line then, for the countryside had not yet been disfigured by progress and shrieking advertisements. There was always time to linger or dawdle at some unscheduled stop along the way, which meant one could divert one's path or even follow the impulse of the minute. No bogey permits or tarmac-to-tarmac timetables impinged and a special pleasure was derived from plans changed suddenly, like impromptu decisions made when a train was missed, or transport broke down, or there was no accommodation for the night and goodness knows what we did next. We were not obliged to fill in endless forms as to *who* we were, or *where* we were going, and *why*. A passport satisfied the most official mind, which also accepted the fact that there was nothing necessarily suspicious in pursuing some undefined route. Adventurous situations were an essential element of travel then, like chance encounters, though these were not the automatic kind now induced by arbitrary seating arrangements on planes. Some of the most memorable were traditionally brought about by sympathetically inclined wagons-lits attendants while the great trains sped softly through the night.

I do not know why I had always longed to go to Bulgaria, or why I had a preference for that country over Serbia or Romania, but so it was. Perhaps some sixth sense told me I would spend some of the happiest days of my life there. In any case Bulgaria spoke to me long before I knew it and ever since I lived there a glowing love for it has remained.

Almost as soon as I arrived in Sofia, busy tittle-tattlers informed me that Nedi Trianova, a beautiful and cultivated young Bulgarian woman who was to become my dearest friend for the rest of her life, had been Romain's mistress before I arrived. I had myself dawdled in Istanbul on my way to join him and so felt indulgently disposed towards the affair. Darling Nedi, she was all goodness and loving kindness; she smoothed our path in a hundred ways during those difficult days when material life in Sofia was a grave problem. We called her *Houbovo* (good, in Bulgarian). She became our most cherished friend and when she had the tact to fall passionately in love with the ambassador of another country, also a close friend, we formed an inseparable quartet to the astonished disapproval of the *corps diplomatique*.

Romain had always hated celebratory fusses, Christmas or birthdays, and so we never exchanged presents. Nevertheless, in Sofia I once received a birthday greeting which I have never forgotten. The day had passed unobserved, I believed, then at midnight a crowd of Tziganes appeared below my window to give me a deliriously seductive serenade. They capered around

singing and fiddling, grinding their curious instruments, *zurnas* and *darbukas* or drums, which they banged ferociously. Laughing and waving little oil lamps recklessly, they refused to go away till I went down and joined them dancing in a ring-o-roses *hora*.

Such a lovely present; I suspected Romain of this gesture, but he shrugged it off as an 'idiot's delight', ever his favourite phrase where the minor pleasures of life were concerned.

Once I was allowed to give him something which he accepted

with genuine pleasure. He had complained that reading the Russian classics in the contemporary Soviet print spoiled everything since he had grown up with the old typography. He mourned in particular an edition of Pushkin which for some unknown reason his mother had given away. Its loss rankled, but by a happy chance, in Sofia, I ran to earth a Russian edition of Pushkin's works, dated if I remember rightly about 1890 and therefore of the proper vintage typographically. This he valued accordingly and it remained with him throughout our many moves.

Many of the *corps diplomatique* found life in Sofia trying. Living conditions were harsh; there was no entertainment except bridge or scandal. But neither Romain nor I longed for worldly diversions. He was absorbed in his day-to-day work at the Legation, providing reports of the political situation both in Bulgaria and in the surrounding countries. I was told later these reports were outstandingly brilliant. He was particularly suited for this type of work; his eye was both shrewd and sympathetic to many problems which the West could only see subjectively as a possible threat to themselves.

While he was so employed, I had acquired some rudimentary knowledge of Bulgarian and made long adventurous sorties about the country, discovering its lovely ancient monasteries and painted churches, its remote villages and strange sects such as the Moslem Pomaks of the little-known Karakachans. And then there were the Tziganes in their *mahallas*; irresistible company to me.

In Sofia we were sometimes invited to very special blini feasts which were held in style, with enormous bowls of caviar supplied by officers commanding the Red Army, then one of the occupying forces based in Sofia, together with the American and British Forces. (We, the French, having been so lately occupied ourselves, had no military representation there, only a Legation, with an Ambassador.) But back to the blini feasts.

They were lovely parties. Nationalities merged, political tensions were ignored – even the most rigid diplomats joined in when the Russians sang together. They sang beautifully: songs of the Red Army or of Old Russia alike; and sometimes Romain's smoky voice would merge with their deep tones. On one of these festive occasions his passion for blini overcame all prudence and he consumed twenty-nine before having to be taken home to recover.

☪

Those were dicey days, a time of dark uncertainties, famine and terror. Beneath a carefully preserved façade of politeness and protocol, the Bulgarians seethed with unrest. At one point, an obscure inter-political crisis threatened to become an international issue when the Minister was away, and Romain was briefly *chargé d'affaires*. A Balkan crisis of some violence had erupted. Waiting for a stream of governmental instructions from Paris to be decoded was nerve-racking. The sinister atmosphere which pressed round was emphasised by sullen crowds agitating, in spite of the heavy snowdrifts which clogged the streets. The snowfall seemed to isolate us. The Legation staff were working furiously, burning certain papers and official documents in the traditional way. Our chimneys blocked up, regurgitating heavy smoke and undigested scraps of official documents, making it increasingly difficult to breathe. Romain was becoming very tense – too tense, it seemed. His ikon-face looked like it had been dipped in vinegar. In vain Raiina, our comforting peasant cook, plied him with her richest pastries. Nothing distracted him, but suddenly I remembered how, during the bombing, he used to enjoy the relaxing qualities of

Peter Rabbit or the Flopsy Bunnies, which he continued to speak of as *La Famille Flopsaut*. But I had not brought any of the little books with me; at the moment of packing they had not seemed essential luggage. Mrs Tiggy-Winkle, a prickly hedge-hog, was one of Beatrix Potter's most endearing heroines. I rang the British Military Mission compound.

'Mary, have your children by any chance got *Mrs Tiggy-Winkle*? Romain would *so* enjoy her just now.'

'Yes, as a matter of fact I think we have. If the snow's not too thick and the mob moves on, I'll send her to you at once.'

There was a distant but distinct click on the line: tapped again. I wondered what the circuitous minds of the Secret Police would make of Mrs Tiggy-Winkle. Some dangerously seductive Mata Hari, no doubt. I imagined the scene at the Deuxième Bureau: 'Who eez Teegee Weenkli? Not on list? *Chort!* Who coming and going? Find! *His own wife* asking for her? Those French!' Romain was delighted by such imaginings that quite took his mind off the crisis, which subsided. I was never connected to some unknown spy-ring.

☪

That Nedi was a spy, or compelled to work for the Bulgarian Secret Service, was generally accepted in Sofia. It was hardly a question one could put directly to her. One either thought she was, and avoided her, or one paid no attention, but was careful of one's confidences. We gradually discovered that she had no choice in the matter. She was beautiful, charming, and as the daughter of an ex-ambassador spoke four or five languages fluently. That she acted as she did was the means by which she saved her family from destitution and banishment to some remote province, for they, and all their class of privileged persons, were beginning to be hounded. Nedi, her mother and father whom she adored and tried to protect, her raffish sister Elie, and a large indulged cat (known as College Boy because of his nice manners) were all crammed into a two-room apartment of a sordid nature.

They were a deeply devoted family and as long as they were together they made the best of the situation. From these uneasy conditions, Nedi would issue forth bravely; *soignée* and delightful she circulated everywhere, no doubt wherever she was instructed to go, picking up such scraps of information as she could. In what we came to consider her time off, she was always with us, a welcome guest, sharing our private life, relaxing by the big wood fire we were able to have (her own family had no heating). We talked on many subjects – the arts, the literature of Russia and Bulgaria and many aspects of Balkan life and history which I found fascinating. Sometimes we were joined by her lover the ambassador, whom I shall not name, and with whom she was passionately involved. Their affair had become very difficult to pursue since his wife showed the most lively jealousy and scandal throbbed. Once the four of us managed to escape to spend some weeks in a rustic house on the then deserted shores of the Black Sea. I am the only survivor of those halycon days and I remember them with love and tears.

It is perhaps not surprising that Romain often roused criticism, even hostility among the more conventional diplomats. Some of the Americans were openly suspicious. The fact that he spoke Russian, had Russian blood, had a wife who danced with the (untouchable) Russian officers, and that *that* woman, Trianova, was never out of their house, who everyone knew was a spy – well it all seemed a bit much, they said. As to his manners! Romain was still sometimes rather uncouth; I occasionally caught glimpses of the brown bear when he seemed lost, in some *mondain* gathering.

Once, I remember, we had been giving a not very refined dinner to a few of the stuffy diplomats and their wives who, as I began to serve the coffee, were standing about like affronted waxworks. Then I saw why. Romain was seated in the corner, his back to the room. Oblivious to all else he was reading his latest book, fresh off the press, which had arrived from Paris that day. I think it was *The Company of Men*, which was dedicated to me. It was hardly something which either of us should have been reading that evening.

Romain had known little happiness and less calm during those war years of violence, of horror; years which were everything his fundamentally idealistic and pacific nature abhorred. Thus he found our new life in Sofia agreeable, cosy and passionately interesting. Bulgaria was still rather remote in its ways and seemed to possess some quality of nineteenth-century Russian life. There was a wild and also rustic air about it. One was alternately lulled by the immemorial calm of the countryside and shaken by the fury of its political climate. Its other climate, in the sense of Fahrenheit and centigrade, was equally violent. Fiery summers were succeeded by almost Siberian winters. There was a small, cultivated society in Sofia which cherished liberal and democratic ideals. But as we watched, the scene slid into chaos, becoming one of persecution and injustice beyond measure. There had been some hope held – though never by Romain – that America might intervene to oppose the Communist takeover, but nothing was done. Romain was profoundly affected by this tragic situation. He could not endure to stand by, a helpless spectator – a diplomat – no longer under arms and able to go into action against oppression. He raged and fretted, becoming more and more morose so that the Bulgarian tragedy became yet another agony which merged with his abiding *Weltschmerz*.

Therefore, when in the winter of 1948 a decree from the Quai d'Orsay arrived, coldly informing him that he was recalled to Paris, he did not take it quite as hard as I did. His sadness at leaving a country in which he felt entangled by his Slav sympathies, his idealism and the friendships he had made, was tinged with guilty feelings of relief. Since there was nothing he could do, it was best to go.

Returning to Paris offered him the opportunity to renew many contacts barely begun in the literary world in which he had now won a rightful place. To move on had become the pattern of his nomadic life.

It snowed hard the night we left Sofia. The whole *corps diplomatique* turned out to see us off at the station, where the Orient Express was waiting in darkness. It was the only train at that time which linked Istanbul with Paris, but it was no longer a luxury legend. No restaurant car – no service or bedding remained. Its once-weekly run transported utilitarian items, baggage, courier supplies and sometimes a few tense pale-faced political exiles who were managing to escape the coming storm. The diplomatic bag was always taken on this train, guarded by embassy personnel. Occasionally it presented a suspiciously bulky form; those were occasions of which no one ever spoke, but which meant that somebody was being smuggled out of the country with the connivance of one embassy or another. Romain's predilection for high adventure had more than once involved him in these risky undertakings. That night at the station, when I felt my heart was breaking at leaving, I too knew a little of what going into exile meant. From a café outside the barrier I could hear that obsessive wailing, feral music of the people's traditional songs; music I loved particularly. Suddenly Raiina, my Macedonian cook, rushed forward and flung herself on the ground, sobbing and clasping my snow boots. I was crying so desperately that

Romain too became overcome and burst into tears – our three-day journey to Paris was a very unhappy one.

## GLOOMY RETURN TO PARIS

On our return to Paris, I mooned about dispossessed and homesick, aching for sight of the Bulgarian mountains, the Black Balkans, longingly repeating their proud, beautiful names: the Rhodope, Musala, Yumrukchal.

Romain was trying to stifle his remembrance of the tragic scenes we had left by breathing the air of freedom round him and combing the art galleries of the Left Bank, where he coveted many paintings.

He longed to possess a Nicholas de Staël, he wanted a Chagall, and one day he returned to our hotel in triumph having chosen a Bauchant, a lovely little still life of fruit in a basket placed on a kitchen table which stood in an innocent landscape. We gloated over it together, but unfortunately, before we could put the money down, we discovered we did not have enough. I still remember Romain's downcast face; 'I never wanted anything so much – I can't bear to see it again,' he said miserably. 'You must take it back to the gallery and explain. You had better say you hate all Bauchant's work and you won't allow me to keep it. That sounds better than our being broke.'

Nina Kacew would not have allowed her son such an admission. I extricated us from the purchase, but it rankled – denying Bauchant.

These were cold penny-pinching days when Romain was working in the central administration of the Quai d'Orsay, that temple of protocol, on minimal pay. Traditionally, the salary a diplomat received was graded according to the rank and the post he occupied. When *en poste* a certain sum was added for expenses incurred, for hospitality and such. When he occupied a post at the central administration in Paris, the pay was not only scrimped but there were no allowances.

For most of his colleagues it was less pinching than for us; they were French, they had a family background and a rooted, centred life. Even if they were not rich, or did not possess an apartment in Paris, they usually seemed able to live with their families, with some aged relative, or to lease something belonging to a colleague *en poste*.

But we were rootless and stood among them like orphaned exiles. The death of Romain's mother in 1941 had left him with no background at all and since the house in Chelsea had gone, my roots lay in the small faraway quarters occupied by my mother in Richmond.

Thus we lived precariously, in and out of modest hotels. A bedroom at the Pas de Calais (which at that time I named le Pas de Confort) was hugger-mugger living; eating in the cheapest bistros, doubling-up in a cramped bedroom, making do with biscuits and cream cheese at night. Romain retreated to the bathroom where he wrote astride the bidet, his manuscript balanced on the taps. He was working on a new book and rewriting *Tulipe* once again, but he had not yet interested Louis Jouvet in the stage play he wished to make of it. Alas! for all the lively interest which Jouvet was later to show in *Tulipe*, and the prospects of it becoming a play that he might have produced, nothing ever materialised.

During that unpleasant time we seemed to have lived, or temporarily alighted, in every arrondissement Paris could offer, in every kind of way. Sometimes it would be an apartment in an historic quarter, perhaps the Ile de la Cité, where one I remember had a strangely terrifying atmosphere from which we fled within days. Later we learned that it was in that apartment the owners had been tortured by the Gestapo before being dispatched to Auschwitz.

Once we leased a very stylish pied-à-terre in the rue St Honoré; it was part of a larger apartment belonging to a fellow diplomat and it overlooked the gardens of the Elysée. There was a lot of red velvet upholstery, but the bed was plank-like and no words of mine could describe the kitchen, a small, dark hole hung with witches' cauldrons and a few blackened utensils with which I tried to prepare our meals. At another, happier time we leased Marguerite Duras's apartment in the rue St Benoît; that too offered little in the way of kitchen facilities and the noise from a celebrated nightclub below was then at its most blasting so that our floors seemed to rock along with the musicians – Claude Luther, Boris Vian and the young Serge Gainsbourg among them, if I remember rightly.

This restless living sometimes spelled only a few settled weeks before we were moving on again. Romain was writing where and how he could. Such constant upheavals were trying for both of us. I was forever piling our belongings in and out of suitcases which overflowed into baskets and bundles resembling gypsy ways. The instability and tensions of those early days gave me a positive dislike of Paris which took me many years to overcome. I remember how Nancy Mitford, the distinguished English writer and a great personality in and around *le gratin*, who was then elegantly installed *entre cour et jardin* in the rue Monsieur, used to say to me in her customary teasing manner, 'Darling, you simply must not go on telling the Parisians how much nicer it was in Sofia, they really won't understand.'

During the rest of the year, Romain lived through a time of great disillusion and bitterness. *Tulipe* had pleased neither the public nor his publisher. Its grinding quality and sardonic idealism fell on deaf ears. He began to doubt his future and the fame his mother had predicted for him.

Yet there were certain glowing friendships to warm the chill tenor of those days. The devotion of his oldest closest friends from Nice, the doctor René Agid and his Swedish wife Sylvia, had never failed in their understanding and support, and now they lovingly invited me, the newcomer, the foreigner, to share their intimacy. There were visits to the veteran Léon Blum to whom Romain had wished to dedicate his first book, or to the coruscating figure of André Malraux in Boulogne sur Seine. There was the admiration of Roger Martin du Gard, of Elsa Triolet and Jeff Kessel, Arthur Koestler, or Albert Camus. The circle of admirers in the world of authors and publishers was widening rapidly.

There were, too, a few occasions which lightened everyday living. They were reminiscent of the Treat Outings of my childhood which might mean being taken to a Christmas pantomime, or a country fair, or a ride in a neighbour's new motor car, then still regarded as excitement and splendour. Romain liked the idea of Treat Outings and enjoyed the phrase, which passed into our private language, but he rarely allowed that any distraction I might suggest (short of the cinema) could justify the phrase.

However, when Marcel Carné invited us to St Germain-en-Laye where he was temporarily holed-up, with some of his team, the better to concentrate on script problems, Romain agreed this might rank as a Treat Outing.

The great French director was then at the zenith of his career, with masterpieces such as *Children of Paradise* or *Daybreak* under his belt. He was not only working on a sticky script, but casting about for new projects, and Romain was a fresh name on the literary scene.

We found Monsieur Carné installed in the luxurious hotel

which stands beside the château, his windows overlooking the beautiful alleyways and shimmering waters of the park: a lovely setting. But both the director and his collaborators were sitting glumly round a long table spread with papers; before each, a notebook and pen. One and all appeared to be in a state of almost marmoreal immobility. It was a scene I came to know well many years later when I was working in Hollywood beside George Cukor at the MGM Studios, and it was about as many years ahead, too, that Romain himself was to be directing and scripting one of his own books in a Paris studio, facing just those same conferences and deadlocks which are an integral part of film-making.

Since the scene before me at St Germain-en-Laye did not look much like a Treat Outing, I crept away to enjoy the park and château on my own terms of pleasure, wandering through the glades of ancient trees outside, then following the adjoining State apartments that opened into one another and which still seemed to breathe the sinister connotations of the past.

Sadly, nothing came of the encounter; even Romain's fertile imagination did not break the deadlock, and any flashes of inspiration were systematically overcome by the rumblings of those dreaded bugbears known to the film world as Costing and Casting.

'So much for Treat Outings,' said Romain as we headed back to Paris and 'Hotel Pas de Confort'. But I observed that he wore that air of quiet satisfaction which he generally reserved for lost illusions.

☪

The French are a Cartesian, or logical, race. They think precisely and prefer to live that way, also, to be able to place others in their precise frame. Romain could never be quite fitted in. A new writer? A diplomat? *Vraiment?* Of Russian origin with an English wife? What was his background? Where did he live? He was *en poste* in some wild place. Well he looked wild anyhow – he was en voyage? Unavailable? *Tiens!*

Although both his personality and his books had been acclaimed by the critics and the literary world of Paris from the start, and he was becoming known to a wider public, I had the impression that he felt, at that time, that he was not well enough known in the small glittering successful milieu called (by themselves) *le tout Paris*; but to be 'known' and to succeed, there needed to be money, a definite base, a showcase perhaps, and at that particular moment Romain did not have one. In a rather touching and secret way, I think he did long to be 'known' and to be claimed among the glitterati. It was something his mother would have certainly thought desirable – a step up along the way she had planned. Even much later, at the height of his fame, when he no longer desired to glitter in that world, I still felt that Romain remained a little apart from Paris – a rare bird to the French. He wrote in French, they proudly claimed him as a French writer, but essentially he wrote in the great tradition of Russian-Jewish literature, the food of his childhood, the core of his inspiration.

☾

In the summer of 1949 we were briefly in Nice. Coming from the disappointing chill atmosphere of Paris, the Côte d'Azur, le Grand Bleu and Romain's old haunts seemed to blaze round us, all colour and garlic and life itself. Even a shattering visit to his mother's grave could not dispel the happiness he felt to be once more in the South of France. Egged on by one of his more untrustworthy friends, known from his schooldays, we bought a ramshackle little dwelling in the hilltop village of Roquebrune. It was a madness, an ill-considered folly. Although its price was ridiculously low, it required an enormous amount of rebuilding and repairs to become only just habitable.

A steep, narrow, tower-like structure of three small rooms required a staircase to link it with some ruined donkey-stables. Until stairs were added, a sheer drop of three metres required gymnastic efforts on some planking to clamber up and down. But each unconnected bit radiated a breathtaking panorama, a vast sweep of Mediterranean blue, of sea, cypress and olive. I calculated that some sort of kitchen and bathroom and, above all, a terrace, could be hacked out of the stones and rubble of the donkey-stables, while the tower-like part, once joined, would provide our bedroom and, most precious of all, a space for Romain to write; in a room of his own. Such calculations swept all other considerations aside. We saw this dilapidated ruin as the roots we hankered after, a refuge in that uncertain future over which Romain liked to brood.

Without more ado we plunged. A notary from Menton, straight out of the pages of Balzac, drew up the papers. Romain signed, we were given the keys and we returned to Paris where his work at the Quai d'Orsay awaited him, whilst the Tower awaited its new owners.


## BERNE AND ROQUEBRUNE

In 1950 we were posted to the French Embassy in Berne, where the lethally dull life of that city was only made bearable by the friendship of the Ambassador, Henri Hoppenot, and his wife Hélène. This became a profoundly enriching friendship. Their eclectic tastes ranged from Chinese paintings to Dada,

Monet, and the works of Klee and Picasso. Their love and understanding of world literature and music was deep. At their Embassy every culture flourished and there Romain felt himself at home and truly appreciated.

The Hoppenots' friendship was, I believe, a privilege not often bestowed and I recall it as a gift from the gods.

☪

The even tenor of those days in Berne gave Romain ample opportunity to write and also feel free to cultivate the society

of any pretty women around. 'I don't fall for real beauty,' he told me, 'it's too awe-inspiring. I prefer prettiness.' In general he enjoyed few things: sex, blini, swimming in the sea and, of course, his writing. This was an organic necessity to him: '*Une évacuation quotidienne*,' a daily excretion, as he said indelicately.

In Berne, Romain's imperious and demanding ways became such that I sometimes accused him of behaving like an insane Roman emperor and often looking the part too, for he spent a lot of time about the house draped in toga-like bath towels. He detested the restrictions of conventional clothing, apart from any aesthetic considerations. Thus the shapeless, all-enclosing kind of dressing gown which Balzac had said should be every writer's garment (one which both he and George Sand adopted for their long hours of work) became his too. I remember he favoured a kimono and I dubbed him Japanese Overlord, with myself as Paper Fan, scuttling about, bowing low and obeying his every command.

We enjoyed many such silly games, along with a sort of private language, and exchanged nicknames according to the minute. He would sometimes address me as Lesloukian in reference to my passion for collecting Caucasian or Armenian rugs, then out of fashion with contemporary interior decorators who favoured all-white wall-to-wall expanses.

'I am married to an Armenian rug dealer,' he once announced to an astonished journalist who was interviewing him, hungry for details of the distinguished author's home life. A statement that was never corrected.

Romain's offstage performances were memorable. Great ham actor that he was, these 'turns' were designed sometimes to amuse his guest, sometimes to intrigue a listener, or to charm a future conquest; most often to relieve his inner tensions. Given the smallest of reasons – household bills, a lost

sock, his own health – or larger issues – world affairs and the
sombre future – he would proceed to lash himself into a lather
of emotion, creating a simmering climate of drama. Having
reduced everyone around him – myself, our Finnish maid, the
dog and an Alsatian secretary – into a corresponding state of
chaos and despair he would abruptly relax. Purged, he posi-
tively bloomed as he surveyed the effects of his performance.

There were few palliatives for living in Berne, but the superb
museums and art galleries and the dazzling quality of private
collections acted as such. Nevertheless, however glowing
the canvas, or rich those mediaeval triptychs of holy figures,
greyness lay all around; heavy and glum like so many of the

citizens. And when the *foehn* raged, that terrible exacerbating wind, there was no escape, indoors or out; nerves were taut and tempers short. It was accepted by the Swiss law courts that when trying criminal cases, or even in divorce proceedings, the calendar should be consulted, for if the *foehn* had raged, this could be taken into account for violent or inexplicable conduct – as it were, an extenuating circumstance upon which the defence might count.

It was in Berne that, pushed to unusual limits of gloom by the daily round, Romain suddenly decided that painting would be a panacea. A lavish supply of paints and brushes were acquired and he selected what I thought was a rather ambitiously large canvas. He waited, champing at the bit, while I explained a few basic facts about the use of turpentine and linseed oil. Then, kicking aside the dustsheet I had prudently spread, mindful of the carpet in our leased apartment, he shut himself away.

From behind the closed door, both lunch and tea were refused and a profound silence reigned. Some seven hours later the door was flung open and he emerged, glowering: 'But it's difficult!' he thundered.

☾⋆

There was a postscript to this experimental effort. He had sloshed about a few more times, seemingly, without much pleasure: dark abstract forms did not satisfy and presently the whole paraphernalia of paint was set aside.

One day, some time later, I heard the dreadful screeching sound of tearing canvas and splintering wood. I remained rooted and, when he came out, it seemed wiser to ask no questions. Only later I found he had destroyed a rather fine, if lugubrious portrait of himself painted by Claude Venard during our life in Paris. One of several Romains had destroyed another.

Curiously, the *foehn* had been raging that day.

C⋆

During our two years in Switzerland, I rushed between Berne and Roquebrune, struggling to bring order out of chaos; battling with the local artisans, the problems of plumbing and the fact that the village was more or less inaccessible at the time.

Roquebrune was not then the smirking tourist trap it has since become. It retained an untamed quality of isolation and primitive living, due in part to the fact it had been evacuated during the war (shelled from the sea coast), and was only slowly resuming ways known earlier, rather than attempting to move forward towards even a minimum of comfort. Few houses had water or electricity or gas. Only the little post office had a telephone. No one had a car. A village bus ran once a day linking this fastness with the coast.

The inhabitants spoke together in a baffling patois of their own which contained many words of Saracen origin and was as unintelligible to the next village as it was to us. This was our first and indeed the only real home we ever knew together. It hung high above the wide sweep of the Mediterranean with faraway Corsica sometimes shimmering on the horizon. We loved our ruin and forgave it all its shortcomings; only slowly did it yield to comfort. While I cooked in a small converted donkey-stable (Butagaz and cold water), Romain wrote in the eyrie above our bedroom. This could only be reached by a perilous wooden staircase, almost a stepladder, but here he wrote undisturbed. In the old Ligurian coast villages such loft-like rooms were generally used for drying the herbs and tomatoes so essential a part of the local cuisine –

thus though most houses had only small, aperture-like windows to keep out both icy winds and searing suns, these loft rooms always had two well-sized windows – glassless of course to admit sun and wind. I don't think we ever put glass in those two windows; Romain liked the room's basic state. A kitchen table, a chair and a truckle bed were about the only furniture, and he preferred it so. He generally wrote seated on the floor, surrounded by large market baskets into which he could hurl the drafts of whatever he wrote, or the pages he had rejected, but kept carefully. The baskets were always overflowing and flurries of paper drifted about the floor which was composed of rotting beams where, sometimes, pages got wedged in the cracks or flew out of a window. But none of that ever mattered to Romain when he was consumed by the *feu sacré*; when he had fire in his belly. He had endured far more discomfort in England during the war while writing his first book in an unheated hangar between operational flights.

Writing, he seemed as one possessed. His head shook violently from side to side, his hair flung out straight all round like one of those frenzied Atan dancers of Afghanistan. Mireille, the child of Ida Dagostin, our housekeeper, still remembers the terror he inspired in her when she was sent to the village bar to get the Gauloises Bleues which he smoked incessantly; she would be obliged to clamber up the perilous ladder and confront this demon figure. He has remained in her memory: one of the strongest impressions of her childhood.

Now become a mature and good-looking woman – the true dark Italianate type of Roquebrunoise – Mireille sometimes conjures up that strange figure. She recalls his slow, silent way of pacing round the village at night, following the steep narrow ways and dead ends, aloof and seeming as if in a trance. She recalls how the villagers of those pre-tourist days used to gather outside their dwellings through the hot summer nights and whisper together as he passed. They thought him an eerie figure.

When Tante Berthe, an aged figure from Romain's childhood in Nice, and before, struggled bravely up the hill to bring us the traditional Russian offering of bread and salt, I felt the seal had been set on our strange little home in the Impasse Scarouget.

It was reached by a noisome dark alley, much favoured as a *pissoir* by the local cats and dogs and quite a few locals too. A large forbidding door was flanked by the broken-down rotting doors of caves used by the Roquebrunois to store their wine or firewood. Such was our uninviting entrance. But once the door opened it revealed a tunnel of jasmine leading to a sweep of sea and sky. I painted this door a faded yet luminous blue and persuaded the local mason to place an eighteenth-century stone angel's head, winged and smiling, above the portal. Many years later, when Garbo came to see me there, she lost her way and went wandering about the village, uttering, like an incantation, 'I am looking for a blue door with an angel's head.' She was wrapped in a nondescript overcoat and wore pink bed-socks inside her espadrilles; she was not recognised in the village.

After Romain and I divorced in 1963, our house there remained in my possession. It was a treasured retreat where I came and went between my travels, and on my return I would sometimes hear of his sudden reappearances in the village. Something still drew him there; I was told he would dash up the hill in a fast car, leave it by the *lavoir* and climb the steep dark ways once again, making unexpected appearances about the place, arriving on the doorstep of the house where Mireille's mother, Ida Dagostin, lived. She had remained a faithful much-loved friend to both of us. I think he found in her, as I did, something of the quality of a loving old family nanny – the *nianya* of Russian tradition; one who knew all the secrets and who remained unchanged.

Many years later, Romain asked me if he might buy back any or all of the many little bits of attic and cellar and terrace that had been gradually expanded and grown into a harmonious whole. I wished to keep one part that I had reconstructed from a couple of cellars acquired later and made into something approximating to the sort of traditional Turkish interior I loved, but I would have gladly ceded him all the rest.

In the summer of 1975 he made several more visits reconnoitring the place, accompanied by our devoted friend Dr Agid, but now he found the rooms too small. I had long sold the loft in which he used to write. Much had been changed; I had pierced some of the hugely thick stone walls to let in light and air. Too many holes 'like Gruyère', he grumbled, but he still hesitated – the past he had lived there, the books he had written there, *Tulipe* and *The Colours of the Day* among them, were jumbled in that eternal *Sehnsucht* known to all who look back.

I still possess a small part of our house in Roquebrune, hardly more than the Turkish room and a bit, but our original terrace still discloses its breathtaking sweep of sea and cypress. Sometimes I sit once more at twilight with a bottle of wine and my manuscript on the table, as once I used to do while waiting for Romain to descend from his eyrie to join me. At times, I fancy his shade keeps me company there and I hear him saying, as he used to do, '*Gros rouge* – that's a killer, much worse than vodka, you'd better look out.' He never drank himself; any wines or spirits brought on violent indigestion, though such killers as pickled cucumbers or salted herring went down without a twinge.

*Quel numéro!* What a character!

## THE WILDER SHORES OF LOVE

The Hoppenots left Berne in 1952. When the Ambassador was appointed to head the French Delegation to the United Nations, he requested that Romain should be officially posted there to accompany them. And so the old enchanting friendship was maintained.

During our life in New York when Romain was acting *porte parole* for the French Delegation, the whole of America was riveted to televised sessions of the Congressional Investigational Committee at Washington, where they were painstakingly exposing the monstrous witch-hunt named Un-American Activities, which Senator McCarthy and Roy Cohen had for years pursued so remorselessly.

These sessions were live and ran throughout the day. When Romain returned late from the UN, I would fill in the picture for him. Although he detested and distrusted the presence of the television, we hired one briefly. It stood there, four-square, at the foot of our bed. There was no other place for it in our cramped apartment. We had agreed it was unthinkable in the living room. 'I tell you – its rays will pollute the very food we eat,' he said. 'And now – now it will make me impotent.' At times he had fanciful notions about mechanical objects or new inventions.

In time he grew to revel in being televised himself. It was another form of theatre – the theatre which, his mother had always reiterated, could be his salvation if things went wrong. 'Remember – the theatre will never let you down.' Such Sibylline utterances stayed with him, along with many more she wove round him, to become a protective carapace when her arms were no longer there.

Thus, if he never trod the boards in a professional sense, his instinct for the dramatic – for all that was *théâtre* – made him a brilliant instinctive broadcaster, possessing a magnetism which professionals might envy.

☪

Many years later, on a night when an American Presidential election was in full swing, I happened to be walking down the Champs Elysées, when to my amazement I saw Romain seated behind an enormous glass window in the offices of some powerful French paper or magazine – perhaps it was *Paris-Match*. There he was, under glaring spotlights, knee-deep in ribbons of tickertape, a running band of electronic headlines above him, while unseen loudspeakers were booming out his comments on the drama then being enacted in Washington, to the crowds outside.

The American friend who was beside me was outraged: 'I don't want your publicity-mad ex-husband to tell me and the French what's going on in America!'

☪

New York was a very heady, colourful city with whole sectors of polyglot groups: Germantown abutting the more spirited Hungarian quarter and further uptown the Puerto Ricans and Harlem; while downtown there was Chinatown and its myriad lanterns next to the dark brooding confines of what had once been the old Jewish quarter.

Between us, Romain and I had a very varied circle of friends in New York. They were perhaps more international than American, while the New Yorkers themselves were a whole climate apart from the rest of the country – a world into which we were, fortunately, admitted, clique within clique. There

were still many Russian émigrés circulating around the last
Romanov echoes – the Grand Duchess Marie, Princess
Natasha Paley, granddaughter of Alexander II, and a mass of
diplomats and journalists, equally polyglot, swanning in and
out of the tall up-ended matchbox building of the United
Nations. There, Romain and the French Delegation sat, hour
after hour in a sort of box-like pen, earphones clapped to their
ears, as the pontiffs droned on, dissecting the latest inter-
national upheaval.

I forget which year it was that André Malraux made one of
his brief visits to New York. We had known him in Paris and
felt ourselves particularly privileged when he invited us to join
him and his wife Madeleine for a weekend in Washington
where he proposed to visit the museums and galleries in which
he was particularly interested. Since those days, thanks to tel-
evision, the French public has become well aware of Malraux's
extraordinary diction; his snuffling, snorting, panting, humming
and muttering – a baffling barrage of sounds which had to be
overcome before his meaning was made clear. Romain had met
him in Paris more often than I and so overcame this barrage,
but for me it was a great challenge. At the same time, in an odd
way, I always found Malraux easy to talk with. He seemed to
know almost intuitively what I was trying to express as he
questioned me about problems to be resolved concerning the
book I was writing about various nineteenth-century characters
set against a romantic, Levantine backcloth. And then, we both
loved cats, and 'talked cat' unreservedly.

One Friday afternoon the four of us set out for the capital
by train, in one of those special saloon carriages where arm-
chairs are grouped round little tables and the atmosphere is a
mixture of club and tea room. The landscape tore past while
attendants rushed about distributing highballs, bourbon old-
fashioneds, coffee, coke or milk shakes as the whim took the

passenger. Malraux's conversation, or rather his particular manner of speech, enthralled all those at nearby tables. They had no doubt that we were a French party, but concluded, I think, that the monumental non-stop monologue to which they were listening was some kind of local dialect they could not be expected to follow, and so went back to their respective drinks, only continuing to cast a respectful eye on what was indeed a marathon performance.

In the taxi on the way to the hotel, this baffling flow continued unabated, ranging over every subject under the sun, fascinating, stimulating and totally absorbing to the black driver, who kept screwing his head round to listen, regardless of oncoming traffic. Reaching the hotel, we went to our room to recuperate our strength for the evening ahead, where we knew this wonderful flow would be resumed, as indeed it was.

After a fevered night spent exchanging our impressions of its highlights, we set off next day to savour the supreme luxury of going round the galleries with Malraux and a number of overawed curators who had arranged that certain rooms should be closed to the public during the time of his visit. Malraux's discursive flow became more comprehensible as we moved from picture to picture and he himself seemed to become simpler, as it were, humanised. When, for example, he stood before Vermeer's *Girl with a Pearl Earring* his absorption and delight in the manner in which the painter had caught the sheen on the pear-shaped drop was positively childish and for ten minutes or so we were treated to his special reflections on Vermeer's eye and brush.

At the end of the morning's delights we repaired to the hotel for luncheon in a state of euphoric exhaustion: Romain (who always found museums extremely difficult to take) was now obliged to lie down before he could rally for sustenance. As I had been brought up from childhood to visit museums regularly, my parents taking me to galleries and exhibitions at least twice a week, I had acquired a built-in stamina which Romain did not possess; but his passionate admiration for Malraux – the man, the adventurer, the thinker, the writer and the politician – sustained him for the rest of the weekend.

On our way home (the flow unabated), Malraux began expounding his fascination with American-Indian Kachina dolls, those ferocious, angular puppet-figures made by certain tribes. He asked me to acquire some for him as he knew I was planning a visit to California and hoped to reach one of the nearby Indian Reservations. At this point I noticed that Romain had sunk back in his seat, with his eyes closed, and I did not think he was taking much interest in the Kachina dolls. But I was wrong: either by some imitative impulse or a new awareness, he was to become intrigued by them; and years later some of these dolls adorned his apartment in Paris.

☪

We seldom quarrelled now – perhaps we both knew how precarious and how precious was the overall calm at which we had arrived; a surprising state considering our separate natures and the restraints they demanded. Thus 'scenes' were few.

However, I do recall one occasion when I hurled a leg of lamb at Romain's head, finding him – I forget why – totally insupportable. We were in the middle of lunch, when, as in some dream, I saw the joint sail across the table, miss Romain's head by inches and slither to a congealing repose under a bookcase. It looked so ridiculous, I burst out laughing.

Not so to *Monsieur Mon Mari*. Rising to his feet, thunderous and silent, he stalked out of the apartment.

An hour or so later his secretary at the French Legation telephoned to say Monsieur Gary would be kept late at the UN –

probably one of those all-night sittings – and it would be better if I cancelled the dinner party we had planned for the following night.

This I did not do, but invited a special friend – I think it was Fulco di Verdura, the Sicilian Duke who designed such luscious jewellery for Chanel – to step in and play host for me. He was the most entertaining person imaginable and we shared a liking for long-winded eighteenth-century Italian operas.

The party was proceeding in a jolly manner when the door

opened and Romain appeared. He was greeted with delighted cries of welcome. His saturnine countenance displayed no surprise as he joined us at the table. Then, eyeing whatever dish I had prepared – probably something exotic, of the kind he regarded as death on the plate, he enquired if there was anything simpler he could eat. 'What about cold lamb?' I suggested, but I did not dare catch his eye. He ate with gusto and the matter was never referred to again.

That same dinner table over which the gigot had been flung saw a lot of service. It was large and round, in an elegant postbellum style, and made of a beautiful coloured wood, no doubt from some North American forest, though its name I cannot recall. I had bought it off a friend leaving New York. Some time later, on my return to Paris, I disposed of its massive bulk to the writer Mary McCarthy who was then setting herself up in Paris.

On one never-to-be-forgotten occasion, our table seated the most remarkable trio. Romain had returned from a particularly trying session at the United Nations and, flinging himself down on the bed, announced, 'I've asked Malraux and Père Teilhard de Chardin to lunch here tomorrow – Gladwyn Jebb* wants to meet them both so he's coming too.' I managed to refrain from saying I thought it very short notice to arrange anything worthy of such notable figures.

In a state of frenzy known to every woman who has had a lunch party flung at her overnight, I decided on a basic menu – no fiddle-dee-dee, no soufflé to rise or fall. The faithful gigot of course, accompanied by yoghurt and aubergines in the Turkish fashion, a dish which I have observed pleases every man and every palate.

---

* Sir Gladwyn Jebb, the British Ambassador to the United Nations.

And so it proved to be. Our guests sat round the table demanding second helpings, always the greatest compliment a hostess can receive. Presently, they settled down to relays of coffee, hot and strong, which I rushed to them throughout the afternoon. The conversation must have been profoundly interesting for it rolled on unabated until 5 o'clock. Unfortunately, I have no clear recollection of what they discussed – much of it was, I think, concerned with Père Teilhard's revolutionary scientific doctrines which were then agitating the Vatican, while Romain was endeavouring to find a way round the ban which forbade their publication.

Even if I had been able to follow such complicated convolutions of thought, I was too occupied cherishing my guests, running between the table and the inconvenient alcove which passed as a kitchen in so many American apartments.

☪

While Romain's conquests were many and easy he did not, as I have said earlier, often discuss them with me. In the classical manner these conquests were growing younger and younger with the years. He had various methods of approach: when playing a mature or more sophisticated game, he had noted that the English language spoken with a slight French accent had a devastating effect, especially on the Anglo-Saxon or American ear. (Maurice Chevalier's *ziss* or *zat* bowled over at least three generations of his fans.) The admired English accent, with all those furry Rs of Russia was an added double enchantment! Romain himself had acquired a perfect English accent; only the timbre of his voice, that deep smoky timbre, hinted at something Slav.

When we were living in America he would assume this 'Chevalier' French accent with great flair and I would watch the effect, across some dinner table perhaps; a lot of *ziss* and *zat* and ve*rry*, ve*rry* rolled Rs soon had the ladies swooning. But if by chance he caught my eye we were both lost, struggling with uncontrollable laughter. Oh yes, Romain could laugh at himself and sometimes did.

In 1954, while in New York, I published my first book, *The Wilder Shores of Love*; biographies of four nineteenth-century women, each from a very different circumstance in life, who fled Western civilisation for the East, and there found fulfilment in adventure, the flesh or the faith of Islam. It was an overnight success, won a book prize in England, was bought for the cinema, was ultimately translated into twelve languages, and is still regularly reprinted. New York buzzed round me, but I dreaded the effect my good fortune would have on Romain. This unexpected success had come at a moment when he was particularly down, suffering a series of setbacks in his own work and relations with his publishers. He had also begun to sketch out the huge canvas of *The Roots of Heaven*. However, he indulged in his usual passion for publicity and published several articles of an ironic nature describing what it was like to be the husband of a successful woman.

☪

When the Hoppenots' term of office in America was finished and they left, there was no further reason for us to remain in New York. I was still giddying around enjoying myself, but Romain was not. He went to London where he had a severe nervous breakdown. When I finally joined him he was alarming the clinic where he was being treated, by constant threats to hurl himself out of the window. I reassured the matron that that was only part of his sense of drama and unless he was actually poised on the window-sill she should not worry. I was not very sympathetic to him at that moment, I know, but I had been advised by the psychoanalyst who was treating him that if I were to show any doting softness it would only make him collapse even further. I did not understand this, but did as I was told, and remained aloof. When Romain had recovered, the Quai d'Orsay appointed him to the French Embassy in London where Monsieur Chauvel was Ambassador. The two men did not appreciate each other and it must also have been hateful for Romain to be introduced everywhere, all that winter, as the husband of the woman who had written *The Wilder Shores of Love*.

This was an unhappy time for both of us. We were no longer living together, having found our side-by-side life untenable, and both of us were at a loss. The Ambassador solved the problem of having Romain on his staff ('I don't want to see that man hanging around my Embassy,' he was quoted as saying), and Romain was given extended leave; a sort of unofficial extended leave. This was a marvellous occasion for Romain to remove himself quietly to Roquebrune to finish the manuscript of *The Roots of Heaven* which had been much interrupted by our personal dramas. Presently, the scene changed and he was nominated Minister at La Paz and left for Bolivia while I remained in London planning a new book.

It should be noted, in passing, that I have never been compelled to write by a burning desire to create. As a journalist, I wrote for a living, nothing more. When I married Romain, I had seen myself leading a pleasant and idle existence, consecrated to the duties of a wife, but apart from two years of carefree life that I had known in Sofia, I soon found it necessary to get back to writing again.

My mother represented a serious financial responsibility for me, and I also realised that if Romain supplied the essentials – a roof over our heads, our daily bread – those additional domestic needs, not to mention my personal expenses, really did not fit into his calculations – if he ever made them. I remember him arriving from the Legation in Sofia with one month's salary in wads of bank notes in his pockets, which fell out across the floor. I often wondered how much he had lost *en route*. I also wondered, during all the years we spent together, how much his salary was and where it all went. He never seemed to have enough, even for our modest lifestyle. So I stopped asking myself questions and continued to write, in order to live with greater ease; which does not mean that I returned to the tyranny of journalism. I was writing books which dealt with subjects of my choice, far from any considerations of a commercial nature. I was lucky that these subjects – one devoted to Imam Shamyl and the religious wars in the Caucasus; and another a biography of Pierre Loti, the French novelist and naval officer who loved both men and women, and who was out of fashion at the time – attracted the interest of a great many readers.

## THE GONCOURT

In December 1956, the Prix Goncourt was awarded to Romain for *The Roots of Heaven*. He was *en poste* in Bolivia while I was in London, so we converged on Paris for that splendid moment and stayed at the Hôtel Port Royal. Like so many other French women of that day I did not then possess a French bank account of my own, and had rushed over from London carrying only a little English money with me. Romain was in turmoil, besieged by journalists and editors, telephones ringing incessantly. Every time I asked him with increasing desperation to let me have some pocket money, he would sweep me aside saying, 'Get it from the hall porter.' This I proceeded to do, and although not given to excessive expenditure, I still ran up a modest bill which, after several days, the hall porter seemed to resent. I found this rather awkward.

Was Romain mean with his money? Yes and no. Like anyone who has known extreme poverty he regarded money with an almost superstitious awe and was horrified at the amount required for the smallest daily expenses. Yet he could be generous to the point of folly sometimes, buying some picture he didn't want, perhaps, to help a struggling artist along the way. Or he would enjoy playing the open-handed host, making grand gestures of hospitality, standing treat for all the scroungers who crowded round. And how many there were in those days directly after he had won the Goncourt, and was a celebrated figure in Paris! A luncheon planned for three or four special friends would soon overflow to a table for fourteen – they 'just happened to be passing by', or 'just wanted to congratulate him'. They just wanted to be in the picture, and eat at his expense. For Romain it was still a new and delicious experience to play the patron. It was as though every plate of food, every glass of wine he offered, was a part of his triumph, a trophy to be laid at the feet of his mother, who in those faraway days had gone hungry so that he might eat.

Although *The Roots of Heaven* had won the Goncourt, some critics found it long-winded and untidily slung together, something they rated above its vast panorama of idealism. But nothing could have exceeded the gross misunderstanding of the theme – the general untidiness, weakness of script and fatal miscasting – which doomed the film Darryl Zanuck made from it. I fancy that John Huston, who directed, was sidetracked by the idea of some big-game hunting while on location and Zanuck was single-minded after another kind of game – the lovely young Juliette Gréco. At any rate, the film – the first of Romain's books to be filmed, was a flop; and Romain grieved for it.

Somewhere I have read that Romain collected elephant fig-
ures; models in china, wood, jade, marble, bronze, or ivory. So
far as I remember he never actively collected any, but he did
receive an enormous amount of such tributes from readers of
*The Roots of Heaven*. How ironic that so many of these trib-
utes should be in ivory, the very material for which so many
unhappy creatures were, and still are, being slaughtered for
their tusks. The hideous truth of these massacres was one of
the main themes of Romain's book. 'Don't my readers read?'
he groaned, receiving yet another ivory memento.

However repetitive and carelessly constructed many of the
pages of this book were, however often I suggested he should
cut or prune, he merely wrote on, a rushing stream, which,
inexplicably, his editors did nothing to check. Such repetitive
passages are the weakness of this fine book; a weakness found
again in some other of Romain's writings.

But then, Romain believed in quantity – bulk – as being the
first essential of success. A curious doctrine. He admired the
enormous output of the nineteenth-century French giants.
'Balzac, Hugo – they had the right idea,' he would say. 'I shan't
rest till I see whole shelves full of my books,' he would add
and I shuddered, for there came a time in his life when quan-
tity had certainly overcome quality.

Looking back over his writing in its fantastic sweep, it can
be divided into three distinct sections. The first: brilliant, fresh,
very personal, which began with *The Forest of Anger* and
went on triumphantly via *The Roots of Heaven* to his master-
piece, *Promise at Dawn*. Then followed a strangely uneven
period which, with certain exceptions – such as that most
touching and fantastic tale of loneliness and a boa constrictor,
*Gros câlin*, and *The Life Before Us*, both published under the
signature of Emile Ajar – often seemed tarnished by banal,
quirky, American-style money-makers. But by the late 1970s,

the original, unmistakable voice was heard again. The inter-
woven pattern of his life and writings can be traced through
those years of achievement, decline and resurgence.

☾⋆

Publicity was something he could never resist. Being inter-
viewed, being photographed, or making appearances on TV,
intoxicated him. He could never have enough of these indul-
gences, for so they became. The quality of his work and his
personal stature needed none of these cheap tricks. But it was
the limelight he sought increasingly.

A time came when, at the most tragic moment of his life, he
must summon the press; he must declaim and denounce or
expose matters concerning his private life. He could not, he
would not, stay out of the limelight; it was a need which came
to override all discretion and dumbfounded even his closest
friends.

He knew my views on publicity, and the value I set on priv-
acy, and I am grateful that he always kept me apart from such
displays.

From the beginning I had known that if Romain and I were
to remain together, I must become like the Three Wise Monkeys:
seeing no evil, hearing no evil, speaking no evil. At least that was
my endeavour where scandals and his innumerable conquests
were concerned. Fortunately, my life was always a very busy
one and left me no time to repine. Romain himself was some-
thing of a handful as nanny would have put it. To follow his
vagaries, his timetables, exits and entrances, extreme disorder
and general unpredictability was totally absorbing. All in all,
my life with him was a happy one and certainly a rewarding
one.

Romain was never much of a one for letters. A few words

scrawled on a postcard, or a telegram, were enough. One such telegram I received went straight to the point, circumnavigating the sort of love letter I should have relished. 'Your letters not loving enough,' it read. Another time, soon after I had been trying to interest him in Wagner's music, and failed, I was in Vienna when a card reached me which merely stated: 'Darling I loathe your Wagner. I spit on his tomb.'

One telegram which I have always kept was sent after he had finished reading my book *The Sabres of Paradise*. He was absent from Los Angeles for a few days and had taken the proofs with him. I was on tenterhooks for he was a severe critic. 'It is an extraordinary book and will remain a classic. Stop. With admiration,' he wired and I breathed again.

C*

Occasionally, when roused to fury over what he considered needless household expenses, he would let fly in long angry letters. 'I have received a bill for six bath towels and four pairs of sheets and pillow things as well as something about an electric kettle. Are you out of your mind? How can I go on if you throw money about. PAY. PAY. PAY. What do we want with new bath towels, I am asking you? You have no conscience. You will ruin me ...'

As he had won the Prix Goncourt and also written a worldwide bestseller, this seemed unlikely, but the outburst reached me in the Caucasus, where I was searching for material for my book on Imam Shamyl, and it succeeded in overshadowing much of my stay there. However, I must add in all honour, he was always generous and understanding about the expensive journeys I made, either to see my mother, or for my work.

There was one lavish ritual which Romain and I kept together for years and for which he never considered the expense. For as long as the famous Russian restaurant Korniloff – the original Korniloff – existed in Paris, we dined there before leaving for a new posting. We flung ourselves recklessly into a last celebratory meal of traditional Russian food: *zakouski* in its plenitude with little pots of *zhulien* and blini, followed by scalding hot consommé, in the traditional manner, then *kulebyaka* for me and *zrazy* with horseradish for Romain, and finally *gogul mogul* just because we both loved the name. 'After the red pottage comes the exceeding bitter cry,' or so the Bible says; but I think these memorable meals made us both so happy that no bitter cry was ever heard.

## PROMISE AT DAWN

1956 found us together again in Los Angeles, or rather Hollywood, where we lived for four years. It was a strange life: a mixture of glitter and glamour among the stars where we made many friends in the cinema world. Romain was, as always, writing furiously, pursuing his amorous conquests across a splendid field and performing his duties as Consul General with his usual careless, but consummate skill. I was also battling to run a large, painfully understaffed household, where much official hospitality had to be dispensed. 'At the least possible expense, you understand,' he would tell me, and I must admit he grudged every penny spent on the upkeep of that post, so that I had to make do with the services of one maid which meant that I was the second and third. I was also writing *The Sabres of Paradise*, a massive book on the Caucasian wars and the struggle of the Moslem tribes for independence from nineteenth-century Russian colonial designs.

Los Angeles, for all its meretricious tinselly charm, was a

place where both of us found we could write well. Other writers also found it congenial: Aldous Huxley and Christopher Isherwood notably. None of us could explain why this should be, but both Romain and myself wrote, I think, our best books there: his *Promise at Dawn*; my *Sabres of Paradise*.

Not only writers, but musicians and painters were drawn to those palmy groves. Stravinsky and his wife Vera, the painter, kept a house there, going frequently between it and their New York base.

As the glow of international fame and financial independence widened it had a curious effect on Romain. The loveable, naive and blundering Romain I had so often likened to a bear was rarely present. But the insane Roman emperor made more and more frequent appearances; moreover, he seemed to be modelling himself on Proust, who wrote, '*Ceux qui ont la possibilité de vivre pour eux-mêmes doivent le faire*' – 'Those who have the opportunity to live for themselves must do so.' In short, the egoism his mother had fostered began to assume disconcerting proportions. His indifference to the reactions of others sometimes bordered on ruthlessness. It was also a form of laziness and self-indulgence which allowed him to ride roughshod towards his objective, while remaining aloof from, or indifferent to, any awkward situation which might ensue.

We were often asked if we were jealous of one another. I think we were, but it was jealousy of an unexpected kind. I was jealous of the adventurous travels he had made in faraway countries before they became part of the tourist circuit. Those glittering horizons haunted me – tormented me, as no remorseless rival could do.

He was jealous of my robust health, my hardy digestion in particular. 'Don't you ever get indigestion?' he would ask bitterly, as I attacked a *brandade*, or a *cassoulet*. Friends told me he often dwelt enviously on the manner in which I could do with little sleep, or never had to resort to pills. '*Quelle santé de fer! Pas croyable! Jamais fatiguée!*' he would say bitterly, although no doubt he did not realise that to keep up with his moods and exigencies, while coping with the practical sides of life, allowed little time for fatigue.

Travelling together we were always in harmony. The fret and fritter of daily life slid away and even Romain, who generally disliked anything approaching sightseeing, joined me looking for the Street of the Necromancers in Prague because the name intrigued him. It breathed all Magic of Magics; but then, with that legion of fabulous grotesque and pathetic characters which he conjured up on every page, was he not something of a magician himself?

Romain was curiously incurious about any strange country or city in which he found himself. If he was to live in it, he did so, but having no sense of direction and no particular desire to explore, he merely continued within his own enclosed world, mollusc-like, scarcely swayed by sun or snow; brooding, writing and decidedly averse to visiting celebrated sites. I think he generally most enjoyed observing the daily life of a city, briefly anchored in a café following the ways of the citizens. In Yucatán, I remember, we were more enthralled watching some iguanas plopping about heavily beside the Mayan temples than in penetrating the terrifying corridors leading to 'El Tigre'.

When we were beside the Muradiye tombs at Brussa (now Bursa), the small Turkish town we loved particularly, he seemed, briefly, content. We would stew in the old Turkish baths at Cekirge which Justinian had built for his Empress Theodora, and were still in use; to us as much a marvel as the Blue Mosque itself. Or, finding a booth where they cooked doner kebab, eat it on the hoof, the gravy dripping down our chins. And if we went to the bazaars or souks (where I at once lost my head), Romain was remarkably patient. Some hours later I would find him seated in a little *kahvehane*, sprawled on a rug, puffing luxuriously at a water-pipe. Asia had claimed its own.

But sooner or later, wherever we were, a cloud would descend and Romain would retreat into that limboland of gloom that was his kingdom. Such incommunicable melancholy usually remained for the rest of the day and sometimes lingered on as a hangover to spoil the following day. Usually this meant that he was struggling with some development of the book he was writing; a block or a problem that obsessed him. There were varying degrees of gloom; some were induced by brooding over the agonies endured by the human race in general. 'Oh do stop worrying about Asia and Africa and help me with the suitcases,' was a cry sometimes wrung from me when he was particularly inert. And then he might laugh and become almost cheerful. Or he might not. At times that profound, more permanent misery concerning his mother could only be lightened by persuading him to recount yet another wildly improbable incident, the sort which always appeared to centre round that extraordinary woman.

☪

That Romain was *un grand coureur*, a tremendous womaniser, was part of the preconceived character his mother had designed for him. It was, too, an unappeasable hunger. Wherever he found himself, the brothel, the pick-up and more rarely the alcove claimed him, though his lifelong terror of disease was to prove rather cramping. The great seducer (and even a putative son of Ivan Mosjoukine, that star of the French silent cinema, could not be otherwise), or the swaggering virile image he always cultivated, something so irritating to other men and so attractive to women, at times gave place to yet another. This was the romantic author-lover, all tenderness for the ideal of fragile womanhood. However, this might be described as a more theoretic and idealised approach, briefly overcoming simpler appetites. If it expressed one of the many Romains, it was certainly an aspect which appealed to a large number of his female readers.

Romain had a very acutely attuned antenna for all that was new in trends, attitudes and fashions; he foresaw the French public's intoxication with all things American, their cowboys, drugstores, blue jeans and tough talk, like their expressive slang or their Kerouac school of hobo literature. He noted it and cultivated it in his own way in some of his books, or in giving interviews to French newspapers about his conversations with Norman Mailer, John Ford and other notables of the American scene. At times he almost seemed to set himself up as interpreter of the United States to the gawping public of France which now appeared to be totally bemused by American living. 'Pop singers, fast cars and film stars are all they want now,' he told me. 'Film stars,' he added, 'have become the new royalty.' That was at a time when European royalty, or what was left of it, still behaved with circumspection and was still admired.

*Promise at Dawn*, a great book and Romain's finest, was begun in Mexico while we were there on holiday in 1958. We had already sampled one Hollywood Christmas with jingle bells and plastic Christmas trees covered in artificial snow, while plastic reindeer were electrically propelled along Sunset Boulevard and carols piped out from every rooftop. We fled to Mexico.

There, we remembered, festive seasons were interpreted in other terms: ghoulish terms perhaps, but both touching and tonic in their macabre way. Sugar skulls, dancing skeletons,

sweetmeat Crucifixions and processions of kneeling penitents, their blood staining the path; but not a trace of jingle bells.

Nevertheless, the American tourist trade had been busy since our last visit. There was a Christmas tree and quite a lot of tinsel to get round before we could sign the hotel register. But once in our room we could trace a vague pearly outline floating far away above the smog. Popocatépetl! Lovely, seductive Mexico awaited us.

I started to unpack. Meanwhile, Romain, with an air of extreme concentration, had placed a large armchair with its back to the window and to the volcano, and called down for a supply of paper, bottles of ink and several pens – spectacular writer's outfit. Before I had finished unpacking he was writing furiously. *Promise at Dawn* was begun. What had no doubt been fermenting in his brain, biding its time, now burst out; flooded out, and was written at white heat. This book was to change his whole life and free him for ever from certain restraints or *pudeurs*. But that freedom lay some years ahead.

For the following week he wrote on, totally immersed in his subject, staring zombie-like if a break or meals were suggested. I left him to it and spent my days wandering about the city with its eternal reminders of José Guadalupe Posada's macabre woodcuts of skeletons or desperate crimes alongside the riotous baroque of churches where Madame Calderón de la Barca has described those sumptuous and sinister ceremonies surrounding a novice taking her final vows. These two extremes of violent emotion are all Mexico.

On one of these expeditions I ran into the giant and picturesque figure of Count Frédéric von Ledebuhr carrying an enormous saddle studded with turquoise, and himself smothered in Indian jewellery. He was driving south-west in his jeep and suggested dropping us off at Taxco. To my astonishment Romain agreed. Perhaps even he needed to draw breath; and he had always enjoyed Frédéric's highly coloured personality and appearance. Thus the three of us set out on a trip which no doubt the stars would not have advised.

☾

Romain was always disagreeably affected by noise. Perhaps it was a legacy of the war years. In any case, no sooner was he removed from the womb-like quiet of room number 184 than he began to complain. A small Mexican city has its own brand of uproar – a yelling population, uncontrollable traffic and blasting mariachi bands as well as ceaseless radio; but the local chemists had never heard of earplugs. That night, supping in a dim little posada, Romain began to fiddle with bits of pneumatic white bread, moulding them, slightly moistened by *pulque*, into quite passable earplugs. We set aside some more bread from the heart of the breakfast rolls, and for two nights it worked perfectly.

Then excruciating earache set in and he was soon roaring and writhing. 'Get me out of here before it's too late,' he moaned, by now green-faced and determined on a brain tumour.

At last a taxi was found and the driver persuaded to drive through the night to reach Mexico City. It was a dreadful journey in this rattling crashing vehicle. Every jolt in the road was agony. Romain lay across the seat, his head on my lap, alternately yelling at the driver to go faster, or giving me last-minute instructions for the care of his manuscripts, for his funeral – by cremation – and the conduct of my widowhood.

On arrival the hotel doctor was sent for. 'Not that he will be able to do anything, it's too late,' said Romain, who had now turned his face to the wall and was awaiting the end.

I suggested that quite a large proportion of Mexicans appeared to be treated satisfactorily in the splendid new hospitals, but he was unconvinced. 'And how will you make them understand my state? Remember, you speak no Spanish ... '

Quite soon the doctor arrived, oozing calm confidence, the traditional opening phrase being uttered in perfect English. 'Now, Signora, what seems to be the matter?' When I told him my husband had been stuffing bread-and-*pulque* pellets into his ear, he asked me to repeat this unusual information. It transpired he had been trained at the Mayo Clinic and all the treatments he prescribed worked perfectly. Two days later Romain was able to go back to *Promise at Dawn*, chapter V, page something or other, with only four days missing from that daemonic impulse which drove him on, throughout the writing of that book.

☪

On our return to Los Angeles I read the manuscript as it progressed, almost hour by hour. He usually gave me large chunks of text to read, as when I was going through the manuscript of *Lady L* which he wrote directly in English – so good an English that once again I marvelled at his acute ear for language.

But now, with *Promise at Dawn*, he would fling me a page or two at a time, sometimes across the dinner table, or as I gardened. It almost seemed as if the pages were smoking with emotion.

Although often hilarious there were certain passages concerning his mother that I thought almost too painful for print. Not that they dishonoured her. That never; she emerges splendidly larger than life, as she was, I believe. Would more discretion have weakened the portrait, I wondered?

Nina Owczyńska was a great woman, however trying as a mother. In writing *Promise at Dawn*, in revealing so much of the raw truth, Romain was not only repaying something of his debt to her love and courage, but revealing that extraordinary link or bond which made him for ever her creation; one half of that indissoluble whole they formed.

I never knew my mother-in-law: she had died in France before I met Romain and I could only envisage her through such glimpses as Romain and a few of his early friends provided.

I have seen several photographs of her: a distinguished, prematurely aged figure, muffled in a shabby overcoat, grey-haired and become almost toothless, I was told. It was difficult to imagine her young and beautiful as Romain said she had once been, before he could distinctly recall her. But one day, not long before we divorced, he suddenly thrust a small packet into my hand. 'You should have these,' he said. 'Keep them safe. Do what you like with them …' There were a few old photographs, scraps of paper, a driving licence, his flying brevet and such. Two of the photographs it contained I treasured especially – the voluptuous, seductively smiling young Nina, the other a fat little Fauntleroy figure, four-year-old Romain: together they showed that indissoluble whole at its very beginning.

Romain could never have been said to mellow with success. Its financial benefits only made him more nervous and irritable. The extreme poverty of his youth was to remain a built-in neurosis, a festering wound which nothing could heal. Thus he lived in a state of permanent apprehension and as his affairs continued to prosper he was still uneasy. Sessions with bankers, brokers or his agent were constantly needed to provide the soothing assurances he craved. Even so, gnawing doubts remained, to cloud that comfortable sense of wealth and achievement he might have enjoyed.

One way or another sex was his driving force, also a neurotic craving, which must be gratified at once (otherwise, he maintained, his writing would suffer). Sometimes it appeared to be a miracle drug both stimulant and sedative, but as Baudelaire said: '*Chaque homme porte en lui sa dose d'opium naturelle*' – 'Each man carries within him his dose of natural opium.'

Water – the element of water – also had a calming effect upon him. Swimming far out to sea, he shed his complexes. Wherever we were he would at once take refuge in the bath tub, spending long hours immersed in steamy concentration on the book of the moment. In Hollywood he also conducted much of the consular business from the bathroom. I would find him wallowing, a large sponge strategically placed and Madame Benedictus, his beautiful and inscrutable Chinese secretary, installed on the lavatory seat, taking shorthand notes with her customary air of imperturbability.

The mechanics of daily living were never taken into consideration. 'I forgot, there are forty fucking *députés* due in from Paris tomorrow. Didn't I tell you? They'll have to have a buffet supper here tomorrow night. Get some starlets for them.' Casual statements which ignored the mechanics of giving a buffet supper with starlets at twenty-four hours' notice might be flung at my head at any time.

Such ruthless disregard sometimes required tact to avoid unnecessary pain. At one time he developed a dislike for certain types of feminine looks. It was not that he was always demanding pretty secretaries in the conventional sense, but rather that a certain cast of countenance, the set of a head, or the colour of the hair could, he said, irritate him beyond measure when dictating. This was difficult to reconcile with the excellent technical abilities of some of the ladies in question.

'I know she's a first-class typist and *bi-lingue*, but she'll have to sit behind a screen,' he once told me; he expected me to provide a screen by the next morning. Much, much more difficult was explaining its presence to the secretary in question.

Such self-centred indifference, call it what you will, combined with stretches of silence which were Trappist in their intensity, could produce unfortunate results. I recall a long, silent drive from Los Angeles heading for Santa Barbara, where, it seemed, some sort of function required our official presence. Romain vouchsafed no further information beyond saying there would be a luncheon afterwards – after what? But he relapsed into one of his silences which one did not break.

It was a chill damp Californian wintry day with the sea mist creeping inland along the Pacific Highway. As usual, Romain drove his convertible with the hood down and I was thankful for the warm coat I was wearing. We were approaching Santa Barbara when he turned and eyed this coat speculatively. 'Mmm – d'you think red is quite right for a funeral?' he enquired, and left me to brave a select gathering of black-clad mourners.

Another searing occasion was when we were giving one of those dinner parties which protocol imposed. Such obligations he had come to regard as intrusions into his life as a writer. The fact that he was Consul General and officially representing France could be swept aside at will. Halfway through this particular evening he showed signs of strain – of unconcealed boredom. I struggled on, conscious of heavy pauses, and turned to him frantically to provide some of those firework-like diversions with which he could at times enchant his audience. But he had vanished.

Muttering something vague, I left the room, to find him in an adjacent bedroom reserved for the ladies' wraps. He had gone to ground – to bed, rather, having inserted himself delicately under a lavish mound of cloaks and furs. There he lay, apparently fast asleep, the mutation mink and silver fox pelts gently heaving as he breathed. There was nothing to be done but to leave him lying there, and return to my guests explaining he had received an urgent call from the Embassy in Washington and was likely to be kept a very long time. I knew better than to try to rouse his social conscience. I made a fevered dash to remove the furs elsewhere, while he slept on, apparently undisturbed, and the evening broke up rather early, exactly as he had intended. After which he emerged, wide-awake and much amused. It was impossible to be angry with him – he was too outrageous.

## LAST YEARS TOGETHER

Towards the end of our years in Los Angeles, Romain began to get restive for Europe and applied for the post of Consul General in Venice. He was determined not to get involved in higher political arenas by returning to Embassy posts. While the question of Venice was open to discussion, I was informed overnight that he wished me to make a dash there and inspect the Consulate General which was housed in a beautiful old palazzo on the Grand Canal – or was it the Giudecca?

'Go and see if it's comfortable and how much space there is. I need a big, light room to work in, well away from the offices. See what the advantages are; see how the land lies and get back here as quickly as possible because I forgot to tell you, the Ambassador and what's-her-name are likely to come down from Washington any day now. You must organise it all so they meet all the big stars – you know that's what they always want.'

I achieved this violent *va et vient*, but when inspecting the palazzo, which occupied the two top floors of a noble building, I found I was more anxiously calculating what sort of a life our two cats would have there, without a garden, cooped up, or taken for uncomfortable walks along some dark alleys.

I need not have worried: on my return, while still panting from the rush, Romain told me he had decided against Venice and would prefer to go to Athens. When I suggested that Tunis or Damascus would also be lovely posts he swept this aside saying, 'I'm not going anywhere where I can't get at the women – it's different for you.'

'Lesley is very eighteenth-century about my affairs,' I was told he had complained to a close friend. Perhaps he regretted there were none of those dramatic scenes and luxurious reconciliations associated with infidelity. But I hated to rock the boat as long as it sailed on over the many cross-currents of our life together and apart. Infidelities, absences, complications, complicities and comprehension: perhaps Romain had the last word when he said, 'No one is a cuckold if they know what's going on.'

Looking back, I think our deepest tie – that which kept us together for eighteen years – was our true friendship. We shared an interest in each other's work (we seldom talked politics together); we shared the same sense of humour; and there was some subtle, Slav ambience that always spelled home to us wherever we were. Above all, it was our deep companionship which came to survive every trial.

I was accustomed to Romain's aching longing for his mother. 'While she was in the room I wanted nothing more,' he once told me, recalling his childhood. But besides this perpetual longing there was also the built-in Slav spleen – *tosca* – and now, almost imperceptibly, I perceived yet another brooding gloom was taking hold. This new misery made Slav sadness, at least, seem almost light-hearted. The age-old Jewish heritage of sorrow which I began to sense in him had, I think, lain dormant, perhaps unconsidered even, through many years; but gradually it was becoming a lurking self-renewing grief from which there was no escape; an inexplicable hereditary or traditional source of guilt for which, it seemed, there was no pardon.

When these despairing, incommunicable moods closed round him they recalled the black tragedies of Elizabethan drama. I remembered Mephistopheles as Marlowe drew him:

FAUSTUS: Where are you damned?
MEPHISTOPHELES: In hell.

FAUSTUS: How comes it then that thou art out of hell?
MEPHISTOPHELES: Why this is hell, nor am I out of it.

The full measure of this haunting only took a real hold towards the end of his life, or so I was told. He seldom spoke of it to me, or would only make an oblique reference which applied to some situation in world politics. Yet it began to cast a long shadow.

I have said earlier that *Promise at Dawn* was to change Romain's whole life; but in more ways than might be expected – in ways that at first were perhaps not observed by anyone but myself. He had won the acclaim of both critics and public; the book had runaway sales and was acquired for the cinema. He had written a great book, a heart-rending book, and it spoke to a public all over the world. But it did something else. It tore away all the subterfuges, the pretences, with which he had carefully fogged much of his background. He had always liked to appear mysterious, but now he had come out with a truth which required cold courage to avow.

The chameleon had shed its protective colouring.

He had begun life in an Eastern Europe slum, a poor little Jew-boy, probably a bastard, baited by his Christian and Polish schoolmates. He had had to face the rat pack alone, except for his mother who fought for them both, accepting any menial task she could find. There was not a home worth calling such and sometimes not enough money for food. Now, he tore away all the comfortable wrappings of mystery, spat on the eclectic stratas of diplomatic life and stood there, or rather strutted, before the whole world. 'That's what I was!' he seemed to shout. 'That's where I came from!' There was a bitterness, an overweening pride together with a curious masochistic pleasure in parading *mis à nu*: exposed. 'Rot the lot of them,' he would say when referring to those persons not in his immediate

favour, adverse critics, or any reminders of obligations per-
taining to the daily round. Sometimes it seemed as if he was
taking his revenge on society in general. But for what, I often
wondered? On fate, perhaps – the tragic fate that had willed
his mother should never know all he had achieved.

This new figure he now revealed had done away with the
last restrictions of any conventions he had observed earlier. He
had lived and fought and achieved magnificently, for Her, his
mother. Now he meant to live another life, his own, and
entirely on his own terms.

On 14 July 1961 Romain's imminent departure from the Los Angeles post had been announced, but now he jumped the gun by refusing to be present at the habitual celebrations. These were held annually at the Consulate General, where the tricolor was run up and a buffet of enormous dimensions awaited the French colony and other citizens of Los Angeles who came to pay their respects and quaff champagne. On this last occasion the French colony were anxious to express their sorrow at Romain's departure and generally to feel themselves in his distinguished company one more time.

But Romain decided not to appear. Having barricaded himself behind closed doors and windows on the far side of the house, he left me, together with the loyal and delightful Vice-Consul Madame Yvonne Petremont, ever a tower of strength, to get through the day as best we could, and lie ourselves into perdition, explaining he had been obliged to leave earlier than planned. Such were the lies, the prevarications and inventions which his implacable egoism sometimes imposed.

I have never been able to reconcile this chill indifference with the profound idealism which spreads through his writings. Oh Romain! How funny, how tragic a figure you were at close quarters! How entertaining, how exasperating a companion! How rare a chance to have known you, loved you and been loved by you.

☪

Our last days in Hollywood were sombre. Romain had come to detest the slightest constraint and had shut himself away to brood. He wanted OUT. His mind was made up: there was to be no more diplomatic life, no more posts abroad. He had requested to be placed *en disponibilité* by the Quai d'Orsay (who were, I must say, always remarkably indulgent to his caprices), and now he was preparing to go forward towards wider horizons as a famous writer savouring that life in Paris for which he had hankered so long.

He began to view the idea of marriage – some conventional sort of marriage, that is – as a panacea for all his ills. He saw it as some remote yet realisable state of grace. That he was essentially a loner, an *égoïste enragé*, was discounted. This shimmering mirage was seen as a halcyon voyage leading towards every fulfilment. 'Besides,' he told me, 'I must have a son. I owe it to my mother.' To be laid at her feet as a last splendid trophy, I wondered?

In 1963 we were divorced. Some years later, although we

*Lesley Blanch in Hollywood in the fifties.*

seldom met, we established a sort of *amitié téléphonique*. These were rare occasions when we could discuss cosily our various problems and sometimes laugh at the madness of the world around us. As certain of Romain's problems became more and more pressing he would call me more often. Oddly he sometimes telephoned from a call box, as if on a sudden impulse, or perhaps seeking its anonymity. At last, I came to imagine this call box, wherever it might be, as some sort of Confessional, our words exchanged through a grille, in that secrecy I knew he desired.

Occasionally he came to see me at my house in Garavan on the French-Italian border. He became fascinated by the still little-known wild yet lush country which rose so steeply behind the house. He asked me to try to find him something in that area: 'Something away from the coast, peaceful, high up, but overlooking the sea,' he stipulated. The Mediterranean – *le Grand Bleu* – was a craving that never left him, and at last his ashes were cast, as he had asked me they should be, into the blue bay lying far below the village of Roquebrune.

☪

When in February 1977 Romain published *Womanlight*, he sent me a copy with a card inside which gave me great pleasure. 'Dearest Lesley,' he wrote, 'When you next come to Paris if you wish you could meet my son, after calling him around one o'clock. He is quite nice. As ever, Romain.'

I was to meet Diego several times; and later under very painful circumstances soon after his father's death. I found him, as Romain had said, nice, very nice, but fate and distances have prevented our friendship from developing, alas. Two or three days before Romain died he telephoned me and seemed, I thought, even more sombre than usual. He spoke of certain new problems that have no place here. *A quoi bon?* What's the use? He chose to solve them in his own way, to vanish in his own way, in his own time; still in his own aura of mystery.

Of one thing I am sure. Whatever the disillusions those last days brought, he would never have wished to remain *en scène* long enough to face the collapse of old age.

'*C'est con* – but Lesley, *tout est con*,' were the last words I heard him say before he rang off.

## POSTSCRIPT

Earlier in these pages I have written of a packet of old photographs and papers which Romain entrusted to my safekeeping: among them one of himself, taken in London in 1944. He is in uniform, on the edge of his first literary success. He smiles, a curious half-smile, as if incredulous of the glowing future that was approaching. This was the Romain who had not yet learned to present himself in that carapace of successive poses which became second nature to him.

Among some faded snapshots of his mother there was one, a studio portrait taken in Warsaw, about 1905 I would judge, and probably the only existing copy. It recalled a young woman, glowing and voluptuously seductive; a woman as her son could never have known her. Any other pictures I have seen only show a worn, shabby, but dignified woman, battered by life. I have often wondered why Romain did not keep this picture beside him. But old photographs make sad looking: perhaps this one was too cruel a reminder of the way life had treated her, as she battled for her Romantchik.

I treasured the packet he had given me and put it away in a little tin trunk: a Victorian child's toy, naively painted with locks and straps. I thought how wryly Romain would have smiled at my choice of a strongbox – something I never possessed, anyhow.

C

One night in April 1994 my house was destroyed by fire. I was awakened by the crash of falling beams and the roar of flames, blinding me as I fled.

By early morning little or nothing remained but piles of soggy debris and ash. My library, with its collection of early travel books on Russia and the Islamic world, had vanished with the rest of my possessions. Ikons, paintings, rugs, manuscripts – all the treasures, trivia and tokens of a lifetime had vanished. Of the lovely room Romain had admired and envied on his rare visits ('Why can't you make me a room like this?') nothing remained.

For several days my friends worked with me, sifting through the charred rubble for anything that might have survived: a hopeless job. On the last day, late in the afternoon as we were about to leave, some sudden impulse made me turn back. 'Let's have one more look – over there in that corner,' I said, though why, I do not know. I must have sounded imperative, for my tired and discouraged companion acquiesced. Mireille Goerand was an old friend and had been that small child at Roquebrune of whom I wrote earlier; the small child who was constantly dispatched to fetch relays of the Gauloises Bleues which Romain then smoked non-stop when writing. But that was forty years ago: since then, she had outgrown her terrors and come to know him on easier terms.

Now, in the fading light, as we once more plunged our hands into the feathery drifts of ash, I saw her draw out something tangible or solid. It was a fragment of charred metal

*Romain and Nina Kacew, mother and son, that indissoluble whole, together.*

stuck together with some blackened papers, curled at the edges. They flaked and scattered as we detached them from a piece of metal that had once been part of a tin trunk. As I touched them two blackened, smoke-blurred photographs emerged from the rest. They were like overexposed prints, dark images, but recognisable still.

As in a dream, I saw those two rare photographs which Romain had entrusted to my care so long ago. There they were: Romain and Nina Kacew, mother and son, that indissoluble whole, together, as ever and just as they would have wished posterity to have recorded them, I fancy. Romain, the Free French aviator, and Nina, the seductively lovely young mother of a *Wunderkind*. They had risen phoenix-like from the ashes of my hearth and they were not going to vanish like all the rest. An extraordinary vitality or life-force seemed to vibrate round their darkened image. They were sole survivors of the disaster and now confronted me in a melodramatic manner. Romain was once more demanding the limelight.

☪

Later, I took the blurred pictures to an expert restorer, a very old person who looked as if he might have worked with Nadar, but who was reputed to perform miracles. He promised nothing and looked doubtful, yet, miraculously, the two pictures were restored, almost as they had been.

And it is here, in these pages, that I feel this dramatic pair should, in the traditional theatrical phraseology, make 'Positively Their Last Appearance Together'.

*Part Four*

# FARAWAY LANDS

# 17. The Lodestar Longing

IF EVER A CHILD was born under the Lilac Star (in Balkan legend that of the traveller) it is myself. As long as I can remember, I have been possessed by a burning craving for far horizons: though this is in no way evasion, for I cherish my home. But my homeland – what is that? I have become a piece of receptive flotsam, at one with each shifting scene. Once attained, each remote land seems home, though some are more home than others, as Orwell might have said. Perhaps I am most at home within the girdle of Islam, in lands where my hours are marked by the muezzin's haunting cry and lance-like minarets soar to radiant skies.

Perhaps this is a predestined pattern, for there is a long tradition of English women who have fallen under the spell of Moslem lands: Lady Mary Wortley Montagu in Turkey, Lady Hester Stanhope in the Lebanon, Lady Anne Blunt in the desert with her magnificent Arab thoroughbreds, Gertrude Bell queening it in Baghdad and Lady Ellenborough who became Jane Mezrabi and a legend in Damascus.

In my case, it all began in the nursery, where my favorite bedtime poem began: 'I'll sing thee songs of Araby and tell of far Kashmir'. The pattern was formed then, and the shimmering oriental image has remained to haunt me, or taunt me, an imperious call, a lodestar, leading me on, into the unknown – for even today it is there for the finding. Other more intrepid travellers than I still seek it. The journeys of Ella

Maillart, Dervla Murphy, Freya Stark and Wilfred Thesiger come to mind.

Travellers fall into clearly defined categories, romantic, intellectual, scientific or commercial, with subdivisions of explorers, exiled wanderers, missionaries, or those shadowy political figures who lurk about frontier zones, still playing the Great Game across the chequerboard of Central Asia and the North West Frontier. Now yet another category has appeared: that of the jumbo-jet tourist. Americans were the first of such hordes. Now the Japanese are snapshotting the Vatican while the Smiths are padding along Papeete's beaches. But it is not travel in the sense of my writing.

Since my motto is ALWAYS TRAVEL HEAVY, air travel is not my choice. Trains still possess a special magic, besides space for one's possessions. Their names alone cast a spell – 'The Acheson Topeka and Santa Fé', the 'Turk Sib', the 'Taurus Express', or the fabled 'Orient Express' on which I travelled, long ago, when I was living in Bulgaria. Those were journeys! A blend of Dietrich and Stroheim, with the lovely Balkan countryside slipping past, an unwinding scroll of gorges, rose valleys and the curious counterpoint of Orthodox monasteries and mosques. Next it was the equally legendary Trans-Siberian which lured me eastward, from Moscow to the Chinese border; later I discovered a local line which rambled about the Ferghana, linking Samarkand to Bokhara and beyond.

Afghanistan, a land I loved passionately, possessed no railways and it was by road that I first came to know something of its savage yet lyrical beauty, scarcely changed since Genghis Khan's horsemen rode there and the Emperor Babur lingered in its gardens. Ah, Afghanistan!

☪

Countries, like people, have each their own individual way of being loveable and hateful. The phenomenon of love at first sight can also exist between a person and a land. One look, one step forward and the heart is stolen away. So it has been for me, throughout my life of emotional journeyings. I have flirted with some countries, Guatemala or India, for example; and had passing affairs with many others, but I was at once lost in love for both Afghanistan and Oman, while Bulgaria holds a place in my heart for ever. By which it will be seen I am one of the more romantic travellers.

I have sometimes been criticised for travelling and writing about countries that are frowned upon politically – Russia for example. But my Russia was not so much the USSR as the eternal Slav land of which Tolstoy wrote, the Russia of Boris Godunov or Dostoevsky. Leningrad still seemed to be St Petersburg when I found Pushkin's house on the Moika Canal, and the Ukrainian collective farms merged with that farm at Dikanka immortalised by Gogol. The magnet pull of Russia derived from my childhood love and admiration for that mysterious Russian known to my family as The Traveller – that strange character who came and went, djinn-like, and fed me the Russian classics and recounted marvellous adventures in the Caucasus or Russian Central Asia; far horizons on which I set my sights.

Very early Europe palled; for all its treasures and *douceur de vivre* it seemed tame. Asia beckoned and I conditioned myself for the wildest shores by gulping innumerable books of forgotten travellers such as those my father – himself an armchair traveller – had collected throughout his life. Thus I had followed Captain Burnaby's famous ride to Khiva in 1875, long before I reached it myself, while the image of Arminius Vámbéry disguised as a Sunni dervish became my familiar, so that when I at last approached the Turkoman encampments I saw their felt-covered *tekkés* through *his* eyes. Everywhere, I have followed some fugitive strain which still echoes the footsteps of earlier travellers: Ibn Batuta in Morocco; Gobineau at Isfahan. Lane's *Manners and Customs of the Modern Egyptians*, although written in 1836, like Lucie Duff-Gordon's enchanting *Letters from Egypt*, written between 1862 and 1869, taught me more about Egypt and the *fellahin* around me as I sailed the Nile, than all the up-to-date guidebooks which revel in Pharaonic data at the expense of much else.

Thus I would advise all voyagers in alien lands to take along the books of earlier travellers. And I cannot praise too highly the information, so richly coloured, of early Baedekers. I have a vintage collection and use them resolutely. Murray's *Handbook for Russia, Poland, Finland and the Crimea*, fifth edition, 1893, is particularly sustaining, for it combines many unchanging aspects of history, geography, the arts and observances, as well as a glossary and mouth-watering information about long-vanished hotels 'fashionably frequented, with Drawing Rooms for Ladies' and 'Special hot-water apparatus' at 3 roubles a night. *Eheu fugaces.*

After such fantastic company, the presence of flesh and blood companions is apt to prove distracting, coming between oneself and one's chosen image. Thus I prefer to travel alone. On the few occasions when I have been joined by friends, they tell me that what I see, search for, or reconstrue bears little relation to fact. The petrol pumps and buses along the route to Timbuctu, I remember, depressed them; but my eyes were fixed on a cloud of dust, raised, I did not doubt, by General Henri Lapperine's sleek *méharis* – those superb fast-running dromedary camels – off to skirmish with the Touaregs. Yes; I shall continue cultivating such romantic perspectives. After all, travel, the act of departure into unknown horizons, is in itself intensely romantic and we should keep it untarnished; seeking the essence, the history and roots beneath the contemporary surface, wherever we wander.

Wandering – and wondering too – is, I believe, the secret of successful travelling. There should be no pre-digested or blasé outings, no rushing from one tourist 'must' to the next. We should leave aside museums and great monuments until we have savoured something of the life in the streets and cafés, and made for both the markets and churches, thus glimpsing both the sacred and profane aspects of a people. We should 'blow where the mind listeth' – preferably on foot, the better to dawdle. To return to my motto: Always Travel Heavy.

## 18. Always Travel Heavy

'TRAVEL LIGHT' IS ONE of those respected, age-old maxims that collapse in the face of reality, along with clichés like 'Blood is thicker than water' (which takes no account of those inter-family feuds so much more ferocious than any others) or 'There's no place like home', a phrase which has a bitter ring to the harassed housewife, whose dream existence is, of course, carefree hotel living. 'Always travel light' was not, as might be expected, a slogan coined by the airlines. It began long, long before, in the ample days of rail and boat travel, when muscular porters, as amiable as husky, were waiting in ranks to fling themselves on as much luggage as one cared to bring.

Even in this day of few porters, fewer taxis, and all the stress of travel, what is described as 'carefree travelling', I have come to the conclusion that it is just as nerve-racking, just as exhausting, to go about with the two or three regulation suit-cases as with ten or twelve. And when you arrive, the extra comforts those other eight or nine contain amply justify the excess baggage rates and all the fuss.

Originally I allowed myself to be conditioned by the idea that it was a nuisance to other people, as well as myself, if I had too much luggage. But now I know it's worth it, for me, and *tant pis* for other people. (If nothing broadens the mind like travel, equally nothing hardens the heart so fast either.) How I wish I could say, like Mr and Mrs Averell Harriman, that I always take along a few good pictures, 'a little travelling collection' like theirs, a Picasso of the Blue period, a Douanier Rousseau, a Gauguin, and a Guardi or two.

This question of a movable *cadre* or transportable personal atmosphere must have been well understood by the Chinese, who by inclination travel with their entire home around them, and who specialised in all sorts of complicated yet simple pieces of furniture which hinged and could be taken to pieces to travel flat; delicate sheets of painted papier-mâché which unfold into hanging cupboards, little tables, or wall brackets. I have several such pieces, once designed as part of a Chinese merchant's caravan, winding across Asia week by week and halting, night by night, to be set up, a little Beijing in the Gobi desert, achieving this very personal *setting* to which I aspire more clumsily today.

In Europe, in the spacious days of the Grand Tour, that magic phrase which set the seal of aristocratic polish on the young gentleman who always voyaged through France and Switzerland to Italy and back, there was no nonsense about travelling light. Then, the great lumbering equipages were made to transport an entire way of life, and as they went lurching up over the St Gotthard Pass, the decanters of port shifted uneasily in their baize-lined mahogany inlaid boxes, the chased silver toilette sets jangled and the copper *batteries de cuisine* clinked; the postilions cracked their whips, the French tutor dutifully extolled the Alpine sunset and the young milord, lolling on the velvet, double-sprung upholstery, thought regretfully of cock-fighting, and yawned his way into Italy.

It must be admitted other ages have not travelled light. I recall the tragicomic accounts of the retreat from Sedan, where the over-choked roads were further congested by the Emperor's chefs and hairdressers and their cumbersome equipment. Lord Byron travelled about with seven servants and an exotic menagerie, some pets, some designed for the table. One Russian nobleman took his private theatre with him when he travelled and beguiled the endless icy *versts* with performances of Molière and Haydn. Other Slavs of substance were installed in sable-lined coaches mounted on sledges, cumbersome as houses, often with a cow or two, to milk *en route*, and an orchestra of serfs, fiddling and scraping through the long dark nights. And we all know the legend of Catherine the Great's journey throughout her realm, not only surrounded by baggage coaches and escorts of Cossacks and various *soupirants*, but confronted, all along the route, by whole cardboard villages, hurriedly thrown up, an hour or two before her passage, to ensure an air of prosperity and population. That was travelling heavy in the grand manner.

Lady Blessington's departure for Italy, with her husband and the dandy Count d'Orsay, was the sensation of Paris in 1827. It was rightly called the Blessington Circus. They had endless baggage wagons and a retinue of servants, as well as a chef and his assistant, with all the egg-whisks, soufflé moulds and pastry-boards necessary to ensure the same Lucullus-like standards the trio had enjoyed at home. Lady Blessington's own carriage, designed by her doting husband, contained, among other things, a small but choice library, a writing-table, satin upholstery, swansdown bedding, a chaise-longue, a gold-fitted dressing table, and a discreet loo. Only forty years earlier, another sybaritic woman's insistence on travelling luxuriously (and heavily) had perhaps caused the death of herself and her family. When Queen Marie Antoinette was a prisoner in the Tuileries in 1791, her adorer, Count Fersen, planned her escape and would probably have achieved it, in spite of postmaster Drouet's dash to call the Republican troops, if the Queen had not insisted on so many fabulous and royal comforts that Fersen had to set about having a special carriage made, a *berline*, 'a stupendous new Coach', Carlyle called it, which delayed the escape by weeks and proved to be both a noticeable and a cumbersome affair, the last thing in which to make a dash over the frontier. Perhaps the ill-fated Queen remembered that luxurious *berline* when she was jolting her way to the scaffold in a tumbril.

My own excess baggage usually includes, besides a few picture books – *éditions d'art* – a favourite ikon, a Sheffield plate teapot (less fragile than china), and a pair of *vermeil* candlesticks found in a Saharan oasis, probably left there by some stylish French officer in the campaigns against Abd-el-Kader. Then, a *toile de Jouy* quilt embellishes any bed, and a rug – gros-point, not the travel kind of course – adorns all floors. I cram these objects, along with a radio, some small cushions and lesser comforts such as corkscrews, string and a magnifying glass into a wicker hamper, in itself decorative, unlike most luggage.

I should like to take a great many of the plants I collect wherever I go, for they, more than anything else, are companionable and beautiful, imparting an atmosphere of repose to even an overnight stop. But after I had tried to cram various examples of trailing and exotic vegetation into my suitcases, and had been told that there were quarantine regulations for plants as well as pets, and later discovered that many a cactus languishes on Ellis Island, I gave up the idea of a travelling greenhouse. But I did contrive to bring back a little pine tree from the Siberian Taiga, coddling it all across the steppes of Central Asia, until it reached my rooftop terrace in Paris where it now thrives.

In spite of my insistence on creature comforts and personal possessions, I do not bother overmuch about insecticides or bedding, things which are a 'must' with many far less demanding travellers whom I have sometimes seen instructing the wagons-lits attendant how to make up the bunk with their own monogrammed, crêpe-de-chine sheets, generously peppered with disinfectant. But then, by the time I have arranged myself in the middle of all my décor, I am so exhausted I can sleep anywhere. To travel heavy is to sleep heavy, too.

# 19. Junking

THROUGHOUT MY LIFE I have collected, though I could not be called a collector in the strict sense of the word. Scavenger would be a better one for my wildly acquisitive nature. This drove me to wander, to search out, and gather round me a heterogeneous mass of objects many of which would be put to use and incorporated into the pattern of daily life, regardless of their origin. Thus a heavy bronze Arabic stirrup encrusted in chips of turquoise, the sort of thing Delacroix's cavaliers would use, I would use to stack important papers through its arch. Russian samovars, of which I had three, boiled water for tea, as they were meant to do, though one massive waist-high primitive metal one, of the type used in Afghan tea houses, made an excellent bedside table as long as its gaping maw on the top was blocked by a tray, which it usually was. Only years later, travelling in Central Asia, did I recognise the double of my great pot-bellied metal block, but by that time I had lost it, in response to the national wartime demand for metal, any metal – to be melted down for use in the munitions factories. The elegant eighteenth-century iron railings and gate to my house in Richmond, along with more railings of elegance round another house in Chelsea, were all part of the way we lost our treasures during the war.

Eighteen years of being a diplomat's wife taught me to carry my precious everything with me, on my back like a snail – I made eleven bases with Romain, which I always had to do very quickly. Confronted by bare walls or, dread trial, the taste of others, it was always due to those things few or many that I carried from from pillar to post that our quarters became more livable. This was not without complications, and required steely resolve to overcome airline strictures and my husband's nomadic preference for travelling light. I adopted 'always travel heavy' as my motto and have lived by it ever since.

Throughout my life – which has mixed an insatiable craving for far lands with an unshakable affection for domestic roots – even my temporary halts in desert tents, hotel rooms, or compartments on long-distance trains such as the Trans-Siberian have been occasions for installing a few favourite objects around me. A pocket-size travelling ikon, a little silver teapot and a gros-point cushion of doves and spaniels have worked wonders, while a small supple Senna rug, on the floor or across the bed, completes the transformation scene.

My rooms are gestures of defiance against every rule of the pundit decorators. My rooms reflect the globe: cultures, races, climates, colours and epochs mix in harmony here, as do bargains and chintz. I was never among the purest band of collectors going for some specific object. My objects told of too many interests covering too wide a field of regions or centuries, the spill of travels in remote lands and the compelling fascination of street markets or sale rooms alike. A Staffordshire rabbit that presided in the nursery sits beside a Tibetan Buddha; a huge Moorish mirror framed in mother-of-pearl reflects a teakwood rocking elephant of baby-Shetland-pony size, gaily painted with garlands and jewels. His history is unknown: I imagine he was made for some turbaned Mughal princeling who, in the palace zenana, pined for one of those classic rocking horses he had heard the memsahib's children possessed. Treasure of treasures to me, my elephant is also useful, for the household keys hang from his tusks. Things like to be used, one way or another, I fancy.

I was gripped from that first fatal day when, aged seven, I acquired, off a barrow in the street, a box crudely painted with tigers and roses, no doubt of Persian or Chinese origin. I gloated over it and kept my week's supply of sweets in its musty interior; it was much nicer than other children's paper bags. Perhaps the fact that my father gave me a Spode teacup to use in the nursery had originally set me going. But his own appreciation for beautiful or interesting objects, seconded by my mother, was not lost on me. A late seventeenth-century cupboard, English, but painted with naive renderings of the chinoiserie then an exotic novelty, speaks to me of my mother, and the conglomeration of beloved objects that overflowed her rooms. Thus, by that intangible magic which cherished objects possess (whether due to historic or romantic connotations, or by their association with ourselves), a personal, private world forms round us.

My accumulation of objects wove themselves into a sort of companionship of fantasy which for me created a barrier between real people and so-called inanimate objects – though they were never inanimate to me, and quite a few people would be better described as inanimate objects themselves. To me, things have always seemed, if not alive in our sense of the word, certainly possessed of some inner nature or presence, some remote derivation of the individual soul. Such, in vague terms, is the Animist belief. It has always seemed to me a true one. Sometimes, from some squalid street market where things were displayed on a sheet spread out on the pavement among a clutter of rubbish, a bicycle pump, old wrist watches and such, some thing, some object would be calling to me. I was aware of this and I knew I would find it, and suddenly it was there, in front of me, and I had to have it. It might be some dirty, grubby little box covered in speckled material, but I knew it was covered in shagreen and delicately hinged, part of an eighteenth-century chatelaine, or it might open to reveal a handy little knife and fork, probably tortoiseshell- or ivory-handled, the sort of necessity once used by early travellers or riders to hounds. I collected these for some time and came to use them myself when travelling, being unenthusiastic about finger-and-thumb eating or tin-ware encountered *en route*. Once, these sorts of objects went for a few shillings, until junking became a modish occupation and the street vendors earned more or gave way to very smart dealers, and it was 'fun' to use the unusual.

Children always endow their toys with a life of their own. There is some powerful imaginative force that unites the living child and its toy which, for the span of their association, comes to life for its owner. Children are not to be foxed by adult phrases such as 'only a toy', and the magic is overcome solely by the bludgeoning process of growing up. Unless that early magic becomes an adult conviction that things do possess a kind of entity to which we respond, and which responds to us – a certain magnetic force, perhaps?

My acquisitive expeditions often occupied a whole day and were planned ahead. I would go junking to one particular market, perhaps the Caledonian in the old days or later to the rather dreggy Portobello Road or some undisclosed area which I felt might yield unknown treasures. Obeying this inner instinct sometimes compelled me to get off a bus at some unpremeditated place and led me zombie-like to the object awaiting me. In this manner I was to acquire a whole portfolio of David Robert's exquisite engravings of Middle Eastern scenes for 18 shillings, cut down from one pound. True, damp had blotted the corner of one or two, but long before I actually saw those deserts, those mosques, those graceful feathery palms and silky waters where camels were tethered, I came to know them by heart, and recognise them when I reached them, as if they had been signposted to put me on my way.

I never knew what would be awaiting me, but I would be suddenly aware that I must go and find it, wandering in London or provincial cities or foreign towns or wherever I happened to be, as if mysteriously led. Not all my findings were ornamental, few were valuable, though seen from today's hindsight, many have become rare, interesting pieces – the carpets and rugs I began picking up for a song when I was living in Los Angeles. At that time oriental rugs were completely out of fashion, well-to-do houses wanted nothing but wall-to-wall carpeting or marble floors. Therefore, beautiful Persian, Turkish and even Afghan carpets were heaped together in obscure little shops that did not know what to do with them. They spoke to me and although I had no definite knowledge of the carpet market then, I began to acquire these for the emotion I felt for them, more than anything else. I instinctively recognised their qualities and defects and began to study their origins, egged on by a few ancient Armenians, who were living downtown in a very sleazy quarter and who were delighted to find an enthusiastic pupil. Often I would come home triumphantly, dragging an enormous piece of carpeting over my shoulder, or heave it out of the boot of my car and try to re-roll it enough to get it upstairs. My husband would observe these activities with a bewildered air and no enthusiasm. But Katousha, my Russian maid, would join me and croon ecstatically over something which reminded her of her Caucasian past.

Churlish as it may seem, I admit to a preference, in general, for *things* rather than people. The affinity I felt for things sometimes developed into a deep relationship. I recall a little carved wooden frog, glimpsed through a fly-speckled window in a gloomy area of Bayswater, standing amidst a number of very ordinary objects, some silver candlesticks, some well-bound books and lamps topped by dreadful lampshades. As I stared in the window, I knew something was waiting for me there and with a violent throb of recognition saw this little frog staring back at me fixedly. In today's jargon, eye-contact was made. The shop was shut; I went away in an agony of frustration, and rushed back the next day with a beating heart as I approached my quarry. A dingy-looking man was lounging about and unwilling to reach into the front of the window, where the frog awaited me. The price was high. 'A lotta people bin after that frog,' said the man, sticking to his price. I paid it and took the frog home, comfortably wrapped in a clean handkerchief, amongst the confusion of my handbag. I was never to discover its origin, though I took it to the V&A for an expert opinion. They were interested but blank. The pale, gleaming wood they could not recognise. The only way to decide was to take a shaving off its stomach and to send it to the tree experts to pronounce on it. But I was not going to have any surgery on this precious companion so I snatched it back. I always thought it had some northern air about it – nothing African anyway. It was about three inches long and four inches wide. A squat little animal, beautifully carved, and in its stomach a little door opened to reveal its inside. Perhaps it had been used by some Baltic sea-captain who stowed his wad of baccie in its belly, I thought. The frog stayed beside me for many years, sharing my life and travels, and when I was sad, I would stare at its round little eyes, for that silent companionship which animals or inanimate objects offer without any ulterior motives. My darling frog perished with all the rest of my possessions when my house was burnt down in 1994. Some years later in some serious magazine of antiques, I found a whole page devoted to the same kind of

carved wooden frogs, varying slightly in colour and wood and their individual expressions, but confirming what I had always imagined him to be, one of the traditional tobacco boxes used by Baltic seamen. I mourn him as I mourn a lost friend.

Whatever the object I pursued, I always recognised it at once, and, meeting its stare, I would feel that strange inexpressible sense of unity with it. I find my things very good company: they are not capricious, or boring, or demanding. They do not have to be entertained, or dined and wined like so much of the human species. By which you will judge me a hardened misanthrope. Quite so. I defend my privacy fiercely.

C☪

By the nature of their contents, my four walls dissolve into far horizons. Beyond that corner where my ikons are gathered traditionally, I reach again the churches of Orthodoxy – magnificent Zagorsk, or the smaller monasteries of the Balkans – Bulgaria, Yugoslavia? No matter; I am once more in their shadowy depths, hearing again those solemn chants.

All Islam, from Cairo to Constantinople, glows for me in that part of the room where a divan is spread with rugs found in Aleppo and cushions of striped *ikkat* silk from Afghanistan, that loved and mourned land. Alongside, a low window is screened by a fretted *moucharabiyeh* from a Tunisian harem. Once the inmates peered out through the latticework, but now bright spangles of sunlight filter inward, recalling for me an Eastern interior painted by John Frederick Lewis.

Now East, now West – my rooms reflect the globe. Thus, like the poet who wrote, 'My mind to me a kingdom is', I find they have gradually become my kingdom, richly peopled by those things that to me could never seem merely inanimate.

# 20. New York: Leo Lerman, Carson McCullers & Others

I HAD A VERY LOVELY LIFE in New York in the early fifties, and was very spoilt. I quickly came to know a large, interchangeable, shifting world which was not America. At that time I was writing my first book, *The Wilder Shores of Love*, which I attacked each night after the gaieties of the evening were over. These might have been sumptuous international dinner parties at our embassy; a downtown dinner at one of the hot-spot restaurants where the press gathered; some piano bar where a pianist was being tried; up town in the new Puerto Rican area to watch one of their overheated dance contests; sometimes stepping out ourselves at some notorious nightclub, or dining quietly in a brownstone house lined with books where the talk and dinner guests were infinitely rewarding; I have in mind particularly the hospitality of that great New York figure Leo Lerman: a bearded, rabbinical figure. He and his companion, the painter Gray Foy, became cherished friends.

☪

They lived in a tall old house way up in the West 90s, edging the Puerto Rican quarter, not far from Harlem. It was certainly not chic, but that particular brownstone was the Mecca of the musical, theatrical, intellectual and artistic world of New York, with many very distinguished foreign visitors besides. I remember one of their famous parties in this house, which was crammed from head to foot with American Victoriana, patchwork, crocheted quilts, dolls' houses, dolls' tea sets, Tiffany lamps – and an entire wall covered in eighteenth-century pastels of Neapolitan scenes, mostly volcanoes in full fire, and another with early photographs and daguerreotypes. There were large numbers of those charmingly grotesque groups of china figures and animals known as English Staffordshire, some of which I had given them from my own collection. It is nearly impossible to describe the atmosphere of this house and the extraordinary contrast and feeling of calm which overcame one when one peered out through the back windows, from where the wide expanses of the East River flowed past and in the foreground could be glimpsed, immediately beside Leo's own backyard, a tiny Jewish synagogue, its little nightlight burning under the porch: the whole atmosphere fused into that of an early Chagall painting. You never knew who you were likely to meet in that early household where Leo and Gray held court – locals like Tennessee Williams, or fascinating figures passing through town like Maria Callas who was an intimate friend of theirs; but she was rarely in New York at that time, so I never had the pleasure of knowing her.

At one party in their brownstone, which I remember in particular, I was sitting on a sofa between Edith Sitwell magnificent in her Priestess robes, and Marlene Dietrich in a glittering black sheath. Stretched across our knees was Truman Capote. As far as I can recall, his head was on Marlene's lap and his feet were held in Edith's exquisite long jewelled hands. Or it may have been the other way round. I only remember getting the middle-cut myself. He was breathing heavily, stentorian, and holding forth above the clatter of teacups, mixed up with glasses full of every kind of liquor. At Gray and Leo's there was always the comforting cup of tea going hot and strong for those who craved it. On my later visits to New York, I was to find them installed midtown where the same tenor of life continued. Wherever they lived, for they made several more moves, they always created the same rarefied atmosphere. On one brief return, long after I had left New York and was living in Europe, I managed to be with them for an Easter breakfast. There was a beautiful early American teapot wreathed in bunnies; painted Russian eggs; nosegays of spring flowers arranged in Victorian mugs, and an enormous fishy-eggy breakfast being cooked by Gray. Their extraordinarily sophisticated yet artless atmosphere was unique. Only they could have created it.

C*

I was also fortunate to be able to go frequently to the ballet or the opera (where I was often given a place in a box at the old Met during rehearsals), and various concert halls, courtesy of the kindness of Lincoln Kirstein, the great patron of the arts, critic and impresario. I had many friends among the Russian colony and Balanchine's ballet world. Then there was the pianist Nikita Magaloff who played Schubert in a manner which, for once, made Romain sit quietly, attending to the music. I felt especially honoured when I occasionally lunched with Countess Alexandra Tolstoy, the Great Man's daughter. She favoured a small Japanese place, and would dwell on her captivity among the Japanese during her escape from Russia. She was a wonderful woman, larger than life, and her work, heading various organisations for the relief of the exiled Russians, is her memorial.

☾

Occasionally, and disregarding all advice, I would go to Harlem on a Sunday evening. I was attracted by the sound of a chapel called 'The Holy Ghost Filling Station'. A knowledgeable friend told me that as long as you were not going there slumming and really wanted to listen to the singing, there would be no objection. The ladies of the choir all wore heavy white crochet halos; some had paper wings attached. The men were more simply attired, but during the process of the service, they sometimes became so carried away in ecstasy that they were almost apoplectic and lay writhing on the floor, and had to be covered with a rug to calm down. The whole atmosphere was very genuine and very kindly disposed to me as a visitor. They tried to persuade me to address them; the Preacher held out a welcoming hand, but I sank back, overcome, whispering with great difficulty that I had throat trouble and could not speak.

☾

Another of my nocturnal sorties was to go down to 42nd Street where there was a celebrated bookshop which remained open all night. I could browse there for the entire evening, usually buying more than I could carry home, which meant I would have no money left for a taxi and so would have to slog back to the Upper East Side 70s on foot. Sometimes I would find that Romain had returned earlier and was in bed, asleep; sometimes I would have the place to myself, and with an energy which I could now not credit, I would get into my dressing gown and slippers and settle down at a small card table covered in exercise books, reference sources and such, and continue to write about the enthralling characters and dramatic scenes which were the subject of *The Wilder Shores of Love*.

☪

Up the Hudson at Rheinbeck there were the Astors. Alice Astor, or Princess Obolensky as she was then, was my particular friend, a wonderful dark beauty; we shared a passion for the Caucasus and its proliferation of fascinating Moslem tribes. Alice thought she had lived there in another life. Gore Vidal had a house nearby; it was curiously built, the front door – or was it the back door – opening directly on to a disused railway line. But Gore was away during the time when I was seeing Alice, and I only came to know him much later in California and then Italy.

☪

One evening, at one of our embassy dinner parties, I was sitting next to an Englishman, Valentine (Nicholas) Lawford, who had been in the diplomatic service and renounced his last appointment as *chargé d'affaires* in Tehran to live his own life in New York, at a house at Oyster Bay which he shared with the world-famous photographer Horst P. Horst. We became a devoted trio and I spent many weekends in the low white house which Horst had built in the middle of a large tract of land, which they were landscaping to transform into a garden paradise. Lawford painted exquisite, Redon-like studies of the flowers they cultivated. Horst had his studio in New York and worked in the city much of his time, but the weekends were always spent at Oyster Bay. It was there that I spent some days correcting my proofs of *The Wilder Shores* which I had been writing a year before in our New York apartment. I remember wheedling Horst to take some photographs of Romain which I wanted for the publicity of a book which he was about to publish. Horst asked me, 'How do you want him to look? Handsome or interesting?' I said, 'Both,' which he was.

I encountered some remarkable personalities through Horst and Nicholas, as Valentine was known. Theirs was a different and more *mondain* set than that of Leo and Gray's. Among these intriguing figures was their immediate neighbour, the aquamarine-eyed beauty Mrs Harrison Williams, who later left New York to become Countess Bismarck and lived in a gorgeous house on Capri. I remember her at Oyster Bay, just down the road from Horst and Lawford, in a fabulous kind of birdcage room of high proportions filled with flowering trees, in which innumerable exotic birds fluttered about. Mona would be draped in some wonderful floating garment based on a *robe de chambre* as worn at the court of Louis XV, or a vast cape of chinchilla pinned by an enormous diamond brooch. I never saw her as anything but the most perfect object of beauty, and I never heard her gossiping idly and unkindly as so many of her contemporaries did. In short, she has remained in my memory as not altogether human in her perfections. The last time I was to see her was at one of Walter Lees's dinners in Paris, many years later, after the death of Eddie Bismarck. Mona had married the Italian doctor who had looked after him and lived across the bay in Naples. They seemed very happy together, but she had changed. She was beyond middle aged and had put on a little weight. The ethereal and legendary creature had vanished, and an extremely elegant, rather roundabout white-haired *grande dame* had taken her place, strictly but perfectly dressed in the latest Balenciaga and adorned by magnificent jewellery. But those wonderful aquamarine eyes still outshone everything else. She was a legend in her time: subsequent generations of beautiful women have never, quite, managed to acquire the quality which she and a couple of her other contemporaries possessed.

Another legend I came to know through Horst and Lawford – my 'pearls' of Oyster Bay – was Madame Balsan. The once celebrated Duchess of Marlborough, she had been a reigning beauty at the court of Edward VII. She was renowned for her immense wealth and her extraordinary slender swan neck, upon which her small, beautiful, dark-haired head rested gracefully. When I knew her in her New York house in Beekman Place, she was in her eighties; now a white-haired beauty. She had the most perfect taste and had filled her home with the most perfect objects that were eighteenth-century in principle: Aubusson carpets, Savonnerie rugs and Chinese screens. Her husband, Colonel Jacques Balsan, older than she, had been one of the ultra chic racing gents round Deauville when the young Chanel was beginning to design hats for the ladies of the turf and Boy Capel was eyeing the young Chanel.

I would try to draw out Colonel Balsan about his youth as a young officer in the Sahara, where he had allegedly served under the renowned Maréchal of that time, Colonel Lyautey. I hoped he could tell me something about Isabelle Eberhardt, one of the more strange characters about whom I was writing in *The Wilder Shores of Love*. It was extremely difficult to find anyone who remembered her as more than a legendary figure, but my host recalled little of that faraway time.

Madame Balsan had a house in Florida, which surprised me, for I could not imagine this sophisticated, urban figure instated amidst sultry crocodile swamps, which was how I erroneously imagined Florida to be. Romain and I were delighted by her invitation and accepted joyously, but somehow either Horst's work, or mine with the Embassy, prevented us from ever making that trip.

☪

I have rarely taken much interest in politics, particularly American politics. But one morning, I woke up to discover that the McCarthy hearings had begun and were being televised. They were of extraordinary interest to anyone who was able to observe from the outside the subtlety with which the legal system and different senators managed to pirouette on the fine line between truth and falsehood. I persuaded Romain that we must hire a TV set. He was working very long hours, sometimes far into the night, at the United Nations, and therefore had little time to watch television. But I could, and so relayed the latest news to him late each night. Our apartment was small and cluttered so there was no space for such a large and clumsy contraption in our living room. The only place for it was to cram it into the bedroom at the foot of our bed. Romain took a violent dislike to the machine. Only the appalling albeit riveting dramas of the McCarthy hearings persuaded him to leave the television in place.

At that time I had a great friend staying in New York who was flat broke. Although a very successful interior decorator in England, he had now fallen on such hard times that he was sleeping in a kind of Salvation Army shelter, and came to us during the day to get a square meal, have his two good shirts washed and generally to keep me company. He was a most entertaining individual and Romain adored talking to him. There was never any question of complicated romantic situations, though no doubt the doorman of our apartment block thought there was, for, every morning, no sooner had Romain left for the United Nations, than Arthur would arrive and rush to join me in the bedroom, curtains drawn, just as the hearings began. Side by side we would spend the day stretched out, following every word, writhing in hatred at McCarthy and Roy

Cohen and applauding the one or two brilliant legal figures who opposed them. I was bewildered and finally dazzled by the emergence of justice which, due to a handful of senators, finally overcame the evil of McCarthyism.

For a brief period at luncheon, Arthur would seize the telephone and ring round his set of elegant New Yorkers, who were his friends but were not aware of the reduced circumstances in which he was living – they always invited him to dine with them in considerable splendour in the restaurants and nightclubs which had been his previous haunts. Our daily, a girl called Heddy, adored Arthur and never found it too much trouble to valet him, leaving me to deal with Romain's wardrobe and my own. As far as I can remember Arthur kept his dinner jacket in one of our cupboards, which once occasioned quite a to-do, when Romain, who was twice his size, tried to get into the wrong suit. Generally this was a happy period, and when Arthur finally left for Madrid, where he was to prosper and become a friend of Balenciaga, we missed him. Life was not easy, despite appearances, but there were always ways of figuring out how to get by.

☪

It was not so much a matter of making ends meet, or putting on a show, as of creating an atmosphere which overcame shortcomings. Fulco di Verdura was a perfect example of this. Born into one of the great Sicilian noble families, his titles would run off the end of any visiting card. But he dropped all that and became known in New York, London and Paris as 'Fulco'. He was a very short, swarthy, roundabout, froglike figure, of enormous gaiety and charm, who became world famous for the fabulous jewellery he designed for the great *bijoutiers* of the moment. He loved precious stones with a greedy sensuous love and would set them in a way that was often audacious and rather oriental. There was a voluptuous quality to his designs and sometimes he could be almost droll: a slab of emerald might be curved over like a wave, to reveal two or three enormous glowering black pearls. His approach to jewels was utterly unlike Fabergé's rather fiddly style. Chanel adored Fulco's work and wore his pieces; she was one of his first patrons, having certain items copied for her *maison de couture*. It is impossible to describe a Fulco jewel, it has to be seen – its special quality can produce a feeling of greed; you want to eat the lovely lump.

Which brings me to dining, and the easy, frankly economic manner of Fulco's *dîners intimes*. He lived in the chic 60s, in a minuscule apartment full of gorgeous and strange *objets d'art*, including his beautiful, tiny landscapes, often no bigger than two postage stamps, yet a whole scene. There he gave very recherché little soirées, largely to listen to music. After a huge plate of spaghetti and sauce spooned on to your plate by Fulco himself – 'The salt's over there, get on with the wine' – he would get going with his endless collection of records, especially Italian opera. We shared a special liking for minor eighteenth-century Venetian composers and I often stayed late, entranced by the baroque strains, as one by one the few guests left. I remember in particular one of the last true Romanovs, Princess Natasha Paley, daughter of Grand Duke Paul, son of Emperor Alexander II. As a child Natasha had escaped to Paris during the Revolution, but she had often played with the unfortunate Romanov children at Tsarskoe Selo before their end in Siberia. She grew up to become known as the greatest beauty in Paris, and first married the couturier Lucien Lelong, but drifted, the muse of many poets, notably Jean Cocteau. She was now married to Jack Wilson, who had been Noël Coward's agent, and worked for her living, like everyone else in Fulco's room that night. At around eleven she stood up, wrapped a scarf around her head, peasant-fashion, saying, 'Well, children, I'm off, I've got to be at work tomorrow at nine.' She would vanish into the night, taking with her some inexplicable aura of palaces and snow and blood. Once, we were speaking of the USSR and Natasha said, 'Well, they shot my father and they killed my brother by throwing him alive down a mine shaft, and they assassinated my grandfather too. I think that's enough!' She worked as a hostess for Main Bocher, one of the few great American couturiers. She lived a very retired life, but loved a Fulco evening, so I sometimes had the pleasure of meeting her at his salon. Another regular there was the stout, burly arch gossip Elsa Maxwell, who bossed everyone and always liked to claim she clinched the Aly Khan–Rita Hayworth wedding; yet she too had another side. Music held her enthralled. We were an odd group, the plates of spaghetti cooling on our laps as we listened to Fulco's selection of music for the evening.

☪

A fascinating, but fiercely different individual whom I came to know gradually, was the writer Carson McCullers – now remembered chiefly for *The Heart is a Lonely Hunter*, *Reflections in a Golden Eye* and *Member of the Wedding*. She was a most extraordinary character. Originally from the deep south, she wrote best about that part of the American world. She was surrounded by a group of southern writers – Tennessee Williams, Truman Capote, Eudora Welty – whom I glimpsed fleetingly but never enough. I did not manage to follow up their invitations to the south, nor did they stop long enough in New York for me to know them as well as I came to know Carson.

She lived with her mother in a rather ramshackle white house on the Hudson River a little way up from New York City. I would cross over the water from the Upper East Side and take a train up the Hudson, and would arrive to be greeted by Carson seated at the tea table, even though it was noon. A cup of tea would immediately be pressed into the hand; as she poured it from the teapot it turned out to be neat gin – or was it vodka? In any case, Carson was a real drinker and looked it – pale and flaccid, often in tears and suddenly oddly gay, easily becoming hysterical and at times so neurotic that it was puzzling how she ever managed to put a line on paper. Her neuroses had affected her right arm and hand to the point of almost complete disability. The atmosphere was not cosy. It was very untidy and draughty. There was invariably a great deal of washing hanging on the line in the garden, which looked out towards the river. Carson was generally collapsed in a sagging cane chair, sometimes dressed or sometimes enveloped in a wrapper. Now and again she would take me deep into her confidence and poured out emotional dramas which had tortured her for a number of years. Around this time she fell violently in love with an experienced older woman, I don't remember who, but it was a period when lesbians were not 'out in the open' and I was disconcerted to hear Carson expounding the strength of her love for this lady. 'Was there ever a woman loved as I loved her! Was there ever, Momma, I ask you?' she wailed, gesturing at her mother with the teapot. 'Was there ever a woman so loved?' 'Sure not, baby,' Mrs McCullers replied soothingly, 'Sure not, baby, you really had it for her.' I was distressed and greatly saddened that Carson ended up destroying herself through drink; eaten up inside by her uncontrollable emotions.

☾⋆

At one time we saw quite a bit of Georges Simenon, whose Maigret novels and other rather sinister stories of over-whelming atmospheres captivated an enormous readership. His recent wife was Canadian by birth – she was sharp, dark and doting. They had built a singularly characterless house outside New York, where deer came to peer in at the windows. It was buried deep in those rather straggly woods which abound in that part of the world, which always gave me a creepy feeling of being stalked by the Redskins whose territory it had once been. The impression was very strong and unpleas-ant. I felt it again in a house occupied by Rebecca West's son, much further upstate. Simenon would talk freely of both his emotions and his sex life; the manner or technique of writing his detective masterpieces and how he would have a nervous broody feeling that a plot was coming on, so he would sharpen his pencils, prepare his study and shut himself up for a week or more, allowing the novel to take form as he went along. But his methods of working have been well recorded elsewhere, along with some of his entirely unabashed descrip-tions of his sex life. Simenon was irresistible to women and bowled them over, as he desired. I found him far from attrac-tive; in fact I had quite an aversion to him. I recall one day at luncheon, neither he nor his wife found the main dish to be satisfactory. 'I really don't know what is the matter with her,' complained Madame S., alluding to the cook. 'Well, I know!' he replied, 'I'll go and give her what she wants,' and he left the table. He returned a short while later, nothing was remarked upon, and the cooking was excellent that evening.

Of course Simenon loved living in America. He loved the American way of life – the freedom and ease he found there which he could not find in Europe. He lived much by routine and would go out every morning in all weathers and walk a mile or two through the open countryside to the nearby village to fetch his post and his newspapers. He was known yet not known. People recognised who he was, but let him be just a neighbour. This easy familiarity, without too close an approach, was typical of people in North America at that time. It reminds me of how, years later, after the revolution in Iran, the Shabanou, or Empress Farah, described how much she enjoyed living peacefully in upstate New York, without any protocol – going to the local grocery store to be hailed by warm greetings, 'Hiya, Farah', but otherwise being left alone. Her lack of pretension does not surprise me, because I grew to know this most wonderful woman quite well when I was writing about her, living in and out of the palace in Tehran, and staying with her on the island of Kish in the Persian Gulf. She was a woman of great simplicity who believed in the mission she was destined to accomplish, but never allowed herself to believe in supreme power, as, unfortunately, her husband the Shah had done.

# 21. Los Angeles: Marlene Dietrich & Others

WHILE I WAS LIVING in New York, I had always hoped that I would travel to California by paddle steamer (as I had so often seen in films) down the Mississippi and on via the Sante Fé Railway. Or else by that great train which heads west through the Rockies to California, with panoramic views and lovely kind retainers who looked after you every inch of the way. I was told they would say, 'We're comin' up to such and such a place. They've real good fresh trout. If I get in touch with them folks we can pick 'em up next stop and you can have 'em fresh for breakfast?' I liked this leisurely attitude towards travel, but I never made that train because at the time air travel had taken over completely.

Later, when we were living in Hollywood, we went to New York either by a very tedious flight, stopping at St Louis or elsewhere *en route*, or, if we could afford it, the night flight, which was the height of luxury. You slept in little curtained bunks, having totally or partially undressed before climbing in. A bell woke you, coffee was served in your bunk and before you had pulled yourself together you were landing at La Guardia. It was a painless way to travel.

I once went on a flight which was made very entertaining and very rowdy because Frankie-Boy Sinatra and his buddies Dean Martin and Sammy Davis Jnr were all aboard. There was also a famous producer, who shall be nameless, but whom they disliked, and, in their own words, were going to 'take the mickey out of him'. On these night flights it was customary to hang your jacket and skirt on a hook beside your bunk and you would find it very neatly pressed in the morning. Men hung their trousers outside their bunks also and found them pressed the following morning. On this occasion, just before we landed, a fearful, shrieking row started up from the disliked producer, who found his pants had been cut to almost crutch length. Frankie and his band of hooligans had been busy in the night. There was nothing for him to do but wear them and descend the steps of the aircraft, in full glare of the photographers who were waiting below to catch Frankie and company, who were rolling about with glee, heightened by their customary liquor intake. Pranks like this were typical of certain Hollywood characters, which might be said to balance the overblown pomposity and wealth displayed by some of the more socialite dwellers in Hollywood.

☪

[Lesley's life in L.A. is evoked in a letter written *circa* 1958 to her friend Cecil Beaton.]

> *Consulat Général de France à Los Angeles,*
> *Monday Sept 8th–9th?*

*Dearest Cecil,*

*I was delighted to hear from you. I couldn't quite read the card – I thought it said 'after ten "embarrassing" days here with T.C.' ! ! ! + then it turned into 'sunbathing' + so I sank back, reassured. I, too, wonder what you are doing … I am unrepentant – I LOVE MY LIFE HERE.*

*Romain is boiling away, has 2 new books done – one
'Lady L' a sort of Pushkinian conte, of which more.
Presently – his Memoirs – coming out in Spring. Vol I. it
is really a heartbreakingly good piece of work ... I can't
bear to read it – he really tells all + doesn't mince or gild.
I remember a conversation we had on that score.*

*I am still on the same book – but I do have a great deal
of domestic intervention – sometimes I can only get 1hr
free, in the day. I am energetic, disciplined – but the
general business, the distances, R's exigencies + the
ceaseless flow of people through this house is <u>terrible</u> for
my own work. Never mind. I am over the halfway mark
now + think, on the whole, not too dissatisfied. I know
some people will like it. You will, I feel sure. But it's not,
really, for all the Harrods readers. No love, no ladies.
Sometimes I get so exhausted, I feel it will be a
posthumous oeuvre. So much research.*

*R. has just returned from 5 weeks in Tahiti + Fiji –
violent contrasts to each other + to Hollywood. He looks
more like Gauguin than ever + has, no doubt, contracted
some dread diseases. He is very interesting about the total
absence of Lotiesque romance – the feeling of the
diabolic, sordid + sinister in this flowery hell ... of course,
he is aching to go back. But Fiji, with Kipling characters
eating curry for breakfast, in pitch-pine 1880 hotels + the
very sumptuous native girls bursting out of cotton frocks,
playing basketball (+ an English games Miss blowing a
whistle) ... straw boaters resting on the pneumatic hair ...
awful. So unimaginative.*

*We leave here any time: we were to have gone some
while ago, when de Gaulle + Malraux wanted R at once –
but I'm personally glad to say it was postponed. I suppose*

*by Xmas, we shall be shuddering in Paris, where R
determines to live for a year or two (if he lives that long,
is his attitude) + I can't imagine where we'll find anything
for ourselves + 5 cats, now. I see myself taking the Polar
Route, with 5 cat baskets … We shall probably try to get
a house just outside the ville, I suppose you don't know
anyone who wants to let?*

*I am probably passing through London around 27th
Sept as I'm going to be in Ireland with Dana Wynter for
10 days 17–27th. She's doing Brando's first production
venture 'Shake Hands With the Devil'. Cagney, Barry
Fitzgerald, maybe Edith Evans. Michael Redgrave, the
Abbey Players – Michael Anderson ('Round The World in
80 Days') directing. Set in Dublin in the Civil War of
1920. I think it will be very good. Sybil Connolly doing
the clothes. As you no doubt know, Dana W. is a perfectly
lovely, most distinguished-looking creature. I wrote to tell
Arlene Talley in case she'd be interested to do a feature on
it – or even Dana, in S. Con latest collection. Are you
interested in doing any pictures? If so, do try + come
before end of month, while I'm there – between 18–30th.
But I am sure you're full up + uninterested. I just suggest
it. Picture goes on for 5 weeks. Can you believe me – I
hate to leave here, + worry over Norman the cat who was
a kitten when you were here. I don't think you ever met
him. But I'm awfully tired, heat very strong here, this
summer 90° + upwards + it also means I can see my
mother for a couple of days, which is wonderful.*

*Listen, dear Cecil, I know I am running on + on but
one more thing. R's new book 'Lady L'. Michael Joseph.
To be published in winter. Literary Guild, here + snapped
up by MGM for Elizabeth Taylor <u>alas</u>, for Mel + Audrey*

*H would have liked to have it, but there was the usual trickiness with agents, 'Swifty' Lazar living up to his name + entre nous I shall be thankful when R has no agent – just a lawyer. Anyhow: it's an odd frivolous, bitter, very entertaining tale, quite unlike anything else of his. Then a coup de théâtre at the end + an undercurrent of 1890 Nihilists, ballrooms, lovers' rendezvous + really points up the tyrannies of love + the seductions of luxury as being far more powerful than any political ideologies.*

*I wrote to Grant at Michael Joseph + said if only you could be persuaded to do the jacket, it would set the whole key for the book. He agreed, wholeheartedly, but said you were very expensive. Now, the real point is – would you care to do it? (You do Nancy's don't you?) Couldn't you both compromise on a fee? He stepping up, you down – a bit? He asked me to approach you + I was just going to brace myself to do so when your card came. I shall tell him I have done so + then he can write to you + you will, I fear, refuse. Anyhow, I have tried.*

*I am just rallying from a week of severe strain: Hervé Alphand + his new wife, adorable, came here for an unofficial, giddy visit – wanted to see the studios, meet the people, bathe, loll … I tried to show them all I could + people were very hospitable. It went off all right, but R was not back (very wisely, en panne, on some outer Pacific isle). Still, it all required a lot of planning; a party for 70 + all the rest. Mary Pickford came + cried loudly as she always does when France is mentioned. Hervé fell for Lauren Bacall + his wife for David Niven! Now they crave a charabanc of stars to be brought constantly, to enliven Washington.*

*No more: really, goodbye. I will ring you as I pass*

*through London: I would like to hear your news: what*
*new books? Plays? Plans? Don't dismiss R's jacket on the*
*first impulse of impatience – but I expect it is a great*
*bother to you, with all your work.*

*Ever, your very admiring + affectionate friend,*

*Lesley*

[Running up left-hand side of page 3 of the letter]: *John*
*Huston changing every day + the original script lost in the*
*jungle.*

*P.S. I am learning the guitar. I have a beauty, of 1820. I*
*learn from a strict classical teacher from Peru. I play like*
*a backward child of 7. It is too, too terribly difficult, but I*
*love it, all of it, wrong notes, or right.*

☪

When discussing Hollywood, certain events in 1954 should
never be forgotten, when that monstrous witchhunt, 'the
McCarthy hearings', destroyed a number of people who were
the target of Senator McCarthy and Roy Cohen. Those who
stood firm to defend their beliefs in liberty risked their own
reputation and jobs, and stormed up to New York to protest
and defend their friends. It took many years before some of
McCarthy's victims were allowed to work again; and some left
America while others committed suicide.

☪

Once, Marlene Dietrich was flashing through Hollywood and
staying at the Beverly Hills, when she telephoned and asked us

to come round and have supper with her. She would cook it herself. We were joined by our friend the French actor Marcel Dalio, who had been a great friend of Jean Gabin, with whom he appeared in many pictures. Dalio was filming in Hollywood, so we saw a great deal of him. I remember him with deep affection; he was one of those brilliant actors who were never sufficiently acknowledged although they achieved considerable success.

Marlene was in a domestic mood. She was occupying a small suite at the Beverly Hills Hotel which contained a perfectly workable kitchenette. Here, she puttered about, beating up eggs and rushing in and out to discuss various aspects of the Hollywood scene, in which she was no longer involved. We did not remind her of some of the awful pictures she had made there, in particular one with Gary Cooper as a Legionnaire, in which there were scenes where she pursued him over the Sahara in a mass of floating chiffon and high-heeled sandals that fell off at every step. But that was before Hollywood began to grow up and occasionally produce works of art. Marlene was very proud of a film she had made recently in England, in which she had to speak what was either Cockney or Welsh or some other accent while playing the role of a spy in disguise. In any case, I believe she did it very well and she was inordinately proud of the accent. A curious sadness hung over that evening. She was no longer the legendary woman who had adored Gabin; he had, she said, really broken her heart when he left her. She made no bones about her grief and was somehow genuinely touching. She returned to the subject several times during the evening as if wishing to keep in contact with it. 'I love to hear the French talking together,' she said, listening to Romain and Dalio in the thick of some discussion. 'It reminds me, it reminds me ...' she said, and went back into the kitchenette to make some more omelettes.

Omelettes were one of the many foods which Romain flatly refused to eat, on account of his liver and his line, which he cherished with particular care; and I myself have always disliked omelettes. I don't know what Dalio felt about them, but as Marlene kept piling them on to our plates as if trying to pinion us down, we ate them, helping her to retrieve one of those domesticated French evenings of a past to which she still clung.

☪

Some years later, when I was living in Paris, I was dining with Brian Ahearn, the English actor who had spent a long time in Hollywood and was now living in Switzerland, at Vevey, where I often saw him when I stayed with James Mason. Both these men would spend a lot of time trying to persuade me to come and live in Switzerland, but there was a certain stodginess which overcame the comfort and I never felt comfortable – although I found Parisian life extremely agitating.

Brian had chosen one of the nicest restaurants on the Ile de la Cité, run by a distinguished French actor, so I was not surprised when my host said, 'It seems Marlene will join us presently.' And so she did, wearing a very large black hat shading her face. Not that she needed its protection for, with those bones, she was indestructibly beautiful. In spite of the fact that it was rather a thespian evening, with a number of French actors and actresses coming up to our table to hail Marlene, our talk somehow turned to cemeteries. Marlene was hunting for somewhere to lay her bones in France, which she considered her adopted country. She explained that her deepest wish was to be buried in a military cemetery, in memory of the wonderful camaraderie she had found among the French

troops for whom she did rousing concerts during the war. She
had encountered General de Gaulle, who had presented her
with signed photographs and, as far as I recall, a Légion
d'honneur in appreciation of her work for France. She asked
me what I thought of approaching him about a grave in a mil-
itary cemetery. 'Your husband was one of his specials, wasn't
he? Isn't he a *Compagnon de la Libération*? Do you think
either of you could help me on this matter?' I replied very cau-
tiously, for I did not imagine that the General would go along
with the idea of any female, let alone a foreigner, having a
place in a military cemetery. Continuing the depressing subject
of graves, whilst eating a delectable, delicious dinner, we went
on to discuss choosing where to be buried. When it came to
my turn, I said that though I'd rather be cremated, I would
choose to lie among the Russians in a small Russian cemetery
at Sainte-Geneviève-des-Bois. This beautiful and simple little
place is just outside Paris, off the road to Orly Airport. It
seems the land was acquired by a mysterious French woman
in memory of some unknown Russian she had deeply loved.
She had constructed a little Russian chapel there and planted
graceful, speckled silver birch trees, the *beryoza* found in every
Russian cemetery, around the graves. And so, after leaving the
main road to the airport, you branch off to the right and sud-
denly find yourself in the outskirts of Moscow or Kaluga or
elsewhere in Russia. A tiny, dumpy, white chapel is topped by
an enormous bell, which rings at various appointed hours, for
the cemetery has a very active life and is run by several
Russian priests. The place is beautifully kept and the graves
endearingly homely in aspect; sometimes just a wooden cross,
the traditional headstone generally in wood with an ikon
attached. Many of them have the equally traditional little
wooden bench alongside, for the family to mourn comfortably
beside their loved and lost, surrounded by those delicate silver

birches. I have always loved the peaceful, even affectionate atmosphere of Russian cemeteries, in which I have spent much time when travelling in Russia. Even on some of my earliest visits there, in the thirties, they did not seem to have suffered the same desecration as many of the churches.

But to return to the dinner table where Marlene was becoming extremely excited about Sainte-Geneviève as I described this endearing spot. 'That's for me! After all, I always feel myself half Russian [she did not say why], and everybody knows I make better blini than anyone else.' I avoided Brian's eye at this point, as she discussed the best way to obtain a grave. 'You must help me. When can we go there?' A day was fixed for me to lunch with her in her apartment, and a car would fetch us later and take us to the cemetery.

I duly presented myself at Marlene's apartment, which contained three large grand pianos she had acquired in Berlin, following one of her tours for the Allied troops stationed there after the war. I suppose this trio was acquired on the principle that 'more' was always better than 'less', although they did take up a certain amount of space in the white salon where red cushions and carpets were echoed by the brilliant scarlet geraniums along her balcony facing the George V. I ventured out on to this narrow strip to admire them and was surprised to find they were artificial, stuck down amid sprigs of privet. 'Much less trouble than the real kind', said this practical woman, who also explained how practical it was to live opposite the George V, since the bellboys could bring her newspapers and anything she wanted, and she could always fall back on their dining room. Dietrich's reputation as a superb cook being widely known, I wondered what was waiting for me. We ate in the kitchen, or rather, I ate and Marlene stood about between the stove and the little table where I was seated. I do not remember the menu, except that it was healthy and slimming. I think there were avocados and lamb chops, but I was so stunned by the whole scenario and being in the presence of this legendary figure in her home, that I recall little else. 'No coffee, it's bad for the complexion,' she said firmly and we repaired to the sitting room where she displayed the framed and signed photographs that occupied the entire surface of one piano. De Gaulle and Eisenhower dominated with Churchill nearby; otherwise it was a mass of distinguished faces and lavish, illegible signatures with a thread of familiar cinematic stars running through, Gabin predominating.

Presently, a chauffeur-driven limousine whipped us off to Sainte-Geneviève. On the way there, Marlene entertained me with accounts of various macabre incidents she had experienced in some other psychic sphere. On arrival, she was as enchanted with the little Russian cemetery as I knew she would be. It was a nostalgic place; Holy Mother Russia was all around us. A few quiet old people were attending the graves, while the wind soughed softly through the birches, scattering the leaves. In one corner a gravedigger was at work, standing deep in the earth. Marlene approached him and, kneeling beside him, in a wheedling manner whispered, 'It would be so beautiful to lie here.' He looked rather surprised but did not answer. 'Do you think you could find me a place here?' she went on. He shook his head. She drew a little closer and, in a voice that would have melted thousands of her fans, said, 'Do you know who I am? I am Marlene Dietrich.' He looked up at me and said in Russian, 'I don't understand her.' I explained who she was and how she longed to be buried there. Unmoved, he simply said, 'Ask the priest,' and, indicating the little doorway at the back of the chapel, went on digging. I knew enough about Marlene to know that she would not let the matter go at that, so I suggested that she might try to talk to the priest. The attendant *baboushka* was, as I had expected, very polite, but quite firm, and made it clear that there could be no question of anyone but a Russian being buried there. I was relieved that Marlene did not tell him that she made the best blini in the world. This highly intelligent woman clearly realised that it was not a reliable opening ploy. She dropped me back at my apartment and, though I was to see her again a few times before I left Paris, the question of her burial was never broached.

## 22. Many Mexicos

THE THEATRICAL ASPECT of Mexican daily life is over-powering: the fierce light beats down, an assault, and the shadows cast by the peons' huge-brimmed sombreros give their faces a skull-like relief, black eyesockets and sunken, fleshless jaws, recalling the apocalyptic woodcuts of Posada, the Daumier of Mexico. Every scene is both convulsive and dramatic. In the shadow of the sumptuously gilded church, a landslide of garbage glows brilliant with rotting fruit and offal. Lean dogs prowl, men fight with knives and a graceful creature, delicately boned as an Aztec princess, draws her *rebozo* about her head – a street Madonna, nursing her child, unmoved.

So many layers of civilisation and brutality here: Aztec, Toltec, Zapotec, Mayan, Spanish, French, American; Maximilian as well as Montezuma. The terrible sacrificial pyramids of Teotihuacan can be seen from the terrace heights of Maximilian's palace at Chapultepec, where Montezuma's giant ahuehuete trees still shade the park. And down in the city, neon lights play across the blistering baroque of a church where Cortés' priests said Mass. Vistas and *aspectos* everywhere.

☾⋆

Across the cactus-studded hills, a cloud of dust resolves into a group of horsemen: bold, centaur figures galloping into town, bent on mischief, by their looks. They rein up abruptly, beside an ambulant photographer's booth and, kneeling before a primitive painted backcloth depicting the Miraculous Virgin of Guadalupe, they strike attitudes of theatrical piety, hands clasped, liquid black eyes rolled heavenwards as if perceiving some ecstatic vision, and are so recorded for their loved-ones, and posterity. Yet, watching them, we shiver: they are cruelty incarnate. It is their Aztec heritage. The sacrificial pyramids of the past are more real, to them, than the archaeologists' Mecca they have now become. The next bend in the road may well reveal that terrible execution scene of Eisenstein's *Thunder Over Mexico*, victims buried up to their necks, their heads ridden down by yelling horsemen.

☪

Prison, like death, is not generally feared, however much, to the stranger's eye, conditions appear those of an engraving by Gustave Doré. Until lately, prisoners carried and perhaps still carry arms – a gun or a knife – as protection against other prisoners. Children are with their mothers and a new women's prison is now being completed where conditions will be very progressive, with crèches and gardens. In many prisons and particularly the penal settlements near Vera Cruz, whole families move in with the criminal, sharing his cell and sentence.

At the Central Prison of Mexico City, an enlightened rule admits the flesh, in the person of prisoners' wives and sweethearts on weekly visits, many hours at a time, behind closed cell doors. The huge noisy crowd of women surges forward through the gates, shrieking like parakeets, gaudy skirts swirling, teeth flashing. Their men are waiting for them, shouting and stamping. One by one the cell doors clang shut on their joys. It is quiet now. The guards lean against the courtyard walls lit by the sinking sun, picking their teeth, looking bored. In the simplicity of human relationships Mexican life recalls that of a more lusty Europe, when camp-followers and *vivandières* marched with the armies.

☾

Elegant, wealthy Mexicans create new standards of luxury living among the black lava fields of Pedigral, where glass and steel architecture seems an organic part of the landscape. There are no trees, no flowers here: only the geometric forms of the villas break the harshness. They are painted astonishingly, lemon or turquoise roofs, one wall salmon, another lilac. Flocks of white doves circle round them, reflecting the colours in an iridescent flash of wings, theatrically brilliant against the lava. When Madame Calderón de la Barca went to Mexico in 1840 as the young Scottish bride of the first Spanish envoy, she described 'the Pedigral' as being an immense formation of ferruginous lava and porphyritic rock, looking as if cursed for some crime committed there.

☾

At dusk, the ilex trees glistened with the first lamplight. Whole families of grey squirrels which had been chittering and frisking in the foliage now darted down to drink the dew from the ornamental flowerbeds below. When they sipped, they shut their eyes, like wine connoisseurs. The markets were closing and the cafés were opening. All along the street beside the fruit market crouched a line of women and young girls, selling off the fruits and food which would not be saleable next day. Each huge basket contained, beside its now dubious wares, an oil lamp lighting the beautiful, stony faces from below, footlight-wise. They preened and ogled the passers-by, shouting bawdily, for they, too, were for sale, along with the melons, aguacates, chayotes, papayas and cherimoyas. Exotic fare.

☪

Behind the convent, a line of black washing, nuns' robes, flaps crow-like and incongruous in the sunlight.

☪

The sound of flute and marimba and a soft, joyous song comes nearer. We stand under the orange trees and watch the procession. It is a baby's funeral. One man carries the shoe-box-sized cardboard coffin on his shoulder. The mourners follow, grave-faced, but not grieving. Life is hard; the baby has escaped; he is with God! They dance, a jigging step, and sing a sort of abstract, stylised expression of joy, in keeping with the Mexican's voluptuous pleasure in death. Hereabouts it is quite customary for a rich family to purchase the corpse from a poor household, thus acquiring a reason for holding an elaborate festival of death – a wake. This way, all are satisfied: the poor, that their dead has a splendid burial; the rich, that they have the occasion to celebrate death worthily.

☪

A luxury hotel is pitched down like an expensive toy, in wildest, richest, loveliest country. The yellow, radioactive pool drips with bougainvillea and roses. Waiters scuttle over from the main building with trays of sustenance. The parakeets shriek and flitter in the eucalyptus groves and the tourists pile their belongings under the sun – parasols, towels, Scrabble sets and small, unobtrusive crocodile jewel-cases. That way they can keep an eye on them. Bandit country! The bare hills quiver in the noonday blaze: rocky, remote, streaked with waterfalls, they are the perfect setting for a brigand's lair. The happy tourists plunge in, surfacing often, like hippos, keeping a wary eye trained on the jewel-cases, boiling away their ailments, their wrinkles, their overweight, their past. And then, a Mexican Indian girl sways down the road, on bare, patrician feet, staring ahead, aloof and indestructibly beautiful in her bone structure, her womanly grace. The tourists watch her out of sight. A shadow seems to have fallen over their play.

'Homer! I guess we'll go in to lunch now,' says a rather fretful voice. One by one, the towels, the Scrabble boards and the crocodile jewel-cases are collected, reassuring symbols of civilisation. At luncheon, most of the visitors bring portable radios to their tables, to croon them through the courses. No more need to talk, to think. No more loneliness, or strangeness. The hearty tones of a 'commercial' rise above the clatter of crockery. No more sense of being far away. They are home.

☪

There are gardenias floating in the yellow-tiled pool of our hotel courtyard and the sheets and pillows are edged with a lovely coarse handmade lace. But Mexicans need little sleep, it seems, for sounds of the most exuberant life are all round us. Romain complains of the uproar, if we leave the windows open; yet how to sleep in this heat, with them shut? Night life in Mexico City reaches its apogee with mariachi bands and revellers around dawn, just as the markets spring to life. Romain has scoured the place for earplugs, without success. Arriving at Taxco, in a room overlooking the little plaza, made golden by the sumptuous cathedral, and shaded by the profound yet sparkling depths of the ilex trees, he is still confronted by the problem of noise, to which is now added the clanging and tolling of bells, almost overhead, and the clatter of mule-hooves.

☪

Leaving Mexico City before dawn, to fly down to the Chiapas Indian country, we saw many peons still sprawled in the booths and tequila bars behind the Thieves' Market. Acetylene flares sharpened the scene dramatically. Noisy mariachi bands were still playing: the more prosperous peons were munching some unplaceable meal – supper, breakfast? It was a dark mess, chocolate and pimento and entrails, oozing from between the eternal tortillas.

Flying southwards, we watched the sky lighten; it burned an electric green; suddenly the sun rose over great Ixctaccihuatl. Our flight followed its snowy flank, over the crumpled brown canyons, on southwards, where nothing lived and where every conical hill was an extinct volcano. Sometimes we traced a thread of track across the desolation, but there were no roads.

'Mont Alban!' shouted the pilot and dipped the little plane sharply, swooping low over the vast Zapotec courts and pyramids lying below us, geometric and grim. Even in our plane (safe in our plane, we felt, by comparison with the legends of human sacrifice and Aztec cruelties), we seemed to hear the ascending shrieks of the victims as their beating hearts were torn from them by the priests' black obsidian knives.

In the Chiapas country of south-east Mexico, towards the Guatemalan border, all is changed. No more exoticism – the tropics give place to Switzerland, pine forests, a chilly, misty upland, inhabited by what appear to be Tibetan monks. The

Chamulas look strongly Asiatic: flat yellow faces, Mongol eyes and a shaggy thatch of hair like black fur – no sleek plumage here. They are gravely civil, but watchful and unenthusiastic towards strangers. They see very few, for their villages lie high in the hills, reached, if at all, by rocky tracks. They are greatly occupied with their own special pagan rituals and medicine.

The traditional Mexican passion for, and belief in, strange drugs, secret spells and herbal concoctions, malefic or curative, continues unabated, but here, besides the necromancers' booths at country markets, where love philtres and darkly powerful powders guaranteed to bring about both births and deaths are sold, there is a purely contemporary aspect too: *INJECIONES* says a roughly printed card in many windows along the cobbled main street. This means that penicillin, hormones and multiple vitamins, as well as less specific kinds of local drugs, are freely obtainable and as freely injected, by the local nurse, the inn-keeper, or the woman across the way.

Among the Chamula Indians, modern medicine is a subject of absorbing interest. In the remote villages set high in the bare, Tibetan-like uplands, they are properly proud of their medical centre. A small, well-equipped clinic is run by a doctor and nurse, whose base it is, between enormous mountain rounds. One or two especially gifted Chamula men, village leaders, were trained as assistants, to act in the doctor's absence. Alas! Having mastered the aseptic technique, their zeal became almost insensate: the limited supplies of rubber gloves, sterilised gauzes, hypodermic needles, surgeons' masks and all the panoply of the operating theatre had been expended on every head-cold, liver complaint or croupy brat brought in for advice. Now, save for real emergencies, a return to more casual curative methods is encouraged.

☾⋆

A bleak, austere land; nothing tropic here. We watch the eagles soaring high above the black forests, where a band of Zinacothék Indians hunt them with crazy flint-lock guns dating from Iturbides' reign. Those Zinacothéks are the fops of Central America; their build, manner and costume mark them as a race apart. They appear to have stepped from some eighteenth-century 'Embarkation for Cythera', a canvas by Hubert Robert, all roses and cupidons, rather than the mountains and gorges that are their home. Their clothes are wildly improbable. The men wear a short – very short – tunic of pink-and-white striped linen, over long, bare legs and elegantly sandalled feet; the whole topped by little straw hats tipped coquettishly over one ear, and bunched with pale-coloured satin ribbons, like a Watteau shepherdess; most of them carry guitars, also ribbon-trimmed, made from armadillo shells. Sometimes we came on groups of them sitting by the road, thrumming their guitars and singing, roadside troubadours. Their women are seldom seen and remain as utilitarian and drab as any hen-bird. These peacock-fops look an idle, seducing lot. It was as if a troupe of strolling players, costumed for one play, had strayed by chance into the scenery of another: some *fête galante* by Marivaux in Pastor Manders' thunderous setting.

☪

Nights are penetratingly cold here. Some of the Indians arrive at the market place in San Cristobal de las Casas before dawn, having walked all night to get there. They watch for the rim of sun to appear over the mountains, *La Capa de los Pobres* – the poor man's mantle, they say, waiting patiently for its rays to warm them through.

But we, guiltily conscious of being *los privilegiados* – the rich ones, the tourists – order our breakfast coffee laced with *eau de vie* before plunging into another day of enraptured wandering.

G*

Zigzagging across the country we reach the Isthmus of Tehuantepec, on the Pacific. *En route*, we are stuck for twenty-four hours at some unpronounceable halt. The only restaurant is a street booth; the menu, tequila or a cup of chocolate, and a local delicacy, reminiscent of potted shrimps, but made of some kind of small worm-like insect – fried. There is no bread other than the pawpaw or breadfruit from trees which grow exuberantly.

G*

At Tapachula, a brazen heat pours down like liquid fire. Above the town the coffee *fincas* quiver in the heat haze. Down below, in the town, it is clammy. All along the wildly cobbled streets, thatched shacks are topped by a line of huge brooding black birds – *zopilotes*, a kind of vulture. Tiny green parakeets, clowns of the bird world, perch on the heads of drowsy dogs, or ride, staggering and lurching, on top of the towering laundry baskets which majestic matrons carry on their heads. Even at noon there is no siesta hush. The voices of women, children and macaws merge into one chattering shriek. The streets peter out into twining coiling jungles, where there are pumas and alligators.

G*

At dusk, the population assemble round one of those tiny, ornate, white-painted iron bandstands that are found in every

Mexican town. They are said to have been inaugurated by the Empress Carlotta and remain a symbol of her refining efforts. A marimba band, opulently dressed in white-and-gold naval uniforms, plays Strauss passionately. Their vigorous bare feet issue from below their richly braided trousers. At the end of each number they applaud each other warmly. Birds stir uneasily in the shining dark depths of the ilex trees. The elaborate street lamps, clusters of incandescent globes, light the lovers, sitting in respectable proximity – but no more. Their beautiful Zapotec faces are grave, aloof in sorrow, in pleasure, in love. The band packs up for the night. The crowd disperses in twos and threes, towards the outskirts, swamps, trailing swags of rubbery vegetation, nothingness.

We walk home through shuttered byways. Outside a last livid-lit *pulquería*, or *pulque*-bar, the peons are sprawled asleep, their machetes beside them. We step over them gingerly. Back at the hotel, we arrive at an unfortunate moment. The night watchman has brought out his pet anaconda, an enormous, bolster-like snake, said to be harmless, but not prepossessing. It is a species much used in the Isthmus of Tehuantepec, as mouser and general household pet. 'He fine on rats,' says the watchman proudly. We hurry upstairs and slam our door.

☪

All night the Berlé-lé shrills its peculiar note, piercing, monotonous. Oddly, this too is regarded as a household pet. Everywhere, the sinister *zopilotes* – those huge carrion birds – sit brooding on the roofs or fences, even along the rail of our balcony, a frieze of doom that flaps down to scavenge in the gutters. 'Make healthy,' said the café waiter indulgently; and maybe they do, in this region of indifferent sanitation. But they are not engaging.

☪

This is our third visit to Mexico. We have fled the tinsel-hung boulevards of Hollywood, the lingerie-pink Father Christmases and the baby-blue reindeer which express the fantasy of

Californians at this season; we will taste again the rough grandeurs of Mexico. From a tinselled and starred airport we emerge into streets hung with grotesque straw figures, carnival puppets, and, in every lighted shrine, rapt, baroque saints. Before the cathedral, the children are forming processions with lanterns and candles bobbing in the dusk. Some mothers carry babies in arms, their midget Murillo faces wondering, their pudgy fists grasping lighted candles, dangerous, but delightful.

Romain and I share Scrooge's detestation of the festive season: we fled its bonhomie in California, yet we find it even here. Along Juarez Avenue, the tourist gift shops are stacked with alligator luggage and silverware labelled (in English) FOR HIM – FOR HER. A straggle of peons put down their bundles and stare. The men have coarse striped serapes over their traditional white cotton clothes, and the women are huddled into their shawls, or *rebozas*, for it is surprisingly cold. The brilliant Christmas star hangs huge and low over the magnolia trees of the Alameda gardens where a troop of mummers are posturing and prancing, keeping Christmas with strange pagan rituals. Christmas everywhere; even here, the hotels rustle with tissue-paper wrappings, Christmas cards, and the inevitable commercial blackmail. Where can we escape it? Cuernavaca will be pullulating with tourists, and the rich polyglot residents will have abandoned themselves to turkey and tinsel. Pueblo? Talapa? Acapulco? Oh no, not Acapulco. It has become the Eden Roc of Central America. There will be Christmas dinner beside the swimming pools.

But Romain settles the question by deciding he will start writing a new book, a memoir of his youth. He sees just how it must go. Mexico can wait, so can dinner. Page 1, Chapter 1, and *Promise at Dawn* is begun. I go out to dine on fiery foods alone and return to find him on page 27. This is the stuff. This is the way we see writers write in the theatre or the films; as painters paint, or, for that matter, people pack suitcases: concentrated action, no hesitations, no indecisions as in real life.

POSTSCRIPT. Before our Christmas holiday was over the first draft was completed. Romain had given himself over totally into the dark grip of memory and had seen nothing at all of the Mexico he loves. But he had escaped Christmas.

G

The feathery pepper trees shade a terrace which overlooks the city far below. Here Carlotta and Maximilian paced, united by their failures as much as their ambitions. He, pouting over some point of Hapsburg protocol to be adapted to the Mexican Court; she, planning where to plant another of those florid little wrought-iron bandstands she strewed about the furthest townlets of her wild domain. They still stand, frivolous monuments to a tragic empress; but when the people gather, solemn in pleasure as in pain, to hear a marimba band whacking local airs or Gershwin, a breath of patchouli and an echo of Offenbach seem to fall on the scene, recalling that Second-Empire Paris which sponsored Maximilian's brief reign.

Proud, ineffectual Carlotta is most clearly seen at Chapultepec, for her private suite is still much as she left it: a series of bourgeois, overstuffed salons, dark, in spite of the brilliant Mexican sunlight outside. Carved ebony furniture, a fusty canopied bed; two rosewood grand pianos, where she and her husband sat back to back, galloping through duets by Meyerbeer, and an inlaid writing-desk where she scribbled away the fateful days. Long-nosed, proud Carlotta, bent over the emblazoned sheets of paper, scribbling her interminable letters to the Empress Eugénie. It was Empress to Empress. 'Madame and good sister,' she wrote, 'We trust in God and are very content. My Mondays are really most successful; small gatherings of guests, fifty or so …' And all the while, the implacable Indian faces were closing in. The fifty guests dwindled to the fourteen ladies in waiting; soon the Court ceased to exist. When the French troops were withdrawn and the last battle lost, only two men stood beside the Emperor, facing the firing squad on the Hill of the Bells, at Querétaro. Even the embalmers failed him. What remained of the Emperor had to be swathed in mummy-like bandages, from head to foot, before it could be returned in state to Vienna.

But as Carlotta had gone mad, some months earlier, when visiting the Vatican to plead her husband's cause, she was spared all knowledge of the final failure.

☪

I crept out of the house very early one morning. I like to watch a village wake. The women were fanning their charcoal braziers, beside the open door. Overhead, brilliant spangled birds flittered in the tall eucalyptus trees. The church bell clanged to the counterpoint of tortillas smacking on the stones, plip-plop, a flabby sound. Along the lake, a group of fishermen were mending their strange looped figure-of-eight nets: they looked like gigantic butterflies settled on the still surface of the water. It was a pastoral scene; a lyric landscape. But brigand-infested too. The men had scowling, blackly beautiful faces. Beside them lay their striped serapes and machetes: these last, murderously curved knives, are as much a symbol of Mexican daily life as the furled umbrella to London. One man, eyeing me stonily, picked up his machete and, licking his thumb, ran it along the blade. As I faltered, he bent forward with a sudden swoop – and began slicing at his toenails. He looked up under his huge straw hat: he was laughing, showing a double row of perfect, broad teeth. But his eyes retained their basilisk stare. Whey-faced ladies should not prowl about alone – even in the morning, he seemed to say.

☾

Here, yet another aspect of Mexico is found – something quite apart, in spirit as in fact. Yucatán remains aloof, almost inaccessible. Ships must lie several miles out to sea, beyond the shallows. Only one track-like road runs through the brush: a plane flies in two or three times a week, stopping there between Mexico and the USA. Once Merida, the capital, was the centre of the world's sisal or hemp trade. Now the forgotten little city lives becalmed in its fabulous archaeological past. The lost splendours of the Mayan cities overpower its modest present. A green web of jungle spreads beyond the ruins of temples, plumed-serpent pyramids and past glories to encroach on the living city. At twilight, the sky turns a pale, bright mauve, and merges in a lilac haze with the deeper mauve of the jacaranda trees. In the cathedral, there is more mauve; the choristers wear parma-violet robes beneath their lace-trimmed tops. Later, we saw them in the main square. They were eating violet ices (*Elegantes y Delicados*) and having their pointed patent-leather boots cleaned by even smaller boys, while a sumptuous middle-aged lady with a lace parasol stood treat, from an open carriage drawn up beside the kerb. I wonder: did Ronald Firbank know Merida? He is recalled at every turn.

☾

Eighty per cent of the local population is Mayan: among themselves Mayan is the current language. Their parrots, too, sound these incomprehensible syllables. Mayan standards of beauty once included bow-legs, receding foreheads achieved by bandages; and a squint, this being arrived at by strings fixed before the babies' line of vision. The present-day citizens, while comely, do not come up to the dazzling standards of the other Mexican provinces: from time to time the diabolic or grotesque masks of Mayan gods are still to be traced in the living Meridans.

☪

Saturday night: the Salón de Bellezza (plugging a line of magenta nail varnish) works overtime preparing the local beauties for the ball tonight. Cantinflas, the Charlie Chaplin of Mexico, is billed at the movie-house. There is *molé* and baby shark on the menu at Pancho Pistoles' restaurant. We will drive there in one of those strange little open carriages peculiar to Yucatán, with cracked, peeling leather curtain-flaps enclosing the passengers with a sort of harem secretiveness. They have an air of sinistry and intrigue and seem at once ambulant confessional box and *maison de rendezvous*. What dark drama lurks within? We imagine some Meridan Emma Bovary rattling to her doom in such an equipage.

☪

A broken-down line of buses runs between Merida and Progresso, in the mangrove-swamp country along the mustard-yellow, brackish Gulf of Mexico. These buses have religious names. Ours was labelled Nostre Dama del Succoro. There were no springs, or glass in the windows either. Furnace heat, weighted by grit, blasted us as we bounced along through the cactus and sisal plantations; a peon sitting next to me had a parrot on his shoulder: like everyone hereabouts, it spoke Mayan: racy talk, I fancy, by the applause.

The journey was enlivened by several stops when everyone drank milk from fresh coconuts. Our driver hacked them open for us with his machete. A blind guitarist paid his passage in kind and everybody requested their favourite tunes, which he obligingly rendered. The driver was after the little señorita in pink on the back seat and kept asking for some song about a dove. What would the French señora like? they asked me, bowing gallantly. My mind went blank. I could only think of Wagner.

☪

In the blood-red waters of the mangrove swamps around Campeché, cormorants waddle intently after fish, hopping from one serpent-like root to the next. They are followed by pelicans, croaking like operatic frogs. Their grotesque beaks are used by the farmers for drilling holes in the ground, when sowing seeds.

☪

We arrive at Chichén Itzá in the blaze of noon – the whole scene quivers. We crawl towards the Astronomers' Palace, the Nunnery, the Warriors' Temple, the Ball Court – steps, steps, walls of steps. We climb, we scramble and climb again. Lost splendours loom over us, plumed serpents and diabolic masks, almost as Catherwood drew them, more than a century ago.

We follow an overgrown track, tick-infested and thorny, through the brush. It leads to the Sacred Well, a brackish pool lying about sixty feet below our path. A sinister silence hangs over the place. No bird sings. All Chichén Itzá is a monument to cruelty. Here some of the sacrificial victims were thrown to their doom. On this curved altar stone, the priests disembowelled others. Down these steps which we climb so painfully they flung the still palpitating hearts of human sacrifices.

And are we not also, in one way, human sacrifices on the altar of culture? Romain and I are not really archaeologically inclined. We begin to flag.

Above us towers the pyramid of El Castillo, constructed at an angle of sixty degrees, making the climb a vertiginous martyrdom. Since Catherwood's day the steps have been cleared of vegetation and their nudity makes the descent more terrifying, for there is nothing to clutch at, or to break one's fall. The Sanctuary of El Tigre, the red tiger, is at the summit of a perpendicular, inter-pyramidal ascent. Pouring with sweat we begin the airless climb, ever higher, till El Tigre is revealed, glowing crimson, studded with jade. How many ages has he lurked in these stone heights? Suppose the door should jam? Suppose a wall should crumble? The accumulated weight of centuries, masonry, and terror closes in.

Enough! We precipitate ourselves down, and out, into the green living world around us.

The perfume of the datura flowers mingles with the smell of bean stew issuing from the guardian's hut. We hear the familiar plip-plop sound of tortillas being patted into shape. No more pyramids! Not one more ruin!

Unrepentant, we will return to Merida, savouring the animation of the collective taxi. We will watch the sun slant behind the palms; we will gorge ourselves on aguacates and chayotes and cherimoyas, fruits of paradise. We will go to the Salón de Billares El Olimpo and watch *los correctos* (the elegant Mexicans) playing chess under the ilex trees in the plaza, while the marimba band is in full whack. Tomorrow we will go and bathe in the opaque mustard-yellow Gulf of Mexico. The ruins must wait. Living, beautiful, seductive Mexico first.

☾⋆

No one told me about the birds. Every province has its own special birds, like its fruit or flowers, a thousand different fluttering, shimmering creatures, fluting, cawing, shrieking. At Purapechas, by the end of the lake, there is a whole world or concentration of humming-birds, where these beetle-sized little beauties zoom and dart about the honeyed trails of vine, 'cup-of-gold', or a plant called *izgujochitl* – 'the flower of the raven'. Pelicans and cormorants in Yucatán. Gaudy macaws and parakeets flashing through the tropic groves round Orizaba. Under the towering ash trees at Tzinzuntzan I heard the nightingale at noon; but it turned out to be a yellow-feathered bird and I recalled that the Emperor Maximilian imported two thousand nightingales from Germany: where they, perhaps, then crossed with canaries? Everywhere, in the mountains, in the valleys, I see those long-tailed black magpie-like birds, so impudently friendly, which seem to address one personally, as they flutter close to perch on the spear-tip of a cactus or on a window-sill. The Mexicans call them *ouraki*; in Mayan, they are *toh*. Their song has the heart-piercing sweetness of a blackbird's trill, with something melancholy added, something which epitomises all Mexico at dusk.

*Part Five*

# THE EASTERN EYE

# 23. Afghanistan

IN MY CHILDHOOD 'Abroad' was a faraway land I must attain; the climate, language or inhabitants were all one to me. My longing for Afghanistan – spelled with two 'ff's as it was in earlier days – ran alongside my obsession with all things Russian, although that had a human deviation. I do not know why, but when poring over that old red atlas which had exotic landscapes and polar regions beside palm trees, that rather small chunk of land between Persia and India seemed to be the quintessential Elsewhere: in one corner I found it marked Afghanistan. Even better, there were exciting-sounding cities: Tashkurgan, Bamiyan, and Kabul. I was determined to visit them all one day. It took me over fifty years to do so, a whole lifetime of longing, but once achieved I made two journeys there within a couple of years, because it was exactly how I'd hoped it would be. I was invited by *The Sunday Times* to write a three-part serial account of journeys about the Moslem world, reporting the position of women. I could choose where I wanted to go and would be accompanied by a photographer. Of course I jumped at it. All my papers and records of these journeys have long perished in the fire which destroyed my house in 1994. I called those years when I was travelling all over the place the 'Years of the Minarets'. Marvellous years: I was in Isfahan and Fez; in Damascus, Delhi and Konya; in Cairo and Bokhara the Noble.

☪

My earlier, dug-in cravings for Afghanistan were in some
measure fostered by the superb drawings of the people by
Jacovleff, who accompanied the Citroën expedition to
Afghanistan in the thirties; and if I remember rightly he con-
tinued across Central Asia to China. His Afghan sketches are
of a particular brilliance, with a draughtsman's incisiveness
and psychological depth. The portraits of tribal characters,
costumes, poses – a foot in or out of a shoe, a hand on a
water-pipe – are an exact record.

☪

Afghanistan, a wild and lovely land, lies at the crossroads of
Central Asia, and if it has remained curiously unknown
compared with its neighbours, it is because it was considered
inaccessible: you could not reach it by boat for there was no
coast; nor by train or aeroplane, for there were no railways
or airfields; and the roads were best left untried. Now,
although there are still no railways, there are magnificent
roads. Russians built the one north, which climbs over and tun-
nels through the Hindu Kush, and Americans the fine highway
south, to Kandahar and beyond. And so the tourists begin to
venture.

Afghanistan is still primarily a pastoral country, and Kabul
a modest little capital: there is poverty, but not squalor; nor
are there any architectural glories. It is in its citizens and its
splendid setting that Kabul enthralls. The city lies in a green
plain ringed by magnificent mountains, the Hindu Kush, the
Koh-i-Baba, the Paghman range; every perspective is glorified
by their towering presence, ever changing – orange in a blaze
of fierce sunlight, violet and sugared-over with snow on

autumn evenings. And always the vast horizons, wild and free like the spirit of the people.

☪

There is an ancient belief that when Satan fell to earth he landed in Afghanistan. I was often reminded of this when I wandered about the strange apocalyptic landscape of convulsive or volcanic rock formations, towering defiles so narrow that no sunlight ever reached the stony paths which lay under the darkling cliffs. I am remembering the Khoord Kabul pass in particular, for there an entire British force, unwisely called the army of occupation, was driven to its doom in 1842. Afghan irregulars – peasants, nobles, the veiled women and their children, ill-armed but united and all fiercely resolved on liberty – massacred the invaders. Only one man survived to tell a tale of horror. It was the most fearful and humiliating disaster of British military history. Two successive punitive expeditions or armies of vengeance could not efface the humiliation which is still told and retold in wayside *chaikhanas*, or tea houses, by descendants of the victors, among whom one finds strangely pale skins and light eyes; these are said to be the marks of some of the women, British army wives, who were seized or acquired, ravished or taken into the harems of the Afghan overlords or of rough tribesmen, according to their destiny. Near Bamiyan in its green and gracious valley, there is a high-placed village known as 'the screaming rock', for it was there that Genghis Khan when passing that way left butchered villagers to rot, while the vultures circled overhead. Certainly much of the history of Afghanistan is blood-curdling as is the depiction of the violent nature of its rulers. Legends abound of the inherent fury of every Afghan against an aggressor, and of the terror of the long Afghan knife, customarily wielded by the women sent out to scour the battlefields for helpless wounded unavoidably left to perish. Even the British at the height of their imperialistic might were unable to hold Afghanistan in fee, and after the third Afghan War in 1919 they gave up trying.

Make what you like of it, but there is a decidedly demonic imprint in the landscape, as if some defiance is hurled at the beholder, yet wholly apart from its inhabitants whom I have not found particularly sinister. On the contrary I found them to be rather aloof and dignified, indifferent to strangers, and not yet on the make or corrupted by Western ways. They are merry, almost childishly so, and love laughing. There is an extraordinary, fatal charm to this strange people. That is how I found them on my first journey there in the sixties.

☪

This rugged lovely country is one vast souk and certainly my favourite, with treasures in every city from Kandahar to Balkh: lapis lazuli and rare antiquities, Graeco-Buddhistic statuary, Nuristan carvings and so on. State-controlled collectors' pieces. In Kabul, splendid carpets, plum-red Bokharans, Turkoman rugs; sometimes rare Samarkands found on junk stalls. Barbaric silver ornaments of the Kuchi tribes; delicious blue glass from Istalif; strange musical instruments, richly decorated weapons, early coins, lengths of turban muslin, velvet, gold-embroidered jackets; semi-precious stones by the bushel.

At Tashkurgan, as if to compensate for the flat sandy wastes, the noisy little souk is ornate, florid even, with fanciful, crudely painted frescoes along the centrifugal arches. It is still much as Marco Polo knew it. The merchandise was very varied and the real old 'Russian' dark blue, rose-flowered

teapots are now collectors' pride, like the naive painted panels – flowers, fruit, lions, or mosques – with which lorry and bus drivers decorate their vehicles.

There from among a pile of Central Asian rainbow silks and *chapans* – those long, striped, cotton-and-silk, padded, dangle-sleeved garments traditionally worn by the men of any tribe – I succeeded in buying a real beauty. Its unusual mixture of Chinese yellow, lilac and rusty pink seemed to glow among the more usual blues and greens. After a lot of haggling, I got it.

I wore it when we headed off down the road to Balkh, Afghanistan's 'Mother of Cities', through vast emptiness broken only now and then by little pointed domed houses like so many upturned bosoms. As the heat mounted I took off my *chapan* and left it at the back of our jeep among the paraphernalia of such come-by-chance journeys.

Much later, after lingering the midday hours in a roadside *chaikhana* where we feasted on kebabs and green tea, we went on our way, belching. Afghans abandon themselves to this practice which I found hard to take until I realised that bouncing about in a jeep over rough tracks it was easier to go along with the Afghan, and belch boldly. Along a stretch of open country nearing Mazari Sharif we overtook a solitary, sauntering turbaned figure who I saw with interest wore a *chapan* with stripes identical to mine; so much for all that salesman's talk about antique rarities. I turned round to look at my own *chapan* snug on the back seat, but it was no longer there. This dawdling figure had pinched it when we were in the *chaikhana* and was now wearing it. In a fury of passion, I told my driver to go back. I flung myself out of the jeep and rushed to confront the thief while my driver shouted warnings. All my few useful phrases in Pashto forgotten, I yelled angrily in English. The man began to laugh, a rollicking, jolly sound, revealing a dazzling mouthful of those large square perfect teeth so often seen in this region. The more I tugged and pulled at the caftan, the more he laughed until, pushing me aside roughly, he took off the coat and, still grinning, in a superb gesture – a sort of elegant *galanterie* – held it open for me to put on. Dumbly, I did so. Feeling rather foolish, I watched him walk away with that curious air of nonchalant detachment I have often remarked among the Afghans, as though they live a succession of vital moments, each one with intensity, at once past, or lost: gone.

# 24. Turkey

ALTHOUGH SO MANY conquerors have eyed Istanbul long-ingly, it has, oddly enough, never really attracted that more modest stratum of humanity, the tourist, until today. Now with that inexplicable urge which makes fashion, it has suddenly become the lodestar of the adventurous; 'To the walls of Constantinople!', once the Crusaders' cry, might now be theirs.

I first went there ten years ago. I have made the journey many ways – by the Orient Express; by lorry, at night, through the desolate frontier zones of Macedonia; by local trains that circle the crumbling walls which once encompassed Constantine's capital. I have flown in, the plane swooping low over the bubble-domed roofs of the Great Bazaar, seeming with every swoop to risk impalement on the spear-like minarets. But the first time, I made the approach by boat, in the classic manner. Only this way can the full impact of Istanbul be obtained. The incomparable silhouette of the city, with its mosques and minarets, watchtowers, cypress trees, and forest of masts, rises suddenly from the pearly distances of the Marmara. Anchored off the Seraglio Point, we were between the two shores, Europe and Asia, at the meeting point of the three legendary waters, Marmara, Bosphorus, and Golden Horn. All the tumult of modern docks and mercantile trade makes the foreground of this historic panorama. Swarms of little caïques skimmed towards us, tugs blasted, loudspeakers blared, and the porters cried their strength in voices at once guttural and shrill. Yet, beneath it all, I caught, borne on the breeze, the faint quarter-tones of oriental music, issuing from the cafés along the waterfront. I thought about those Turks who stormed Vienna, accompanied by their military band, the Mehter, whose curious rhythm *alla Turca* of drums and bells was to influence both Mozart and Beethoven.

Perhaps the most outstanding characteristic of the Turkish scene is space – emptiness – stillness. In spite of the teeming alleyways, the pullulating bazaars, the charging trams and uproar of Pera (a section of Istanbul), the ramshackle houses of Stamboul are dumped about open waste ground like some transitory camp, with wild flowers, rubbish, and rough pasture ground for goats between the encampments. At Brussa, on the slopes of Bithynian Mount Olympus, while the boys spend their evenings playing football, there are still large numbers of inhabitants who just sit – in the traditional manner of Eastern contemplation. Beside the splendours of the Sublime Porte, its palaces and mosques and treasure houses, lie the plains of Asia, those limitless distances stretching to the steppes, to the north wind and beyond.

There is, too, behind the superficially glowing Near-Eastern beauty, a sombre thread, an enclosed, almost sinister note, which remains from other days, giving a character which leaves its mark on man as well as land. Just as Turkey is not truly (except round Izmir) that smiling landscape we see on a box of figs, so the Turk is not that supple plump Levantine merchant of legend. The first Turks swept across Asia to become a military aristocracy, and then found the Seljuk dynasty. They were a horde of lean, hawk-faced men, with dark slit eyes: ferocious warriors. And today, those who have fought beside the magnificent Turkish brigades in Korea know the breed has remained uncorrupted.

In spite of this increasing awareness of, and interest in,

Turkey, it remains singularly remote in the Western mind. Ask the man in the street what he knows of it, and he will speak vaguely of Turkish delight, carpets, baths, coffee, and trousers, but he won't be very precise. Those who, like myself, enjoy collecting useless pieces of information recall it was the Turks who first imposed cafés – coffee houses – on besieged Vienna, which subsequently became celebrated for these same cafés; know that when Britain was an obscure Roman colony it was administered from Constantinople, then the Eastern capital of the Roman Empire; that the mysterious prevalence of elastic-sided boots among the citizens of any big Turkish city is due to the fact that it enables them to be removed easily on entering a mosque for the daily sunset and sunrise prayers; that the tulip is the national flower, its shape woven into a thousand decorative motifs, and that the English word 'tulip' was inspired by the form of the huge turbans we see in the early portraits of pashas painted by Van Loo or Rembrandt. The more informed will tell you that modern Turkey is an agricultural country with a population of 21,000,000; that four years ago it was importing wheat, and now, due in part to American aid, it exports around 2,000,000 tons. That there are 16,000 miles of new all-weather roads, and that 40 per cent of their budget is earmarked for the US-trained-and-equipped armed forces. That there are six hundred or more Turkish students in American universities and technical colleges, mostly studying engineering or medicine. These are facts and figures. I must confess to a muddle-headed preference for the legendary Turkey of my mind's eye; to me it is still the land of Loti's *mystique impression d'Islam*. To me, the cry of the muezzin still mingles with the song of the *bulbul* (or nightingale) in fountain courts.

In reality, it is another, more brisk, more reassuring scene. Across the Galata Bridge, bright new taxis nose through crowds; past and present, always this counterpoint. Byzantine cupolas topped by Moslem minarets, and these, in turn, topped by the crescent of the pagan goddess Diana. History and myth. Beggars, hotel touts, pedlars, bearded Greek priests and turbaned imams; behind the Spice Bazaar, perfumes and petrol; camels unload beside jeeps. Trim typists patter along, as in any American city; bunchy, black-shawled women, the more conservative matriarchs, are returning from an agreeable day's outing to the cemeteries of Scutari or Eyub, where they have picnicked and dallied, in the traditional Moslem manner, beside the graves of their departed loved ones. One and all seem to be clutching baggy black umbrellas, poor substitute, it must be admitted, for those plumed horsehair wands once carried by Three-Tailed Bashaws.

Umbrellas or no, Istanbul has a sharpening effect on the imagination, a way of dramatising the everyday scene. But then, Turkey conjures so many scenes, so many characters. It is impossible for the most frivolous tourist, downing a Martini at the Park Oteli bar, to remain unaware of the texture of history all around. Even the most sternly contemporary mind must range back over, say, the massacre of the Janissaries in the Meydan where, today, the Turkish nursemaids air their charges, pet lambs accompanying them in the manner of dogs; or those violet-hung porphyry rooms of the Paleologi, designed for the birth of princes, from which our phrase 'born to the purple' derives. Or, in softer mood, plunge into the delicious nostalgia of *Aziyadé*, Pierre Loti's masterpiece, the story of his love for the ill-fated Circassian odalisque. Loti is out of fashion now, but one day his wonderful evocation of a mood, a landscape, or the essence of a country will be revalued. Of Turkey he wrote: 'The Orient is the dream of land and legends. Turkey is the eye, the tongue, the light and the truth of that magic land.'

Everyone who visits Turkey should try to snatch a few days in the interior of the country. Brussa, with its Green Mosque, its elegiac beauty; Edirne, Smyrna (or Izmir), the little ports along the Black Sea; the thrusting, eager vitality of Ankara, Amasya, pretty and provinicial, Erzurum, the historic fortress set in savage, magnificent scenery; or nearing the Syrian coast, Tarsus and Antioch with their Biblical echoes. So, too, no one should even spend a weekend in Istanbul without crossing to the Asiatic shore. Pera, on the European shore, is not typical. It is the quarter where it is probably expedient to stay, though not necessarily to eat. Old Stamboul, across the Galata Bridge, and Scutari across the Bosphorus, are far more rewarding. Pera is, as it were, the midtown Manhattan section of Istanbul. Here, the best hotels, the international restaurants, art galleries, shops and night-life are found. Here, the great families of Turkey live, for the most part in modern apartment houses that look over the Bosphorus – their rooms have far fewer divans than the most contemporary Western interiors. The women are dressed by Paris, or after Dior. They play canasta and tennis, enjoy cocktails, boogie, and other manifestations of Western culture. (Flying is the present passion, and many Turkish women hold pilot licences.) But traces of exoticism remain, I am glad to say. Their voluptuous good looks recall the Circassians from whom many descend. Their jewels have an opulence unknown to the West. And the family portraits are all of beetle-browed, turbaned Grand Viziers or melting Sultanas.

Perhaps the best way to savour Istanbul's variegated panorama, its layers of life (and I do not speak, here, of the regular tourist round of mosques and museums), is to zigzag up the Bosphorus in the ferry-boat, going from side to side, from one age to another, from Asia to Europe. At Scutari, Florence Nightingale engaged in her heroic struggles, and there the cypress alleys shade the tombs of the Sultan's favourite charger, among the vast concourse of ornamental tombs. Some are topped by a turban, others by the tools of a man's trade, a sword, a brush, a hammer – some more modern ones bear an almost visiting-card precision. 'Doctor Zāti: Specialist in diseases of the ear, nose and throat, snatched from his patients in the flower of his wisdom.'

At Rumeli Hisari, Xenophon and his ten thousand Greeks are said to have crossed – the battlements of its castle are dominated by Robert College, an American institution which for ninety years has wielded so profound an influence on Turkish life and thought. The Sweet Waters of Asia, it must be said, do not live up to their name: a creek, a bridge, huge plane trees; where once the harems so joyously dallied on their rare outings. The ferry chugs on, past bathing beaches and fishing villages and the crumbling splendours of the *yalis*, or summer houses, whose carved wooden façades overhang the water. Some are historic palaces; others in the 1890 villa style, corresponding perhaps to some Newport establishments. Their balconies were a window on to life, on to the stream of boats that passed below. Only a generation or so back, the last of the harems languished there, craving the latest thing from Paris, unsuitable plumed hats, or button boots, maybe, which they delighted to adorn with real ruby or diamond buttons. At Kanlidja, the little cafés bask in the westering sun, beside the huge yacht where once Kemal Atatürk enjoyed a few moments of leisure from his Herculean labours. On the European shore again there is Therapia, a summer resort where the various foreign embassies have hot-weather palaces hidden among the tropic luxuriance of their gardens. They look across to the forests of Belgrade, where there is boar-hunting and quail-shooting.

Now the Bosphorus widens and merges into the Black Sea.

Its inky hue does not belie its name, though it was called 'black' in reference to its treacherous nature. All at once, we sense the north – the wind from the steppes hurls across these intervening waters and can transform Istanbul into a snow-bound winter city. (It is said that there is no climate in Istanbul, only the north wind and the south wind.) Suddenly, we see why the samovars and curious bell-hung arches across the horses' heads, which recall old Russia, belong in this oriental landscape too. It is all part of the counterpoint. The violent contrasts: north and south, East and West, new and old, legend and myth, that go to make up the Turkey I love.

## 25. The Turquoise Table: Traditional Persian Food

PERSIA, THE TURQUOISE KINGDOM of legend and history, is now called Iran, though we still continue to speak of Persian carpets and Persian miniatures (or the Persian Gulf, for that matter). I always think of the lovely land I knew as Persia, and ask indulgence to write of it thus.

My introduction to traditional Persian food took place many years ago, in a country house on the slopes of the Elburz mountains, deep in the woods north of Tehran. It belonged to an aged general, and all was tradition there. The rather ramshackle house, with its tall pillared and recessed veranda or *talah*, where a samovar purred ceaselessly, recalled those nests of gentlefolk which Turgenev describes. It was a patriarchal life, at once rural and intellectual. One of the finest private libraries of the Middle East was housed a few steps from the cowsheds. The atmosphere was both careless and welcoming, with a sort of battered luxury added. There were big iron stoves to heat the rooms, ancient rugs and worn scraps of rare embroideries everywhere, and a piano stacked with the scores of Russian operas. There were horses in the stables, and cows in the pasture, for my hostess (of English origin) had been the first to introduce fresh cow's milk to Iran: earlier there was only goat's or ewe's milk (the latter makes what is unquestionably the richest, most suave yoghourt). There were also twenty or more dogs, for any stray animal always found a home there.

Once, before my time, there had been a wolf cub who grew up among the dogs, wagged his tail and did not know he was otherwise. When the family left on a long journey, they gave the gardener money and instructions to feed the wolf well. Needless to say, the gardener pocketed the money and left the wolf to fend for itself. Resourcefully, the wolf made a meal of the gardener's child. The child recovered, but the wolf was shot. On his return the general sacked the gardener – it was the least he could do to defend the wolf's memory.

☪

Cooking in this household was strictly traditional, like the placing of the kitchen or cookhouse, a building apart, in the garden. There the cook had all his equipment and cool, stone-hewed larders. Everything was prepared on big wood fires outside, under the trees, with huge iron and copper cauldrons and racks suspended over the flames. In the heavy snows of winter, a lean-to shed sheltered the fire, and the cook crunched about, muffled and swearing vigorously.

But no one ever thought of an indoor kitchen. In summer our table was laid in a clearing of the woods, sunlight or starlight dappling through the branches while the dogs sat hopefully at a respectful distance and the samovar hummed. Samovars are a salient feature of domestic life in Iran, as in Russia, and glasses of amber-coloured tea are drunk as constantly. I loved those meals, the patriarchal atmosphere and the family servants of two or three generations, who looked after us. They had poetic names, Moon-Fairy, or Jewel of Delight, and they spoke poetically. If I returned from a short walk they would say, 'Your footsteps are on my eyes' or 'Your shadow has been missed', and if given an order, would reply, 'May I be your sacrifice!' meaning, 'I will sacrifice myself to execute your order.' Oh! happy days when no one felt they lost caste by domestic labour, and no one's conscience pricked if they gave an order.

Yet even while I was rejoicing in those traditional ways – ways already remote from the West – progress in terms of modernisation was being pushed forward at an increasingly giddy pace. Everywhere about the Turquoise Kingdom giant supermarkets were springing up, stacked with 'convenience' contraptions – deep freezes, push-carts, moving stairways, and tinned goods from faraway sources. Fewer and fewer of the small street-corner bakeries were to be seen about the expanding cities, and their excellent bread was giving place to cellophane-wrapped spongy white loaves obtained in chain-stores. They were the kind I used to see in America labelled 'factory fresh'; though there today good bread is reinstated and homemade loaves are seen as a status symbol.

One of the charms of walking about Persian cities used to be the smell of freshly baked bread and the singular sight of those large dappled sheets of *sangak*, curiously spotted dark and light brown, so that it seemed as if the population were always carrying a leopardskin about with them.

Today, with a return both violent and mystical to all things traditional, no doubt the original dispossessed breads, like other local foods, are reinstated, while the tin-opener has become a symbol of Western degeneracy. It is a point of view hard to criticise.

☪

That exquisite sense of design which is found in Persian carpets, like the intricate brickwork of the ancient mosques (I am remembering particularly the Friday Mosque at Isfahan) or the shimmering blue-tiled work of a thousand other holy shrines, was also to be traced more simply in many other aspects of life. Even the presentation of some everyday dish echoed this profound or atavistic sense of decoration. As in Japan, you might say. Certainly; but I will not embark on comparative niceties. Persian food, whether for a feast or daily life, was invariably pleasing to the eye by the manner in which it was presented. By that I do not imply all kinds of pretentious fiddlededee which swells out the *cuisine minceur* considered chic today. Rather, a basic sense of display, and what best suited the material to hand, however modest. It is an Eastern trait.

Thus an encampment of the nomad tribes on the desolate plains beyond Shiraz, the Kashgai, let us say, would offer the plainest dish of rice – but it was no accident that it was piled into a huge bowl of coarse turquoise blue pottery. There would have been a white tin basin somewhere to hand, no doubt, but that would spoil the effect of the snowy rice, and this they instinctively knew.

Shop windows, like booths in the bazaars, or along the streets, used to display ranks of pickle jars, and piles of melons or aubergines which recalled the intricate geometric patterns of a rug. Even the simple wooden spoons still in use (although many are now regarded as museum-pieces) were gracefully shaped; the best, called 'sherbet spoons', being of wafer-thin pearwood, delicate as curved petals, had long stem-like handles perhaps eighteen or more inches in length. Such far-reaching spoons were strictly practical when everyone, from courtier to farmer or merchant, sat round on the floor and reached for one central dish; but a shorter form has remained, to grace the now more general Western-style table.

At those elaborate Persian banquets we see portrayed in

miniatures, or that entrancing school of early nineteenth-century painting known as Qadjar (from the dynasty of that name), the most voluptuous luxury is apparent. Thirty-seven courses were *de rigueur*, we are told, and indeed, such largesse was maintained well on into the twentieth century. Seventeenth-century travellers and diplomats who succeeded in reaching the glittering Safavid court of Shah Abbas at Isfahan were dumb-founded, for after many wearisome months struggling across the barren wastes of Central Asia they were confronted by unparalleled splendours. Their memoirs also recorded a curi-ous custom designed to refresh revellers at the Shah's table. Between the courses, by way of diversion, a basket of kittens (Persian of course) was often circulated, the guests fondling the little creatures ecstatically. Cats were ever the Persians' especial delight, and at the banquets they provided a kind of furry variation to the customary undulating *houris* or their rivals, the painted dancing boys. All of them were seen as a *détente* between the sumptuous sequence of gold, jewel-studded dishes the Shah, 'Allah's Shadow on Earth', offered the assemblage crouched before him on silken rugs beside pearl-tasselled bolsters.

Returning to a more modest scene, at the kind of Persian table I once knew, a typical Persian dinner always began with *sabzi* (green), which consists of tiny spring onions, chunks of cucumber, parsley, mint and radishes. Every stratum of Persian society loves *sabzi*, and I never noticed anyone had hiccups, or recked of onions, so my more queasy readers should take heart and put aside the heartburn mixtures and 'breathalators' of effete living.

*Ashe* is Persia's basic soup, a thick mixture of every imagin-able vegetable, and often accompanied by *kofte* (meat balls), heavily spiced and marble-sized. I came to know *ashe* well, when staying in the province of Mazanderan in a house beside

the curiously sullen, greyish waters of the Caspian. There winter comes down early. An incessant fine, damp mist swirled mysteriously through the lush groves of orange and mulberry trees, and then *ashe* came into its own. We consumed it beside a fire of scented apple boughs, and as the autumnal gales tore round the wood-tiled roof, blowing straight in from the

Russian steppes northwards across the Caspian, our appetites were keen. In that house, the cook, a gifted boy from the region, finding us enthusiastic, offered us a different kind of *ashe* each of the six days we lingered there. In more southerly regions, in great heat for example, there are cold versions, equally sustaining, with yoghourt as a base. *Ashe* in one form or another has always been a staple nourishment for the various peoples of Central Asia.

Rice, innumerable vegetables, fruit and yoghourt, or *mast*, are the country's staple diet. In many households, the main dish, or even the only one, was inevitably rice; but rice made intriguing by a series of intricate sauces (*khoresh*), either sweet or sour. These subtle but daring mixtures are the secret and the glory of traditional Persian cooking; as contradictory and complicated as the race itself. When deep in such delights as rice with *khoresh fesanjan*, I used to speculate as to its composition – the rice was transformed, the palate stimulated; what exactly were the ingredients? A small amount of meat, mixed with fruit and vegetables – but which? – were the the basis of every *khoresh*. The stewy sort of sauce which resulted was transformed by such surprising additions as rhubarb or pomegranates, as in the case of *khoresh fesanjan*, or oranges, spinach and cinnamon, for *khoresh sak*. Such sauces might be described as the Persian equivalent of Italy's tomato-based accompaniment to pastas.

*Chelo kebab* is the quintessential Persian dish, found throughout the land, in private houses, wayside caravanserais, modern hotels or the small eating houses of the bazaars. *Chelo* is steamed rice, *kebab* grilled meat, and they are served with a sauce, which is something in the nature of a *coup de théâtre*. Beside each plate of rice and meat (lamb or beef) stands a raw egg in its shell, some powdered brown *sumak*, grated from the bark of the sumak tree, and a chunk of butter. But where is the sauce, you may ask? Where? – in its shell. You seized the egg (boldness and speed are essential to this operation), then, making a deep hole in the mound of rice, you cracked the egg open and stirred it into the rice along with the butter. All had to be done while the rice was blazing hot; a divinely rich yet simple sauce resulted, colouring the rice to a pale gold on to which was then sprinkled the tawny *sumak*. The accompanying salad was invariably tomato and raw onion. I know of no better feast.

The Persian menu seldom included cheese as in so much of Europe and America. *Panir* was a very tough, very salty goat cheese, rustic in nature and eaten with melon or sprinkled with one of the innumerable spices of the Persian cuisine; it was also sometimes eaten with beetroot. In winter, cooked beetroot was sold smoking hot from street barrows and, whenever I was afoot in the bazaar quarter of Tehran (which I much preferred to the characterless modern city), I found the beetroot a wonderful snack.

On the subject of snacks – if such a phrase can be applied to caviar – I always thought it ironic that the rare golden kind, reserved by tradition for the Shah alone, was seldom served at the Palace, for the monarch was allergic to caviar in any form; thus my curiosity and the cravings of other guests were seldom fully gratified.

Persian desserts – *shirini* (or sweets) – were not only extremely sweet, but *très parfumés*. The puddings and tarts of our Western world were not favoured. *Shirini* are lighter, a cross between honeyed pastries and meringues, mostly flavoured with rosewater. A water ice of crushed mint, almost a sherbet, such as the sorbets we know, was popular and called *sharbat*, but which was the original, sherbet or *sharbat*, who knows?

Fruit was abundant, of all kinds, while a certain small, very delicate cucumber ranked as such, and was eaten with sugar.

Pomegranate juice was drunk in large quantities for its health-giving properties, much as we take orange juice. It was sold bottled, and gushed from street soda-fountains, pressed and de-seeded, or the fruit was just cut open and sucked noisily, messily, deliciously.

Finally, delicacy of all delicacies to me, there was *sekanjaban*; a most elegant Persian extra, which I have never encountered anywhere but in Iran. This dish – though perhaps I should call it a dip – first seduced me with its subtle, minty-sour sweetness when I encountered it at a picnic in the palm groves of an ancient royal garden on the island of Kish (Sinbad's island according to legend), a small sandy hump rising from the azure waters of the Persian Gulf. Long spears of crisp Romaine lettuce were served with the syrupy vinegar dip, and as I struggled to master the technique of eating this elegantly, I thought that nursery bibs would have been a practical accompaniment. This nation's innate sense of decoration might have made each bib and tucker a work of art like tiles or Kalamkar cotton prints.

When at last the picnic was over, and the sun sank behind the snake-like limbs of the giant banyan trees, carpets were spread beneath them, and we were invited to listen to the nightingales. In the sultry dusk we waited, while I wondered how much of the delicacy and elegance of this Persian feast I could transpose to my own house. There, bamboo thickets, jacaranda, jasmine, cypress and fig replace the banyan. True, there are nightingales to sing for me and carpets galore – what then is missing? Simply this: my setting is the South of France – Europe – and nothing can impose that curious ambience, at once sophisticated and primitive, all age-old Asia, which makes up the arts and crafts, traditions and gastronomy of Persia.

## 26. The Joys of Comfort

IT HAS BEEN SAID (and it is a point of view still held by some) that to seek comfort, physical or moral, is a sign of weakness; an inability to take life's rough with the smooth. 'All strange and terrible events are welcome, but comforts we despise' runs a heroic line from Shakespeare with which, as an unrepentant hedonist, I cannot agree. To cultivate comfort, to offer it to others, seems to me a very proper endeavour.

Comfort has been defined as that stealthy thing which enters our lives as our slave, and becomes our master. The dictionary defines it as 'well-being, ease'. Comfort is not necessarily luxury, nor is luxury necessarily comfortable. (Sometimes quite the contrary.) It takes many forms, shifting according to climate, century and environment; according to personal taste and the dictates of fashion.

Since heat and cold represent the two basic poles of comfort, their control has always been man's preoccupation as he seeks shade or warmth. Once, the dwellers in the jungle knew comfort in terms of a nakedness – alas! – ultimately overcome by missionary clothing. For Slav serfs, comfort was probably seen as one of those high stone stoves upon which they climbed to snore away their miseries through the long icy nights. Nineteenth-century sahibs sweltering under Indian skies, like American southern gentry, thought the languid to-and-fro of the punkah fans the first essential of comfort, as the glowing hearth of Dickensian tradition appeared to the chilly

English. But those proven comforts are no more, like the shadowy figures who made them work – the punkah wallahs, the persons who stoked the fires and such. (And, all moral issues apart, let us admit that the presence of some ministering attendant must have been the *ne plus ultra* of comfort.)

Today, what is called Progress has equated heat and cold with central heating and air conditioning, with electric fans and that charmless object, the radiator. But all these innovations are susceptible to sudden breakdowns, requiring the service of experts, costly and seldom on hand. Thus I have learned that comfort is often more assured in less progressive lands, where old ways die hard.

The tandour, for example, once used extensively about the Middle East, especially in Turkey and Iran, is still found in remote areas. A brazier of glowing charcoal is placed under a low table covered with a heavy coverlet or rug. The assembled company sit round, their knees and feet tucked snugly inside. Although backs are left to freeze, the tandour is considered *le tout confort* – which is so, if you are wearing the sort of sheepskin garment indigenous to the area.

In my own home, while avoiding most mechanical devices, I have acquired, or continued to use, numbers of rather out-of-date objects upon which I can rely to feel comfortable at all times. These creature comforts, these fans, hot-water bottles, tea cosies, parasols, footstools, screens, shawls and even mittens lap me round. Mittens may sound far-fetched, but no, they warm the hand while leaving the fingers free to cook, garden, or – as I do now – write.

Fans, for example, too long regarded as museum pieces, flutter into action against airless, centrally overheated rooms, fierce suns, foul odours or the forays of insects. Fans are always objects of beauty and elegance, whether of painted silk, scented sandalwood, pleated paper or woven straw. I collect them wherever I go, finding them, also, essential adjuncts to comfortable travel.

Likewise the shawl: with three or four of these, every circumstance, sartorial or climatic, can be met comfortably. Wrapped close, they become an overcoat or dressing gown; draped, an elegant cloak. Spread out, a rug; rolled, a pillow; worn over the head, a hood against sun or storm. Cashmere shawls, derived from the wool of Kashmir goats, were often woven so fine they could pass through a ring. Throughout the East they were considered *grand luxe*, the most lavish of gifts, exchanged between sultans and emirs. Worn chiefly by men, they also served as hangings for a princely tent, or trappings for those glittering ceremonial occasions held in lofty palaces, where their intricate patterns could be displayed to advantage. And now – O desecration! – I see them cut up by careless designers to cover cushions and *banquettes*.

It was Empress Josephine who first popularised cashmere shawls among European ladies. Her Creole blood curdled in the chill splendours of Malmaison and, after Napoleon presented her with one – a spoil of battle from some eastern campaign – she soon acquired several hundred more, draping them about her graceful figure with that incomparable elegance that was her secret. Napoleon grew to dislike them – perhaps they hid too much of that graceful figure. There were scenes. He flung one on the fire. But she just smiled and went on enjoying her comfort.

Fifty years later shawls reached their apogee, worn by women of all degrees, for they draped easily over the crinolines of that era. Then, gradually, they fell from favour, to become the badge of peasants or poor folk. They lingered on, however, in the form of those small tippets of crocheted wool, black or grey, until lately uniform wear for every Paris concierge. These formidable figures, mostly viragos or vigilantes who still observe our comings and goings with insatiable curiosity, were traditionally housed in dank courtyard quarters and could count on few comforts other than their shawls.

My own cherished collection, amassed over the years and across many lands, is housed in a camphored cupboard that is known as my *châleiothèque*, counterpoint to my *bibliothèque* (and the books are not nearly so well housed).

Another form of comfort to which I have become addicted is the footstool, since it so perfectly removes one's feet from cold floors, just as the screen functions against draughts. Then there are parasols, which are far more comfortable than sun hats, for they do not clamp down on one's head or blow away with a puff of wind. As I live in the South of France, under a strong sun, I use them constantly, preferring those antiquated, toylike affairs, often shaped like little pagodas. They belong to that era forever associated with the drawings of Constantin Guys, the era of fine *équipages* bowling along the Bois – all luxury. But such little treasures are also practical; for, being light to hold, with their ivory or carved wood handles cunningly hinged, they can be stowed away in the smallest space – a handbag or even a pocket. The latter is, for women, a sadly neglected aspect of comfort, forcing them to fall back on handbags. Couturiers should take note and devise at least four or five pockets for every garment they design. I am reminded of Queen Mary, whose regal appearance was never marred by a handbag, but who commanded her dressmakers to put discreet pockets into even her most magnificent robes of state.

Thus members of royalty – embalmed, it might seem, in some remote and rigid limboland of a decreed lifestyle – sometimes break out to impose their own particular comforts. Another great queen, Victoria (whose idea of well-being was to live in rooms where the temperature was scarcely above freezing), displayed a singularly down-to-earth ingenuity to obtain her breakfast tea at precisely the temperature she wished. The queen, in august defiance of the climate, favoured alfresco breakfasts. Nevertheless, finding the first scalding sip of tea uncomfortable, and being too imperiously impatient to wait for the brew to cool, she ordered two cups to be placed side by side. The tea was poured first into one cup, and from that into the second, by which time it suited Her Majesty.

Which illustrates my point that comfort, like taste, must always be a purely personal matter, interpreted individually.

*Epilogue —*
## Georgia de Chamberet

A TRAVELLER'S TALE typical of Lesley: although great numbers of the clergy and religious believers were shot or sent to forced-labour camps during Stalin's purges, some survived. During a visit to a dilapidated Russian Orthodox Church, a priest materialised from its hidden recesses. Lesley began to discuss the ikons with him, and he took her on a tour of the church. He was erudite and appreciated talking to a knowledgeable foreigner. Votive offerings had been left by the Orthodox faithful. She admired a brooch of violet-coloured stones (possibly coloured glass) suspended over a painting. The priest took it down and pressed it into her hand as a memento. Lesley was touched and a little taken aback, but accepted the gift as a souvenir of a special encounter. She kept it on her desk and would say: *it has whatever value you give it.* When she escaped in her night-dress from her burning house in 1994, she took it with her, leaving behind a diamond brooch that had been given to her by a lover. The priest's gift now hangs over a precious Turkish family prayer rug on the wall in Lesley's beloved house in Roquebrune.

# Acknowledgements

FOR THEIR SUPPORT and belief in this project over the last five years I wish to thank: Susan Train, Stephen Pickles, Alan Williams, Ben Fiagbe, Laure de Gramont, Elie Schulman, Eileen Horne, Adam and Nelly Munthe, Hugo Vickers, Philip Mansel, Philip Ziegler, Frances Wilson, Linda Kelly, Rosanna Gardner, Carol Russell Wood, Morgan Mason, Belinda Carlisle, Joan Bailey, James Hill, Bettina McNulty, Katia Aubry de Peyer, Alfredo Gonzalez and Lex Aitken, Mitchell Crites, Naomi Vanloo, Jemma Jupp, Mallery Roberts Morgan, Lindsey Thurlow, Harriet Wilson, Robin Muir, Leigh Montville, Tom Gunther, Mary Esdaile, Anne Solange Noble, Elisa Segrave, Duncan Fallowell, Anthony Verschoyle and Ruthie Burgess at Gurr Johns.

Special thanks also to those who were kind enough to grant access to archive material and for answering my queries: Ian Moore at the British Library (Reference Team, Newsroom), The Academy of Motion Picture Arts and Sciences, 333 South La Cienega Boulevard, Beverly Hills, California 90211 (George Cukor Papers). UCLA Library, Special Collections, Charles E. Young Research Library, Los Angeles 90095-1575 (Anaïs Nin Papers), and Tree Leyburn Wright. Arike Oke at The Rambert Archive near Waterloo Bridge and the Estate of Diana Gould. Emmanuelle Toulet and Pauline Girard at the Bibliothèque Historique de la Ville de Paris. Matthias Auclair at the Bibliothèque-Musée de l'Opéra. The librarians at Arts du spectacle, Bibliothèque Nationale de France, rue Vivienne, Paris. The Literary Executors of the late Sir Cecil Beaton who granted access to his papers at St John's College Library, Cambridge. Martin Stone at Forgotten Shelf Ltd, and George Houle at George Houle Rare Books & Autographs, 7260 Beverly Blvd, Los Angeles, California 90036, USA.

The excellent interviews given to me by Yves and Olivier Agid, and Roger Grenier, are appreciated. In the last years of their life, Mireille Dagostin and Dana Wynter were kind enough to give me fresh insights into the Blanch–Gary marriage via email and interview. All are valuable contributions to the Lesley Blanch Archive.

The advice of my publisher, Lennie Goodings, has been an education in itself, and the enthusiasm of her team inspiring. I am especially grateful to Carol MacArthur at United Agents for helping bring this unruly project to a satisfactory conclusion.

# Source Notes

Page ix – Lesley Blanch – 'I don't write fiction because I can't invent. [...] doesn't mean that you don't use your imagination.' Lesley Blanch interview with Shusha Guppy, *Looking Back: A Panoramic View of a Literary Age by the Grandes Dames of European Letters*, Simon & Schuster, London 1993, p. 22.

*Lesley Blanch Remembered – Georgia de Chamberet*

Bibliographical Resources

Victor Borovsky, *A Triptych from the Russian Theatre: An Artistic Biography of the Komissarzhevsky Family*, C. Hurst & Co. Publishers Ltd, London 2001.

Théâtre des Champs Elysées and Théâtre Pigalle programmes and posters from the twenties and early thirties held at the Bibliothèque Historique de la Ville de Paris, 24 rue Pavée, Paris 75004.

Page 1 – 'my title [...] on a new fashion.' Website www.lesley-blanch.com content created by Lesley Blanch and author and posted in 2006. © Georgia de Chamberet, 2015.

Page 1 – 'four women escaping the boredom of convention'. Ibid.

Page 6 – 'To the historian Philip Mansel [...] a true original'. Lesley Blanch interview with Joe Boyd, 'Time Traveller', the *Guardian*, July 2005.

Page 8 – 'loved him in spite of themselves, [...] desperately aware.' Lesley Blanch, *Journey into the Mind's Eye: Fragments of an Autobiography*, Eland Publishing Ltd, London, PB 2005, pp. 29–30. © Lesley Blanch, 1968.

Page 8 – 'A great *metteur en scène*, an inspiring teacher, and a master of theatrical orchestration'. John Gielgud, 'Mr Komisarjevsky', *The Times*, 21 April 1954.

Page 9 – 'As Wagner had done with opera and Diaghilev with ballet, Komisarjevsky dreamed of creating a universal model of theatre with drama.' Victor Borovsky, *A Triptych from the Russian Theatre: An Artistic Biography of the Komissarzhevsky Family*, C. Hurst & Co. Publishers Ltd, London 2001, pp. 249–50.

Page 9 – 'Mysterious and cynical [...] fascinating character.' John Gielgud, 'Mr Komisarjevsky', *The Times*, 21 April 1954.

Page 9 – 'heart-warming through hard times'. Lesley Blanch to author in May 2007.

Page 9 – 'The Traveller acted disgracefully, [...] practised care.' Lesley Blanch, *Journey into the Mind's Eye: Fragments of an Autobiography*, Eland Publishing Ltd, London, PB 2005, pp. 72–3. © Lesley Blanch, 1968.

Page 9 – 'Peggy Ashcroft took him off me.' Lesley Blanch to author in May 2007.

Page 11 – 'Everything about her was abundant; [...] cornucopia of personality.' Anne Scott-James, *In the Mink*, Michael Joseph, London, 1952, p. 61.

Page 12 – 'It was a *coup de foudre*, and it was mutual.' Caroline Baum, 'The Wild One', the *Spectator*, May 2007.

Page 12 – 'wrote in *Vogue*, in January 1945, about his first novel, *Forest of Anger*'. Extract from 'Reading Matter', *Vogue*, January 1945, pp. 151–8. Lesley Blanch / British *Vogue* © The Condé Nast Publications Ltd.

Page 13 – 'They were both of them capable [...] luckily, it was the former.' Anne Scott-James, *In the Mink*, Michael Joseph, London, 1952, p. 67.

Page 13 – 'we knew everybody: Aldous and Maria Huxley [...] was one of the few intriguing women there at that time.' Website www.lesleyblanch.com content created by Lesley Blanch and author and posted in 2006. © Georgia de Chamberet, 2015.

Page 14 – 'I'm madly in love with him, but he's unbearable!' Lesley Blanch to author's late mother, Gael Elton Mayo.

Page 14 – 'I met his wife Lesley Blanch [...] Don Juan.' Anaïs Nin Diaries 1957, Collection name and number 2066 Anaïs Nin, box 28, folder 5 at the UCLA Library, Dept of Special Collections, A1713 Young Research Library, Box 951575, Los Angeles CA90095-1575. Handwritten manuscript (7 pp.) read on 26 January 2011. Photocopies received on 15 February 2011. © The Anaïs Nin Trust. Special thanks to Tree Leyburn Wright.

Page 15 – 'he was Russian [...] The Traveller again in him.' Philip Mansel, 'Lesley Blanch: My Life on the Wilder Shores', *Cornucopia*, issue 37, 2007.

Page 15 – 'to escape the boredom of convention'. Website www. lesleyblanch.com content created by Lesley Blanch and author and posted in 2006. © Georgia de Chamberet, 2015.

Page 15 – 'learning how to deal with pain is the most important thing in life'. Lesley Blanch to author in May 2007.

Page 16 – 'Wallis was a very nice person and I don't mind what anyone said, he was highly intelligent.' Lesley Blanch interview with Maureen Cleave, 'A Mystery Woman Lifts the Veil', *Daily Telegraph, Weekend*, 1987.

Page 16 – 'The arrival of the jet plane in the sixties [...] new horizons.' Author interview with Susan Train, Paris, 27 April 2013.

Page 16 – 'American *Vogue*'s April 1965 issue [...] Vreeland wrote in her "Editor's Note": "Lesley Blanch is an adventurous woman, [...] and her understanding of love."' American *Vogue* © The Condé Nast Publications Ltd.

Page 16 – 'For [Lesley Blanch], the veil [...] the mechanics of male domination.' Philip Mansel, 'Lesley Blanch: My Life on the Wilder Shores', *Cornucopia*, issue 37, 2007.

Page 17 – 'Always explore a new town on an empty stomach, [...] the monuments commemorate.' Lesley Blanch, *Journey into the Mind's Eye: Fragments of an Autobiography*, Eland Publishing Ltd,

London, PB 2005, p. 129. © Lesley Blanch, 1968.

Page 17 – 'Scratch any of [...] Nancy Mitford and Rebecca West.' Michael Ratcliffe, *The Times*, December 1968.

Page 17 – 'Romain Gary's quip [...] very eighteenth-century!' Lesley Blanch interview with Mary Blume, *International Herald Tribune*, 1986.

Page 17 – 'always detested conventions, [...] iconoclastic and traditional', 'wild and free'. Lesley Blanch to author during 2001–2004.

Page 18 – 'secrecy was with him [...] for its own sake'. Lesley Blanch, *Journey into the Mind's Eye: Fragments of an Autobiography*, Eland Publishing Ltd, London, PB 2005, p. 59. © Lesley Blanch, 1968.

Page 18 – 'People didn't know much in the fifties [...] which was disconcerting.' Yves Agid interview with author in Paris, 25 April 2013.

Page 19 – 'I liked having adventures [...] and yes, I did have lovers too.' Lesley Blanch interview with Shusha Guppy, *Looking Back: A Panoramic View of a Literary Age by the Grandes Dames of European Letters*, Simon & Schuster, London 1993, p. 11.

Page 19 – 'Delicious tea was served [...] found one for herself.' Hugo Vickers interview with Lesley Blanch, Friday, 17 September 1981.

Pages 19-20 – 'Shirley Conran tells me [...] King of Jordan' Shirley Conran, telephone conversation with author, 31 October 2014.

Page 20 – 'Lesley was the Queen of the Middle East. She was divine.' Gore Vidal, telephone conversation with author, 6 April 2011.

Page 20 – 'I first met her when I was fifteen. [...] These transgenerational relationships are rare. I have had really only one or two.' From Turi Munthe's commemorative speech at the memorial, 'Remembering Lesley – A Celebration of the Life of Lesley Blanch', Wednesday, 19 September 2007.

Page 21 – 'Do I have to just sit and take it?' Author interview with Susan Train, Paris, 31 July 2010.

Page 21 – 'quite happy to own up [...] shadow of the suburbs'. Lesley Blanch interview with Jeremy Round, the *Independent*, July 1989.

*Far to Go and Many to Love – Lesley Blanch*

Typed-up introduction to Lesley Blanch's memoirs written 2001–2004. © Georgia de Chamberet, 2015.

## PART ONE – SCENES FROM CHILDHOOD

Typed-up childhood section of Lesley Blanch's memoirs written 2001–2004. © Georgia de Chamberet, 2015.

Page 118 – 'She also liked to tell me how my great-grandmother, [...] in love, in London, in 1852.' Lesley Blanch, *Pavilions of the Heart: The Four Walls of Love*, Weidenfeld & Nicolson, London, 1974, pp. 16–17. © Lesley Blanch, 1974.

Page 127 – 'the baroque Villa Ombrellino on the hillside across the Arno, where Mrs Keppel, King Edward VII's last and most cherished charmer, lived in regal splendour.' Lesley gave me Mrs Keppel's prayer book before she died; it was given to her by Violet Trefusis.

Page 149 – 'There were shortages of butter and sugar. Face cream was scarce so I nourished my face with lard and then washed it off; otherwise it went rancid and smelled.' Mireille Dagostin, interview with author, Roquebrune, 27–28 April 2012.

*A London Life – Georgia de Chamberet*

Page 150 – 'T. S. Eliot at Faber & Faber: a very grave, quiet, polite, nice man.' Website www.lesleyblanch.com content created by Lesley Blanch and author and posted in 2006. © Georgia de Chamberet, 2015.

Page 150 – 'Sometimes advances were made, [...] books for me to read and illustrate.' Handwritten notes for Lesley Blanch's memoirs. © Georgia de Chamberet, 2015.

Page 152 – 'popular with actors [...] Victorian songs and ballads.' Ibid.

Page 152 – 'coveys of flappers danced until dawn, [...] *Battleship Potemkin* made an impact.' Ibid.

Page 153 – 'A fast-paced, carnivalesque version [...] clockwork toys.' Clive Barker, Maggie Barbara Gale (editors), *British Theatre between the Wars, 1918–1939*, Cambridge University Press 2007, p. 143.

Page 153 – '*Macbeth* was performed [...] swirling light effects.' Michael Mullins, 'Augurs and Understood Relations: Theodore Komisarjevsky's *Macbeth*', *Educational Theatre Journal*, vol. 26, no. 1 (March 1974), The Johns Hopkins University Press, p. 20.

Page 153 – 'Komisarjevsky's interpretation of the play was as a psychological drama.' Victor Borovsky, *A Triptych from the Russian Theatre: An Artistic Biography of the Komissarzhevsky Family*, C. Hurst & Co. Publishers Ltd, London 2001, p. 395.

Page 153 – 'The costume designs by Mrs Lesley Blanch for Komisarjevsky's [...] robot-like appearance of the players.' Written beneath the costume design by Lesley Blanch. From a Private Collection.

Page 156 – 'dingy little flat in an unfashionable part of London'. Sarah Bradford, Robin Gibson, John Pearson, *The Sitwells and the Arts of the Twenties and Thirties*, University of Texas Press, Austin 1996, p. 74.

Page 157 – 'stone-built hall [...] road from Oxford'. Ashley Dukes, *The Scene is Changed*, Macmillan & Co. Ltd, London 1942, p. 65.

Page 157 – 'Freddie was offered up on stage [...] Admirers liked my baroque curtain.' Handwritten notes for Lesley Blanch's memoirs. © Georgia de Chamberet, 2015.

Special thanks to Arike Oke, Rambert Archivist, The Rambert Archive, 99 Upper Ground, London SE1 9PP for all her help. Marie Rambert's autobiography *Quicksilver* (Macmillan, 1972), pp. 141–3, provided invaluable background information about the Ballet Club and The Mercury Theatre for page 157.

Page 157 – 'a woman with the morals of the cat and the manners of a highly cultivated kitten'. *The Times*, 15 January 1934.

Page 158 – 'Marry first for love [...] with love or money.' Lesley Blanch, *Journey into the Mind's Eye: Fragments of an Autobiography*, Eland Publishing Ltd, London 2005, p. 145. © Lesley Blanch, 1968.

Page 158 – 'Lesley married [...] for love of a house.' Lesley Blanch interview with Karen Robinson, *Sunday Times*, August 2006.

Pages 158 – 'epoch William & Mary [...] lost by my fault and gained by that too.' Handwritten notes for Lesley Blanch's memoirs. © Georgia de Chamberet, 2015.

Pages 158 – 'It was a lovely room with its big bow windows [...] rickety summer-house overhanging the wall.' Ibid.

Page 160 – 'it was a great moment for advertising firms, it was the beginning.' Ibid.

Page 160 – 'instructed to write on everything [...] books, people.' Ibid.

Page 161 – 'le gratin versus café society: rich Americans, idle aristocrats, film and theatre celebrities, gigolos and hangers-on'. Ibid.

Page 161 – 'a new kind of caricature-portrait [...] everything I have put in.' Ibid.

Page 161 – 'Lesley told Beaton's biographer, [...] Underneath there was great understanding.' Hugo Vickers' interview with Lesley Blanch, Friday 17 September 1981.

## PART TWO – SCENES FROM THE HOME FRONT

### Vogue *Remembered*

Typed-up section of Lesley Blanch's memoirs 2001–2004. © Georgia de Chamberet, 2015.

### *'Spotlight': Writing from the* Vogue *Years*

Lesley Blanch / British *Vogue* © The Condé Nast Publications Ltd.

*The Years Between* – British *Vogue*, September 1941, pp. 115–19.

*A Babel of Tongues* – 'Spotlight', British *Vogue*, November 1939, pp. 119–20.

*Living the Sheltered Life* – British *Vogue*, October 1940, pp. 120–3.

*To Have or to Hold* – British *Vogue*, April 1941, pp. 123–5.

*War on Winter* – British *Vogue*, November 1941, pp. 125–7.

*Blitzed Britain* – 'Spotlight', British *Vogue*, October 1941, pp. 127–8.

*Noël Coward's New Medium* – British *Vogue*, November 1942, pp. 54, 72.

*The True Story of Lili Marlene* – British *Vogue*, April 1944, pp. 142–6.

*Some of All the Russias* – British *Vogue*, March 1942, pp. 31–2, 86.

*Russia: Landscape of the Heart*

*First Travels* – Typed-up section of Lesley Blanch's memoirs 2001–2004. © Georgia de Chamberet, 2015.

'*Sweet chance that led my steps abroad . . .* ' – Handwritten notes for Lesley Blanch's memoirs 2001–2004. © Georgia de Chamberet, 2015.


PART THREE – SCENES FROM A MARRIAGE

*Romain Gary: A Private View*

Originally published in France by Actes Sud, 1998, translated into French by Jean Lambert. Written in English but unpublished. © Georgia de Chamberet, 2015.

Page 272 – 'Many years later, when Garbo came to see me there, [. . .] she was not recognised in the village.' During my interview with Mireille Dagostin in Roquebrune, 27–28 April 2012, she told me that M. Borla, a municipal employee, was a huge fan of Garbo and recognised her stranded in the village café, so he showed her the way to Lesley's house.

Page 307 – 'He asked me to try to find him something in that area'. Romain Gary committed suicide on 2 December 1980. The following extract from a letter to René Agid (the original is in French), dated 10 March 1981, throws light on Lesley's enduring relationship with her former husband. © Georgia de Chamberet, 2015.

*Dear René,*

*[. . .] Had I known R. was in <u>such</u> a low mental state I would have telephoned, or written, just to say, once again, that I remained his loyal friend. Nothing more. I have no illusions as to R.'s emotions, or*

*his nature: he always preferred to avoid difficult encounters which evoke the past, even when he said, during one of his brief visits here, that he played his cards wrong and probably the happiest period of his life was in Bulgaria. (With or without me?) I did not answer – what's the point?*

*Clearly a rather singular friendship remained between us, particularly a little before, and after, the death of Jean [Seberg], when we <u>often</u> spoke on the telephone. I believe we fully understood our 'relationship' – a matter of distance – but very <u>real</u>.*

*R. was a man exhausted by life and by his emotions, he did not want to be flayed alive by exasperations and misunderstandings. Or by everyday problems. On this, I understood him very well.*

*I was always surprised when he called me, even. And, at the time, I did not understand his last letter, or the sinister significance behind his lines. Did you know that, on a few occasions, R. invited me to stay with him in rue du Bac, if I happened to be going through Paris?*

*In any case, I preferred to stay with a friend, Susan Train, who was nearby. I wanted to avoid it being the slightest effort, for him or for me. And, René, his invitations were not in <u>writing</u>, if you doubt my word?*

*During the last years, well before Jean died, I became accustomed to having dinner with R. on the rare occasions I came through Paris. Much of the time I briefly saw Diego too. But I <u>never</u> thought I'd become part of his domestic inner circle. At any rate, it's pointless to go on about this.*

*I am perfectly aware that my presence was embarrassing for you where R. was concerned. Remember how, from the moment we were divorced, I kept away, <u>expressly</u> to avoid any embarrassment on your part. It was Sylvia who took the first step, when R. was thinking about an apartment at Roquebrune. How happy I was to be with you again! I always thought of you as my closest, my nearest and dearest, in France.*

*Things are not going well here.*

*I hope you will understand what I have written so very badly.*

*I am, as ever, your loyal friend, Lesley*

PART FOUR – FARAWAY LANDS

### The Lodestar Longing

Article (undated) found amongst Lesley Blanch's papers. © Georgia de Chamberet, 2015.

Reasonable efforts have been made to find out if this article has ever been published. An appropriate acknowledgement can be inserted by the publisher in any subsequent printing or edition.

### Always Travel Heavy

From *Under a Lilac-bleeding Star, Travels and Travellers*, originally published by John Murray in 1963. © Lesley Blanch, 1963.

### Junking

From typed-up sections of Lesley Blanch's memoir 2001–2004. © Georgia de Chamberet, 2015.

### New York: Leo Lerman, Carson McCullers & Others

From typed-up sections of Lesley Blanch's memoir 2001–2004. © Georgia de Chamberet, 2015.

### Los Angeles: Marlene Dietrich & Others

From typed-up sections of Lesley Blanch's memoir 2001–2004. © Georgia de Chamberet, 2015.

Page 348 – Letter: Lesley Blanch to Cecil Beaton, Monday 8–9? September [*circa* 1958]. Special thanks to Hugo Vickers / the Literary Executors of the late Sir Cecil Beaton who were kind enough to grant access to his papers at St John's College Library, Cambridge. © Georgia de Chamberet, 2015.

### Many Mexicos

From *Under a Lilac-bleeding Star, Travels and Travellers*, originally published by John Murray in 1963. © Lesley Blanch, 1963.

## PART FIVE – THE EASTERN EYE

### *Afghanistan*

From Lesley Blanch's handwritten rough notes for her memoir 2001–2004. © Georgia de Chamberet, 2015.

### *Turkey*

American *Vogue*, 1 November 1954. Lesley Blanch / American *Vogue* © The Condé Nast Publications Ltd.

### *The Turquoise Table: Traditional Persian Food*

From *From Wilder Shores: The Tables of My Travels*, John Murray, 1989. © Lesley Blanch, 1989.

### *The Joys of Comfort*

'Guest Speaker', *Architectural Digest*, April 1985.

Lesley Blanch / *Architectural Digest* © The Condé Nast Publications Ltd.

### *Epilogue*

This anecdote is from Mireille Dagostin's interview with the author in Roquebrune, 27–28 April 2012, Tuesday 13 November 2012; and on the telephone 21 March 2013. © Georgia de Chamberet, 2015.

# Illustration and Photograph Credits

Endpapers: Sketch by Lesley Blanch: Round the World in Tea. Copyright © Georgia de Chamberet, 2015. From *Round the World in 80 Dishes*, Grub Street Publishing, London, 2011.

## LESLEY BLANCH REMEMBERED

Lesley Blanch and Georgia de Chamberet, Garavan, 1971. Photo by Gael Elton Mayo. Copyright © Georgia de Chamberet, Stephen Gebb, Guislaine Vincent Morland, 2015.

Lesley's desk in Garavan, *circa* 1981. Photo by Gael Elton Mayo. Copyright © Georgia de Chamberet, Stephen Gebb, Guislaine Vincent Morland, 2015.

Scenic design by Lesley Blanch for Komisarjevsky's production of Cimarosa's *Giannina et Bernardone*, Théâtre Pigalle, Paris, May–June 1931. Copyright © Georgia de Chamberet, 2015.

Lesley with Smiley, Garavan, *circa* 1981. Photo by Gael Elton Mayo. Copyright © Georgia de Chamberet, Stephen Gebb, Guislaine Vincent Morland, 2015.

## FAR TO GO AND MANY TO LOVE

The Nancy Mitford memorial window, Garavan. Photo by Georgia de Chamberet. Copyright © Georgia de Chamberet, 2015.

## SCENES FROM CHILDHOOD

Martha Mabel Blanch née Thorpe.

Lesley Blanch, aged three.

Walter Blanch.

Lesley Blanch's great-grandfather, John Stewart, who brought up her mother Martha Mabel Thorpe, leaving her most of his fortune.

Lesley Blanch in 1925.

Illustration (Lavinia Blythe): *Songs and Poems by John Dryden*, The Golden Cockerel Press, 1957. Copyright © Georgia de Chamberet, 2015.

Costume design by Lesley Blanch for Shylock in Komisarjevsky's *The Merchant of Venice*, 1932. Copyright © Georgia de Chamberet, 2015.

Costume design by Lesley Blanch for two male characters, French Farce. Copyright © Georgia de Chamberet, 2015.

SCENES FROM A MARRIAGE

Lesley Blanch in Hollywood in the fifties. Photo by Gael Elton Mayo. Copyright © Georgia de Chamberet, Stephen Gebb, Guislaine Vincent Morland, 2015.

Romain and Nina Kacew, mother and son, that indissoluble whole, together. Photo Studio Modense Vilna, Warsaw.

Sketches by Lesley Blanch on pages 30, 65, 74, 116, 164, 222, 266, 268, 279, 304 and 380: copyright © Georgia de Chamberet, 2015.

Sketches by Lesley Blanch on pages 252, 294, 314, 331, 368, 385, 399: copyright © Georgia de Chamberet, 2015. From *Round the World in 80 Dishes*, Grub Street Publishing, 2011.

# Index